T. D. & SERITA ANN JAKES

Speak to Women

Books by T. D. Jakes

Lay Aside the Weight (with workbook & journal)

Loose That Man & Let Him Go!

Loose That Man & Let Him Go! (with workbook)

So You Call Yourself a Man?

T. D. Jakes Speaks to Men!

T. D. Jakes Speaks to Women!

Woman, Thou Art Loosed!

SIX PILLARS FOR THE BELIEVER

Celebrating Marriage

Experiencing Jesus

Intimacy With God

Life Overflowing

Loved by God

Overcoming the Enemy

Devotionals

Loose That Man & Let Him Go! Devotional

Woman, Thou Art Loosed! Devotional

To contact T. D. Jakes, write:

T. D. Jakes Ministries

P.O. Box 5390

Dallas, Texas 75236

www.tdjakes.org

T.D. & SERITA ANN JAKES
Speak to Women

THREE BESTSELLING BOOKS IN ONE VOLUME!

Woman, Thou Art Loosed!
The Princess Within
T.D. Jakes Speaks to Women

BETHANYHOUSE
MINNEAPOLIS, MINNESOTA

T. D. and Serita Jakes Speak to Women
Copyright © 1996, 1999
T. D. Jakes and Serita Jakes
Previously published in three volumes:

Woman, Thou Are Loosed! © 1996, 2004 by T. D. Jakes

The Princess Within © 1999 by Serita Ann Jakes

T. D. Jakes Speaks to Women! © 1996 by T D. Jakes Ministries

Cover design by Jennifer Parker

SCRIPTURE CREDITS:

Woman, Thou Art Loosed!

Unless otherwise identified, Scripture quotations are from the King James Version of the Bible.

Scripture quotations identified NIV are from the HOLY BIBLE, NEW INTERNATIONAL VERSION®. Copyright © 1973, 1978, 1984 by International Bible Society. Used by permission of Zondervan Publishing House. All rights reserved.

The Princess Within

Unless otherwise identified Scripture quotations are from the HOLY BIBLE, NEW INTERNATIONAL VERSION®. Copyright © 1973, 1978, 1984 by International Bible Society. Used by permission of Zondervan Publishing House. All rights reserved.

Scripture quotations identified KJV are from the King James Version of the Bible.

Scripture quotations identified AMP are from the Amplified Bible. Old Testament copyright © 1965, 1987 by the Zondervan Corporation. The Amplified New Testament copyright © 1958, 1987 by the Lockman Foundation. Used by permission.

Scripture quotations identified NKJV are from the New King James Version of the Bible. Copyright © 1979, 1980, 1982 by Thomas Nelson, Inc. Used by permission. All rights reserved.

Scripture quotations identified NASB are taken from the NEW AMERICAN STANDARD BIBLE®, © Copyright The Lockman Foundation 1960, 1962, 1963, 1968, 1971, 1972, 1973, 1975, 1977, 1995. Used by permission. (www.Lockman.org)

Published by Bethany House Publishers
11400 Hampshire Avenue South
Bloomington, Minnesota 55438

Bethany House Publishers is a division of
Baker Publishing Group, Grand Rapids, Michigan.

Printed in the United States of America

ISBN-13: 978-0-7642-0301-5
ISBN-10: 0-7642-0301-0

T. D. JAKES, founder and senior pastor of The Potter's House Church in Dallas, Texas, is a celebrated speaker and author with many bestselling books to his credit. His weekly television broadcast is viewed in millions of homes nationwide. Featured on the cover of *Time Magazine,* he is known around the world for his message of freedom to be found in Christ.

SERITA ANN JAKES has been involved in ministry all her life. God was preparing her for the responsibility of carrying out God's vision for his people with her husband, Bishop T. D. Jakes. She is known among women from all walks of life and is in demand as a speaker by organizations throughout the country. Serita is faithful to the care and nurture of her family and can be found close to her husband and her children. The Jakes family lives in Dallas, Texas.

Woman,
Thou Art Loosed

HEALING THE WOUNDS OF THE PAST

by
T. D. Jakes

CONTENTS

CHAPTER ONE

Infirm Woman

It is important to remember that for every person, there will be a problem. Even more importantly, for every problem, our God has a prescription!

And, behold, there was a woman which had a spirit of infirmity eighteen years, and was bowed together, and could in no wise lift up herself. And when Jesus saw her, he called her to him, and said unto her, "Woman, thou art loosed from thine infirmity."

LUKE 13:11–12

The Holy Spirit periodically lets us catch a glimpse of the personal testimony of one of the patients of the Divine Physician Himself. This woman's dilemma is her own, but perhaps you will find some point of relativity between her case history and your own. She could be like someone you know or have known; she could even be like you.

There are three major characters in this story. They are the person, the problem, and the prescription. It is important to remember that for every person, there will be a problem. But even more importantly, for every problem, our God has a prescription!

Jesus' opening statement to the problem in this woman's life is not a recommendation for counseling—it is a challenging command! Often much more is involved in maintaining deliverance than just discussing past trauma. Jesus did not counsel what should have been commanded. I am not, however, against seeking the counsel of godly men. On the contrary, the Scriptures say:

Blessed is the man that walketh not in the counsel of the ungodly, nor standeth in the way of the sinners, nor sitteth in the seat of the scornful.

PSALM 1:1

Where no counsel is, the people fall: but in the multitude of counsellors there is safety.

PROVERBS 11:14

What I want to make clear is that after you have analyzed the condition, after you have understood its origin, it will still take the authority of God's Word to put the past under your feet! This woman was suffering as a result of something that attacked her eighteen years earlier. I wonder if you can relate to the long-range aftereffects of past pain? This kind of trauma is as fresh to the victim today as it was the day it occurred. Although the problem may be rooted in the past, the prescription is a present word from God! The Word is the same yesterday, today and forevermore (Hebrews 13:8). That is to say, the Word you are hearing today is able to heal your yesterday!

A PERSONAL WAR

When Jesus said, "Woman, thou art loosed," He did not call her by name. He wasn't speaking to her just as a person. He spoke to her femininity. He spoke to the song in her. He spoke to the lace in her. Like a crum-

4

bling rose, Jesus spoke to what she could, and would have been. I believe the Lord spoke to the twinkle that existed in her eye when she was a child; to the girlish glow that makeup can never seem to recapture. He spoke to her God-given uniqueness. He spoke to her gender.

Her problem didn't begin suddenly. It had existed in her life for eighteen years. We are looking at a woman who had a personal war going on inside her. These struggles must have tainted many other areas of her life. The infirmity that attached to her life was physical.

However, many women also wrestle with infirmities in emotional traumas. These infirmities can be just as challenging as a physical affliction. An emotional handicap can create dependency on many different levels. Relationships can become crutches. The infirm woman can place such weight on people that it strains a healthy relationship. And many times such emotional handicaps will spawn a series of unhealthy relationships.

> *"For thou hast had five husbands; and he whom thou now hast is not thy husband: in that saidst thou truly."*
>
> JOHN 4:18

Healing cannot come to a desperate person rummaging through other people's lives. One of the first things that a hurting person needs to do is break the habit of using other people as a narcotic to numb the dull aching of an inner void. The more you medicate the symptoms, the less chance you have of allowing God to heal you.

CLINGING OR LOVING?

Another destructive tendency that can exist with any abuse is the continual increasing of dosage. So avoid addictive, obsessive relationships. If you are becoming increasingly dependent upon anything other than God to create a sense of wholeness in your life, you are abusing your relationships.

Clinging to people is far different from loving them. It is not so much a statement of your love for them as it is a crying out of your need for them. Like lust, it is intensely selfish. It is taking and not giving.

Love is giving. God is love. God proved His love not by His need of us, but by His giving to us.

> *For God so loved the world, that he gave his only begotten Son, that whosoever believeth in him should not perish, but have everlasting life.*
>
> JOHN 3:16

The Scriptures plainly show that this infirm woman had tried to lift herself. People who stood on the outside could easily criticize and assume that the infirm woman lacked effort and fortitude. But that is not always the case. Some situations in which we find ourselves defy willpower. We feel unable to change. The Scriptures say this woman "could in no wise lift up herself." This implies she had employed various means of self-ministry.

SPIRITUAL AILMENTS

Isn't it amazing how the same people who lift up countless others, often cannot lift themselves? This type of person may be a tower of faith and prayer for others, but impotent when it comes to their own limitations. This type of person may be the one others rely upon. Sometimes we esteem others more important than ourselves and we always become the martyr. It is wonderful to be self-sacrificing, but watch out for self-disdain! If we don't apply some of the medicine that we use on others to strengthen ourselves, our patients will be healed and we will be dying.

> *I shall not die, but live, and declare the works of the Lord.*
>
> PSALM 118:17

Many things can engender disappointment and depression. In this woman's case, a spirit of infirmity had gripped her life. A spirit can manifest itself in many forms. For some it may be low self-esteem caused by child abuse, rape, wife abuse or divorce. I realize that these are natural problems, but they are rooted in spiritual ailments.

One of the many damaging things that can affect us today is divorce, particularly among women, who often look forward to a happy relationship. Little girls grow up playing with Barbie and Ken dolls, dressing doll babies and playing house. Young girls lie in bed reading romance novels, while little boys play ball and ride bicycles in the park. Whenever a woman is indoctrinated to think success is *romance*, then experiences the trauma of a failed relationship, she comes to a painful awakening.

PUTTING PERSPECTIVE ON THE PAST

Divorce is not merely separating; it is the tearing apart of what was once joined together. Whenever something is torn, it does not heal easily. But Jesus can heal a broken or torn heart!

> *"The Spirit of the Lord is upon me, because he hath anointed me to preach the gospel to the poor; he hath sent me to heal the broken-hearted, to preach deliverance to the captives, and recovering of sight to the blind, to set at liberty them that are bruised."*
>
> LUKE 4:18

Approximately five out of ten marriages end in divorce. Those broken homes in which it occurs leave a trail of broken dreams, people and children. Only the Master can heal these victims in the times in which we live. Only He can treat the long-term effects of this tragedy.

One of the great healing balms of the Holy Spirit is forgiveness. To forgive is to break the link between you and your past. Sadly, though, many times the person hardest to forgive is the one in the mirror. Although many rage loudly about others, they secretly blame themselves for a failed relationship. But regardless of who they may be holding responsible, there is no healing in blame!

When you begin to realize that your past does not necessarily dictate the outcome of your future, you can finally release the hurt. It is impossible to inhale new air until you exhale the old.

I pray that as you continue reading, God will give the grace of releasing where you have been, so you can receive what God has for you now. Exhale, then inhale; there is more for you.

LET THE LITTLE CHILDREN COME TO ME. . . .
MATTHEW 19:14

Perhaps one of the more serious indictments against our civilization is our flagrant disregard for the welfare of our children. Child abuse, regardless of whether it is physical, sexual or emotional, is a terrible issue for an innocent mind to wrestle with. It is horrifying to think that little children who survive the peril of the streets, the public schools, and the aggravated society in which we live, come home to be abused in what should be a haven.

Recent statistics suggest that three in five young girls in this country have been or will be sexually assaulted. If that many are reported, I shudder to think of how many are never reported and are covered with a shroud of secrecy.

THE ABUSED ARE IN OUR MIDST

If by chance you are a pastor, please realize that these figures are actually faces in your choir, committees, etc. They reflect a growing amount of our congregational needs. Although this book focuses on women, many men also have been abused as children. And I fear that God will judge us for our blatant disregard of this need in our messages, ministries and prayers. I would even suggest that our silence contributes to the shame and secrecy that Satan attaches to these victimized persons.

So whenever I think on these issues, I am reminded of what my mother used to say. I was forever coming home with a scratch or cut from school-yard play. When I did, my mother would take the band-aid off, clean the wound and say, "Things that are covered don't heal well." And mother was right. Things that are covered do not heal well.

Perhaps Jesus was thinking on this order when He called the infirm woman to come forward. It takes a lot of courage even in church today to receive ministry in sensitive areas. But the Lord is the kind of physician who can pour on the healing oil. So uncover your wounds in His presence and allow Him to gently heal your injuries. One woman even found healing in the hem of His garment (Mark 5:25–29). There is a balm in Gilead! (Jeremiah 8:22).

THE DEATH OF TRUST

However, even when a victim survives, there is still a casualty. It is the death of trust. Surely you realize that little girls tend to be trusting and unsuspicious. But when those who should nurture and protect them violate that trust through illicit behavior, multiple scars result. It is like programming a computer with false information; you can get out of it only what has been programmed into it.

When a man tells a little girl that his perverted acts are normal, she has no reason not to believe that what she is being taught is true. She is devoted to him and allows him to fondle her and further misappropriate his actions toward her. Usually the abuser is someone very close, with access to the child at vulnerable times. But fear is also a factor. Many children lay down with the cold taste of fear in their mouths. They believe the abuser could and would kill them for divulging his liberties against them. And some, as the victims of rape, feel physically powerless to wrestle with the assailant.

What kind of emotions might this kind of conduct bring out in the later life of this person? I am glad you asked. It would be easy for this kind of little girl to grow into a young lady who has difficulty trusting anyone! Maybe she will learn to deal with the pain inside by getting attention in illicit ways. Drug rehabilitation centers and prisons are full of adults who were abused children needing attention.

INTIMIDATED BY INTIMACY

Not every abused child takes such drastic steps. Often their period of behavioral disorder dissipates with time. Still, the abused child struggles with her own self-worth. She reasons, "How can I be valuable if the only way I could please my own father was to have sex with him?" This kind of childhood can affect how later relationships progress. Intimidated by intimacy, she struggles with trusting anyone. Insecurity and jealousy may be constant companions to this lady who can't seem to grasp the idea that someone could love her.

There are a variety of reactions to child abuse. Some avoid people who really care, being attracted to those who do not treat them well. Relating to abuse, they seem to sabotage good relationships and struggle for years in worthless ones. Others have become emotionally incapacitated to the degree that they need endless affirmation and affection just to maintain the courage to face ordinary days.

UNPROGRAMMING LIFE'S
POORLY PROGRAMMED EVENTS

The pastor may tell this lady that God is her heavenly Father. But that doesn't help, because the problem is her point of reference. We frame our references around our own experiences. If those experiences are distorted, our ability to comprehend spiritual truths can be off center. I know that may sound very negative for someone who is in that circumstance. But what do you do when you have been poorly programmed by life's events? I've got good news! You can reprogram your mind through the Word of God.

Do not conform any longer to the pattern of this world, but be transformed by the renewing of your mind. Then you will be able to test and approve what God's will is—his good, pleasing and perfect will.

ROMANS 12:2 NIV

The Greek word *metamorphoo* is translated as "transformed" in this text. Literally, it means to change into another form! You can have a complete metamorphosis through the Word of God.

It has been my experience as a pastor who does extensive counseling in my own ministry and abroad, that many abused people, women in particular, tend to flock to legalistic churches who see God primarily as a disciplinarian. Many times the concept of fatherhood for them is a harsh code of ethics. This type of domineering ministry may appeal to those who are performance-oriented.

MORALITY OR LEGALISM?

I understand that morality is important in Christianity. However, there is a great deal of difference between morality and legalism. It is important that God not be misrepresented. He is a balanced God. He is not an extremist.

The Word became flesh and made his dwelling among us. We have seen his glory, the glory of the One and Only, who came from the Father, full of grace and truth.

JOHN 1:14 NIV

The glory of God is manifested only when there is a balance between grace and truth. Religion doesn't transform. Legalism doesn't transform. For the person who feels dirty, harsh rules may create a sense of self-righteousness. But God doesn't have to punish you to heal you. Jesus has already prayed for you.

"Sanctify them through thy truth: thy word is truth."

JOHN 17:17

Jesus simply shared grace and truth with that one hurting woman. He said, "Woman, thou art loosed." Jesus our Lord was a great emancipator of the oppressed. It does not matter whether someone has been oppressed socially, sexually or racially; our Lord is an eliminator of distinctions. Anyone can believe the Word of God and be free.

There is neither Jew nor Greek [racial], there is neither bond nor free [social], there is neither male nor female [sexual]: for ye are all one in Christ Jesus.

GALATIANS 3:28

I feel it is important to point out that this verse deals with unity and equality in regard to the covenant of salvation. That is to say, God is no respecter of persons. He tears down barriers that would promote prejudice and separation in the Body of Christ. Yet it is important also to note that while there is no distinction in the manner in which we receive any of those groups, there should be an appreciation for the uniqueness of their individuality.

CULTURAL RAPE

There is a racial, social and sexual uniqueness that we should not only accept, but also appreciate. It is cultural rape to teach other cultures or races that the only way to worship God is the way another race or culture does. Unity should not come at the expense of uniqueness of expression. We should also tolerate variance in social classes. It is wonderful to teach prosperity as long as it is understood that the Church is not an elite organization for spiritual yuppies only, who exclude other social classes.

And if uniqueness is to be appreciated racially and socially, it is certainly to be appreciated sexually. Male and female are one in Christ. Yet they are unique, and that uniqueness is not to be tampered with. Let the male be masculine and the female be feminine!

It is a sin for a man to misrepresent himself by conducting himself as a woman. I am not merely speaking of homosexuality. I am also talking about men who are feminine in their mannerisms. Many of these men may not be homosexual in their behavior, but the Bible says they must be healed of feminine mannerisms, and vice versa.[1] It is equally sad to see a masculine woman. Nevertheless, God wants them healed, not hated!

> *Know ye not that the unrighteous shall not inherit the kingdom of God? Be not deceived: neither fornicators, nor idolaters, nor adulterers, nor effeminate, nor abusers of themselves with mankind.*
>
> I CORINTHIANS 6:9

I realize that these behavioral disorders are areas that require healing and prayer. My point is simply that unity does not negate uniqueness. God is saying, "I don't want men to lose their masculine uniqueness." This is true racially, socially and sexually.

God can appreciate our differences and still create unity. It is like a conductor who can orchestrate extremely different instruments into producing

---

[1] *Effeminate:* Strong's #3120 "*malakos* (mal-ak-os'); of uncertain affinity; soft, i.e. fine (clothing); figuratively a catamite: effeminate, soft" (*Strong's Exhaustive Concordance of the Bible,* Hendrickson Publishers, n.d.)

a harmonious, unified sound. Together we produce a sound of harmony that expresses the multifaceted character of God.

Having established the uniqueness of unity, let us now discuss some aspects of the uniqueness of the woman. By nature a woman is a receiver. She is not physically designed to be a giver. Her sexual and emotional fulfillment becomes somewhat dependent on the giving of her male counterpart (in regard to intimate relationships).

A CERTAIN VULNERABILITY

There is a certain vulnerability that is a part to being a receiver. In regard to reproduction (sexual relationships), the man is the contributing factor while the woman is the receiver. And what is true of the natural is true of the spiritual. Men tend to act out of what they perceive to be facts, while women tend to react out of their emotions.

If your actions and moods are not a reaction to the probing of the Holy Spirit, then you are reacting to the subtle taunting of the enemy. He is trying to produce his destructive fruit in your home, heart, and even in your relationships.

So *receiver*, be careful what you *receive!* Moods and attitudes that Satan would offer, you need to resist. Tell the enemy, "This is not me, and I don't receive it." It is his job to offer it . . . and your job to resist it. If you do your job, all will go well.

Submit yourselves, then, to God. Resist the devil, and he will flee from you.

JAMES 4:7 NIV

Don't allow the enemy to plug into you and violate you through his subtle seductions. He is a giver, and he is looking for a receiver. You must discern his influence if you are going to rebuke him. Anything that comes and any mood that is not in agreement with God's Word, is Satan trying to plug into the earthly realm through your life. He wants you to believe you cannot change. He loves prisons and chains!

ACCEPTING LIPS

Statements like, "This is just the way I am," or "I am in a terrible mood today," come from lips that accept what they ought to reject. So never allow yourself to settle for anything less than the attitude God wants you to have in your heart. Don't let Satan have your day, your husband, or your home. Eve could have thrown the devil out of Eden!

Neither give place to the devil.

EPHESIANS 4:27

It is not enough to reject the enemy's plan. You must nurture the Word of the Lord. You need to draw the promise of God and His vision for the future to your breast. It is a natural law that anything not fed will die. And whatever you have drawn to your breast is what is growing in your life. So, breast-feeding holds several advantages for what you are feeding. First, it hears your heartbeat. Second, it is warmed by your closeness. And third, it draws nourishment from you.

But be cautious. Be sure you are nurturing what you want to grow, and starving what you want to die. As you read this, you may feel that life is passing you by. You may be experiencing success in one area, and gross defeat in others.

15

You need a burning desire for the future—the kind of desire that overcomes past fear and inhibitions. You will remain chained to your past and all the secrets therein until you decide enough is enough!

THERE IS AN EARTHQUAKE COMING INTO YOUR PRISON!

I am telling you that when your desire for the future peaks, you can break out of prison. I challenge you to sit down and write thirty things you would like to do with your life and scratch them off, one by one, as you accomplish them. There is no way you can plan for the future while dwelling in the past at the same time.

I feel an earthquake coming into your prison! It is midnight—the turning point of days! It is your time for a change. So praise God and escape out of the dungeons of your past!

And at midnight Paul and Silas prayed, and sang praises unto God: and the prisoners heard them. And suddenly there was a great earthquake, so that the foundations of the prison were shaken: and immediately all the doors were opened, and every one's bands were loosed.

ACTS 16:25-26

Have you ever noticed how hard it is to communicate with distracted people who will not give you their attention? They almost seem weird. They do not respond! There is a principle to learn here. Paul and Silas were completely preoccupied with God in the midst of their pain. Pain will not continue to rehearse itself in the life of a preoccupied, distracted person.

Every woman has something she wishes she could forget. Forgetting isn't a memory lapse; it is a memory release! Like carbon dioxide the body can no longer use, exhale it and let it go out of your spirit. Set your mind on God, and let God set you free.

Brethren, I count not myself to have apprehended: but this one thing I do, forgetting those things which are behind, and reaching forth unto those things which are before, I press toward the mark for the prize of the high calling of God in Christ Jesus. Let us therefore, as many as be perfect, be thus minded: and if in any thing ye be otherwise minded, God shall reveal even this unto you.

PHILIPPIANS 3:13–15

Jesus set the infirm woman free. She was able to stand upright. The crippling condition of her infirmity was removed by the God who cares, sees and calls our infirmities to the dispensary of healing and deliverance. You can call upon Him even in the middle of the night. Like a 24-hour medical center, you can reach Him at any time. He is touched by the feeling of your infirmity.

For we have not an high priest which cannot be touched with the feeling of our infirmities; but was in all points tempted like as we are, yet without sin.

HEBREWS 4:15

In the name of our High Priest, Jesus Christ, I curse the infirmity that has bowed the backs of God's women. I pray that as we share together out of the Word of God, the Holy Spirit will roll you into God's recovery room where you can fully realize that your trauma is over.

And I am excited to say that God never loosed anybody that He wasn't going to use mightily. May God reveal His healing and purpose as we continue to seek Him.

CHAPTER TWO

Broken Arrows

Children are living epistles that should stand as evidence to the future that the past made some level of contribution.

Lo, children are an heritage of the Lord: and the fruit of the womb is his reward. As arrows are in the hand of a mighty man; so are children of the youth. Happy is the man that hath his quiver full of them: they shall not be ashamed, but they shall speak with the enemies in the gate.

PSALM 127:3-5

The birth of a child is still the greatest miracle I have ever seen. Standing in the sterile white environment of that hospital maternity ward with the smell of disinfectant strong on my hands like some strange new cologne, they handed me my link into the future. They handed me my ambassador to the next generation. Blinking, winking, squirming little slice of love, wrapped in a blanket and forever fastened to my heart . . . we had just had a baby! To me a piece of heaven had been pushed through the womb of our consummated love.

LIVING EPISTLES

Children are living epistles that should stand as evidence to the future that the past made some level of contribution. The psalmist David wrote a brief note that is as loud as an atomic bomb which speaks to the heart of men concerning their attitude toward their offspring. Remember, this was David, the man whose indiscretion with Bathsheba had produced a love child.

Though inappropriately conceived, David's baby was loved nonetheless. David loved it so much that he laid upon the ground in sackcloth and ashes, praying feverishly for mercy, as his child squirmed in the icy hands of death. Then, suddenly, a cold silence slowly grew in his tent. The squirming stopped. The crying stilled. David's baby had gone into eternal rest.

ARROWS IN OUR HANDS

If anybody knows the value of children, it is those who just left theirs in the ground. *"As arrows are in the hand of a mighty man; so are children of the youth,"* says King David, whose arrow they lowered into the ground.

So why did David compare children to arrows? Maybe it was because of their potential to be propelled into the future. Perhaps it was for the intrinsic gold mine that lies in the heart of every child who is "shot" through the womb. Or maybe he was trying to tell us that children go where we, their parents, aim them. Could it be that we, as parents, must be responsible enough to place them in the kind of bow that will accelerate their success and emotional well-being? I think so. How happy I am to have my quiver full of arrows!

AN ARROW SHOT

If someone must be hurt, if it ever becomes necessary to bear pains, weather strong winds, or withstand trials and opposition, let it be adults . . .

not their children. I was my father's arrow and my mother's heart. My father is dead, but his arrows are yet soaring in the wind. You will never know him; he is gone. However, my brother, my sister and I are flying, soaring, scientific proof that he was, and through us, continues to be.

So don't worry about me; I am an arrow shot. If I don't succeed, I have had the greatest riches known to man. I have had an opportunity to test the limits of my destiny. Whatever happens will happen. I can accept the fate before me. But whether preferred or rejected, let the record show: I am here. My father aimed me, and now I pray, "Oh, God, let me hit my target!" If I miss and plummet to the ground, then at least I can say, "I have been shot!"

BROKEN ARROWS

It is for the arrows of this generation that we must pray. We must pray for those who are being aimed at the streets and drugs and perversion. Not all of them, but some of them, have been broken in the quiver!

I write to every empty-eyed child I have ever seen sit at my desk with tears and trembling lips struggling to tell their unmentionable secret.

I write to the trembling voice of every caller who spoke into a telephone the secret they could not keep and could not tell.

I write to every husband who holds a woman every night who was a child lost in space, a rosebud crushed before you met her, a broken arrow shaking in the quiver.

And I write to every lady who hides behind her silk dresses and leather purses a terrible secret that makeup can't seem to cover, and long showers will not wash.

Some people call them abused children. Some call them victimized. Some call them statistics. But I call them broken arrows.

Whose hand is this that fondles the bare, flat chest of a little girl? Whose fingers linger upon the flesh he helped to create? Why has the love that should be mama's come to snuggle under daughter?

"Can someone tell me how to rinse the feeling of fingers off my mind?" This is the cry of little children all over this country. This is the cry of worried minds clutching dolls and riding bicycles. Of little girls and even little boys sitting on school buses who got more for Christmas than they could ever show and tell.

MENDING ARROWS

Today the Church must realize that the adult problems we are fighting to correct, are often rooted in the ashes of such childhood experiences. How delicate is the touch of a surgeon's hand. Who needs surgery under a butchering hacksaw? So it is in the ministry. There is a different prerequisite for effectiveness than what the textbooks alone can provide. Ours is not a medicine that can be mixed by a pharmacist. Our patients' wounds are in the heart. We don't need medicine; we need miracles.

I always laugh at the carnal mind that picks up books like this to critique the approach of the prophet. They weigh the words of divine wisdom against the data they have studied. Many have more faith in a textbook written by a person whose eyes may be clouded by their own secrets, than to rely upon the word of a God who knows the end from the beginning.

Whatever a psychologist learned, he either read in a book, heard in a lecture, or discovered in an experiment. I do appreciate the many who have been helped through these precious hearts. Yet I know that, at best, they are practicing an uncertain method on people as they ramble through the closets of a troubled person's mind. What they need is divine intervention!

If there is something minor wrong with my car, like a radiator hose needing replacement or a tire that needs to be changed, I can take it almost anywhere. But if I suspect there is serious trouble with it, I always take it to the dealer. The manufacturer knows his product better than the average mechanic. So like the dealership, ministers may work with, but need not be intimidated by, the sciences of the mind! Child abuse is no radiator hose.

God is not practicing. He is the manufacturer. He is accomplished. We need to share God-given, biblical answers to troubling questions as we deal with the highly sensitive areas of sexually abused children.

COMPASSION AND CHANGE

I earnestly believe that where there is no compassion, there can be no lasting change. As long as Christian leadership secretly jeers and sneers at the perversion that comes into the Church, there will be no healing. Perversion is the offspring of abuse! As long as we crush what is already broken by our own prejudices and phobias, there will be no healing. The enemy robs us of our healing power by robbing us of our concern.

Compassion is the mother of miracles! When the storm had troubled the waters and the disciples thought they would die, they didn't challenge Christ's power; they challenged His compassion. They went to the back of the ship and said, ". . . Carest thou not that we perish?" (Mark 4:38). They understood that if there is no real compassion, then there can be no miracle.

Until we, as priests, are touched with the feelings of our parishioners' illnesses rather than just being turned off by their symptoms, they will not be healed. Also, to every husband who wants to see his wife healed and to every mother who has a little girl with a woman's problem: The power to heal is in the power to care.

ARE YOU A BROKEN ARROW?

If you are a broken arrow, please allow someone into your storm. I know you usually do not allow anyone to come to your aid. And I realize a breach of trust may have left you leery of everyone. But the walls you have built to protect yourself have also imprisoned you.

BE LOOSED!

The Lord wants to *loose* you out of your dungeon of fear! He does care. No one would take hours away from themselves and from their family praying for you, preaching to you, or even writing this to you if they didn't care. *Rise and be healed in the name of Jesus!*

What happened to the disciples as their ship was tossed and they questioned the Lord's concern? Jesus rebuked the storm! How could they have thought that the God who was sailing with them didn't care about the storm? When Jesus said, ". . . Peace, be still. . . !" (Mark 4:39) there was a great calm. Jesus does care. He is full of compassion. And to you today, He is still saying, "Peace, be still!"

> *But when he saw the multitudes, he was moved with compassion on them, because they fainted, and were scattered abroad, as sheep having no shepherd.*
>
> MATTHEW 9:36

> *And Jesus went forth, and saw a great multitude, and was moved with compassion toward them, and he healed their sick.*
>
> MATTHEW 14:14

> *And Jesus, moved with compassion, put forth his hand, and touched him, and saith unto him, "I will; be thou clean."*
>
> MARK 1:41

> *And Jesus, when he came out, saw much people, and was moved with compassion toward them, because they were as sheep not having a shepherd: and he began to teach them many things.*
>
> MARK 6:34

"Then the lord of that servant was moved with compassion, and loosed him, and forgave him the debt."

MATTHEW 18:27

Preceding miracle after miracle, compassion provoked Christ's power. We can build all the churches we want. We can decorate them with fine tapestry and ornate artifacts. But if people cannot find a loving voice within our hallowed walls, they will pass through unaltered by our clichés and religious rhetoric.

LOOKING CHILD ABUSE IN THE FACE

We can no longer ostracize the victim and let the assailant escape! Every time you see some insecure, vulnerable, intimidated adult who has unnatural fear in her eyes, low self-esteem or an apologetic posture, she is saying, "Carest thou not that I perish?"

Every time you see a bra-less woman in men's jeans, choosing to act like a man rather than to sleep with one, and every time you see a handsome young man who could have been someone's father walking like someone's mother—you may be looking child abuse in the face. If you think it's ugly, you're right. And if you think it's wrong, you're right again. But if you think it can't be healed, you're dead wrong! If you look closely into these eyes I've so feebly tried to describe, you will sense that something in this person is weak, hurt, maimed or disturbed, but fixable.

PAIN ISN'T PREJUDICED

These splintered, broken arrows come in all colors and forms. Some are black, some are white. Some are rich, some are poor. One thing about pain, though . . . it isn't prejudiced. Camouflaged, behind the walls of otherwise successful lives, successful people often wrestle with secret pain. So we must not narrow the scope of our ministries. Many people bear no outward signs of trauma as dramatic as I have described. Yet there are tragedies in their lives severe enough to have destroyed them, had God not held them together.

To God be the glory. He is a magnificent Healer!

Each person who has been through these adversities has their own story. Some have been blessed by not having to experience any such circumstance. Let the strong bear the infirmities of the weak! God can greatly use you to restore wholeness to others who walk in varying degrees of brokenness. After all, every car accident doesn't have the same assessment of damage. Most of us have had some degree of cracking, submitting to the ineffective narcotics of a sinful and often perverted lifestyle.

But to those who have fallen prey to Satan's snares, we must teach righteousness. The fact that we have persevered is a testimony to all who understand themselves to be broken arrows.

And they brought young children to him, that he should touch them: and his disciples rebuked those that brought them. But when Jesus saw it, he was much displeased, and said unto them, "Suffer the little children to come unto me, and forbid them not: for of such is the kingdom of God. Verily I say unto you, Whosoever shall not receive the kingdom of God as a little child, he shall not enter therein." And he took them up in his arms, put his hands upon them, and blessed them.

MARK 10:13–16

It is interesting to me that just before this account took place in Scripture, the Lord was ministering on the subject of adultery and divorce. When

He brought the subject up, someone brought the children to Him so He could touch them.

BROKEN HOMES PRODUCE BROKEN CHILDREN

Broken homes often produce broken children. It is the little ones who are often caught in the crossfire of angry parents. It reminds me of a newscast report I heard on the Gulf War. It was a listing of the many young men who were accidentally killed by their own military. They were killed innocently in the confusion of the battle. The newscaster used a term I had not heard before. He called it "friendly fire." I thought, *What is friendly about bleeding to death with your face buried in the hot sand of a strange country? I mean, it doesn't help much when I am dead!* Many children are wounded by the friendly fire of angry parents.

I wonder who these nameless persons were who had the insight and wisdom to bring the children to the Master? They brought the children to Him that He might touch them. What a strange interruption to a discourse on adultery and divorce. Here came these little children dragging dirty blankets and blank gazes into the presence of God while He was dealing with grown-up problems. When He saw them, He took time from His busy schedule, not so much to counsel them, but to touch them. That's all it takes.

A HIGH CALLING

I salute all the wonderful people who work with children. Whether through children's church or public school, you have a very high calling. Don't forget to touch their lives with a word of hope and a smile of encouragement. It may be the only one some of them will receive. You are the builders of our future. So be careful, you may be building a house that we will have to live in!

What was wrong with these disciples that made them angry at some nameless person who aimed these little arrows at the only answer they might ever have gotten to see? Jesus stopped teaching on the cause of divorce and marital abuse to touch the victim. He stopped to minister to the effect of the abuse and told them to suffer the little children to come. Suffer the suffering to come!

It is hard to work with hurting people, but the time has come for us to suffer the suffering to come. Anything, whether an injured animal or a hospital patient, if it is hurt, is unhappy. We cannot get a wounded lion to jump through hoops! Hurting children as well as hurting adults can carry the unpleasant aroma of bitterness. But in spite of the challenge, it is foolish to give up. So they brought the "ouch" to the band-aid, and He stopped the message of His mission.

Imagine tiny hands outstretched, little faces upturned, perching like sparrows on His knee. They came to get a touch, but Jesus always gives us more than we expect. He held them with His loving arms. He touched them with His sensitive hands. But most of all, He blessed them with His compassionate heart!

I am concerned that we maintain our compassion. How can we be in the presence of a loving God and not love these little ones? When Jesus blessed the children, He challenged the adults to become as children. Oh, to be a child again! To allow ourselves the kind of relationship with God that we may have missed as a child!

Sometimes we need to allow the Lord to adjust the damaged places of our past. I am glad to say that God provides arms which allow grown children to climb up like little children to be nurtured through the tragedies of early days. Isn't it nice to toddle into the presence of God and let Him hold you in His arms? In God, we can become children again. Salvation is God giving us a chance to start over again. He will not abuse the children that come to Him.

CLIMB INTO YOUR FATHER'S ARMS

It is so important that we learn how to worship and adore our God. There is no better way to climb into His arms. Even if you were exposed to grown-up situations when you were a child, God can reverse what you have been through. He will let the grown-up person experience the joy of being a child in His presence!

Through praise, I approach Him like a toddler on unskillful legs. In worship, I kiss His face and am held by the caress of His anointing. He has no ulterior motive. His caress is safe and wholesome.

> *"Because thou shalt forget thy misery, and remember it as waters that pass away: and thine age shall be clearer than the noonday; thou shalt shine forth, thou shalt be as the morning. And thou shalt be secure, because there is hope; yea, thou shalt dig about thee, and thou shalt take thy rest in safety. Also thou shalt lie down, and none shall make thee afraid; yea, many shall make suit unto thee."*
>
> JOB 11:16–19

It is inconceivable to the injured that the injury can be forgotten. However, as I mentioned in chapter one, to forget isn't to develop amnesia. It is to reach a place where the misery is pulled from the wounded one's memory, as a stinger is pulled out of an insect bite. Once the stinger is gone, healing is inevitable.

The above passage in Job points out so eloquently that the memory is as "waters that pass away." Stand in a stream with waters around your ankles, and the waters passing by at that moment, you will never see again. So it is with the misery that has challenged your life: Let it go, let it pass away. And he says, the brilliance of morning is in sharp contrast to the darkness of night. Simply stated, it was night, but now it is day.

Perhaps David understood the aftereffects of traumatic deliverance when he said, ". . . Weeping may endure for a night, but joy cometh in the morning" (Psalm 30:5b). There is such a security that comes when we are safe in the arms of God. It is when we become secure in our relationship with God that we begin to allow the past to fall from us as a garment. We may remember it, but we choose not to wear it!

RESTING IN HIS PRESENCE

I am convinced that resting in the relationship we have with God heals us from the feelings of vulnerability. It is a shame that many Christians have not yet rested in the promise of God. Everyone needs reassurance. Little girls as well as grown women need that sense of security. In the process of creating Eve, the mother of all living, His timing was crucial. In fact, God did not unveil her until everything she needed was provided. From establishment to relationship, all things were in order. He knew the woman would tend to need stability. It is innate. He knew she would want no sudden changes that would disrupt or compromise her security.

MEANT TO BE COVERED

Woman was meant to be covered. Originally Adam was her covering. He was to nurture and protect her. My sister, you were made to be covered even as a child. If someone "uncovered" you, there is a feeling of being violated. Even when these feelings are suppressed, and they often are, they are still powerful.

I think it is interesting that when the Bible talks about incest, it uses the word *uncover*. Sexual abuse violates the covering of a family and the responsible persons whom we looked to for guidance. This stripping away of right relationship leaves us exposed to the infinite reality of corrupt, lustful imaginations. Like fruit peeled too soon, it is damaging to uncover what God had wanted to remain protected!

Who among us can re-peel a banana once it has been peeled? The Bible says, ". . . With men it is impossible, but not with God: for with God all things are possible" (Mark 10:27).

> *"None of you shall approach to any that is near of kin to him, to uncover their nakedness: I am the Lord."*
>
> LEVITICUS 18:6

To molest a child is to uncover them. It leaves them feeling unprotected. Do you realize that one of the things the blood of Jesus Christ does is cover us? Like Noah's sons who covered their father's nakedness, the blood of Jesus will cover the uncovered. He will not allow you to spend the rest of your life exposed and violated.

God spoke a message through Ezekiel to the nation of Israel with an illustration of an abused woman. He spoke about how, as a child, this little girl was not cared for properly. But that He passed by and swaddled and cared for her as a baby. He also said the baby would have bled to death if He hadn't stopped the bleeding.

> *"Then I passed by and saw you kicking about in your blood, and as you lay there in your blood I said to you, 'Live!' I made you grow like a plant of the field. You grew up and developed and became the most beautiful of jewels. Your breasts were formed and your hair grew, you who were naked and bare. Later I passed by, and when I looked at you and saw that you were old enough for love, I spread the corner of my garment over you and covered your nakedness. I gave you my solemn oath and entered into a covenant with you, declares the Sov-*

ereign Lord, and you became mine. I bathed you with water and washed the blood from you and put ointments on you. I clothed you with an embroidered dress and put leather sandals on you. I dressed you in fine linen and covered you with costly garments."

EZEKIEL 16:6–10 NIV

Did you know that God can stop the bleeding of an abused child? Even as you grow older, He still watches out for you! He will cover your nakedness. Reach out and embrace the fact that God has been watching over you all of your life. My sister, He covers you, He clothes you, and He blesses you! Rejoice in Him in spite of the broken places. God's grace is sufficient for your needs and your scars. He will anoint you with oil.

GOD'S INTENSIVE CARE

The anointing of the Lord be upon you now! May it bathe, heal and strengthen you as never before. For the hurting, God has intensive care. There will be times in your life when God nurtures you through crisis situations. You may not even realize how many times God has already intervened to relieve the tensions and stresses of day-to-day living. Because every now and then, He does us a favor. Yes, a favor—something we didn't earn or can't even explain except as the loving hand of God. He knows when the load is overwhelming. And many times He moves (it seems to us) just in the nick of time.

The Bible instructs men to dwell with women according to knowledge (1 Peter 3:7). It will pay every husband to understand that many, many women do not deal easily with such stress as unpaid bills and financial disorder. Because of the way God created women, a feeling of security is a plus, especially in reference to the home. That same principle is important in our relationship with God. He is constantly reassuring us that we might have a consolation and a hope for the soul, the mind and emotions, steadfast and unmovable. He gives us security and assurance.

*Because God wanted to make the unchanging nature of his pur-
pose very clear to the heirs of what was promised, he confirmed it
with an oath. God did this so that, by two unchangeable things in
which it is impossible for God to lie, we who have fled to take hold of
the hope offered to us may be greatly encouraged.*

HEBREWS 6:17–18 NIV

BROKEN ARROW FEAR

"Also thou shalt lie down, and none shall make thee afraid . . ." is the
Word of God to you (Job 11:19). God wants to bring you to a place of rest,
where there is no pacing the floor and no glaring through frightened eyes at
those with whom you are involved. Like a frightened animal backed into a
corner, we can become fearful and angry because we don't feel safe. So
Christ says, "Woman, thou art loosed!"

There is no torment like inner-torment. How can you run from yourself?
No matter what you achieve in life, if the clanging, rattling chains of old
ghosts are not laid to rest, you will not have any real sense of peace and
inner joy. God says, "None shall make thee afraid." And ". . . perfect love
casteth out fear . . ." (1 John 4:18).

It is a miserable feeling to spend your life in fear. Many grown women
live in a fear that resulted from broken arrow experiences. This kind of fear
can manifest itself in jealousy, depression and many other distresses. As you
allow the past to pass over you as waters moving in the sea, you will begin
to live and rest in a new assurance. God loves you so much that He is even
concerned about your rest. So take authority over every flashback and every
dream that keeps you linked to the past. Even as we share together here,
the peace of God will do a new thing in your life. I encourage you to claim
Job 11:16–19 as yours.

SIMPLER DAYS

I was raised in the rich, robust Appalachian mountains of West Virginia where the plush greenery accentuates the majestic peaks of the rugged, mountainous terrain. The hills sit around the river's edge like court stenographers, recording the events of the ages without expression or interference. I learned as a child how to entertain myself by running up and down the trails and scenic paths of our community, splashing in the creek beds and singing songs to the wind. This kind of simplistic joy is, to me, characteristic of that time when children were not as complex as they are now.

If you know much about the Appalachian mountains, you know they were the backyard for many, many Indians in days gone by. During my childhood, occasionally my classmates or I would find old Indian memorabilia in the rocks and creek beds in the hills. There are many large, man-made hills that the Indians called mounds, which served as cemeteries for the more affluent members of the tribes.

The most common things we found were discarded arrowheads that were carved to a point and beaten flat. Perhaps an Indian brave from the pages of history had thrown away an arrow, assuming he had gotten out of it all the use that he possibly could. Though worthless to him, it was priceless to us as we retrieved it from its hiding place and saved it in a safe and sacred place.

GOD GATHERS BROKEN ARROWS

In the same way, I believe God gathers discarded children who, like arrows, have been thrown away from the quiver of vain and ruthless people. If children are like arrows in the quiver of a mighty man, then broken arrows thrown away by that same man belong to our God. He is forever finding treasure in the discarded refuse of our confused society.

> *And they shall be mine, saith the Lord of hosts, in that day when I make up my jewels; and I will spare them, as a man spareth his own son that serveth him.*
>
> MALACHI 3:17

Please, Holy Spirit, translate these meager words into a deluge of cleansing and renewal. I pray that you who have been marred, would allow the reconstructive hand of the Potter to mend the broken places in your lives. Amidst affairs and struggles, needs and incidents, may the peace and calmness of knowing God cause the birth of fresh dreams. But most of all, may it lay to rest old fears.

CHAPTER THREE

That Was Then

Many have more faith in a
textbook written by a person
whose eyes may be clouded by
their own secrets, than to rely
on the Word of God who
knows the end from the
beginning.

M any Christians experienced the new birth early in their childhood. It is beneficial to have the advantage of Christian ethics. I'm not sure what it would have been like to have been raised in the Church insulated from worldliness and sin. Sometimes I envy those who have been able to live victoriously all of their lives. But most of us have not had that kind of life. My concern is the many persons who have lost their sensitivity for others and who suffer from spiritual arrogance. Jesus condemned the Pharisees for their spiritual arrogance, yet many times that same self-righteous spirit creeps into the Church.

UNHOLY HOLINESS

There are those who define holiness as what one wears or what a person eats. For years churches displayed the name "holiness" because they monitored a person's outward appearance. But they weren't truly looking at character. Often, they were carried away with whether someone should wear makeup or jewelry when thousands of people were destroying themselves on drugs and prostitution. Priorities were confused. Unchurched people who came to church had no idea why the minister would emphasize outward apparel when people were bleeding inside.

The fact is, we were all born in sin and shaped in iniquity. We have no true badge of righteousness that we can wear on the outside. God concluded all are in sin so He might save us from ourselves (Galatians 3:22). It wasn't the act of sin, but the state of sin, that brought us into condemnation. We were all born in sin. Equally and individually we were shaped in iniquity without one race or sociological group escaping the fact of Adam's sinful heritage.

MAJORING ON THE MINORS

No one person needs any more of the blood of Jesus than the other. Jesus died once and for all. Humanity must come to God on equal terms. Each individual is totally helpless to earn his or her way to Him. When we come to Him with this attitude, He raises us up by the blood of Christ. He doesn't raise us up because we do good things. He raises us up because we have faith in the finished work on the cross.

Many in the Church were striving for holiness. What we were striving to perfect had already fallen and will only be restored at the second coming of the Lord. We were trying to perfect flesh. But flesh is in enmity against God, whether we paint it or not.

The Church frequently has, and still does, majored on the minors. When that begins to happen, it is a sign that the Church has lost touch with the world and with the inspiration of the Lord. It is no longer reaching out to the lost. A church that focuses on the external has lost its passion for souls. When we come into that position, we have attained a pseudo-holiness. It's a false sanctity.

WHAT IS HOLINESS?

To understand holiness, we must first separate the pseudo from the genuine, because when you come into a church, it is possible to walk away feeling like a second-class citizen. Many start going overboard trying to be a super spiritual person in order to compensate for an embarrassing past. You can't earn deliverance. You have to just receive it by faith. Christ is the only righteousness that God will accept. If outward sanctity had impressed God, Christ would have endorsed the Pharisees.

However, there is a sanctity of your spirit that comes through the blood of the Lord Jesus Christ which sanctifies the innermost part of your being. Certainly, once you get cleaned up in your spirit, it will be reflected in your character and conduct. You won't dress like Mary Magdalene did before she met the Master. The Spirit of the Lord will give you boundaries. On the other hand, people must be loosed from the chains of guilt and condemnation. Many women in particular have been bound by manipulative messages that specialize in control and dominance.

THE ONLY HOSPITAL FOR WOUNDED SOULS

The Church must open its doors and allow people who have a past to enter in. What often happens is they're spending years in the back pew trying to pay through obeisance for something in the past. Congregations are often unwilling to release reformed women. Remember, the same blood that cleanses the man can restore the woman also.

The Bible never camouflaged the weaknesses of the people God used. God used David and God used Abraham. We must divorce our embarrassment about wounded people. Yes, we've got wounded people. Yes, we've got hurting people. And sometimes they break the boundaries becoming lascivious and out of control. When they do, we have to readmit them into the hospital and allow them to be treated again. But that's what the Church is designed to do. The Church is the only hospital for wounded souls.

The staff in a hospital understands that periodically people get sick and they need a place to recover. Now, I'm not condoning the sin. I'm just explaining that it's a reality. Many of those in Scripture were unholy. The only holy man out of all the characters in the Bible is Jesus Christ, the righteousness of God.

FOCUSING ON HURTING PEOPLE

We have all wrestled with something, though it may not always be the same challenge. My struggle may not be yours. If I'm wrestling with something that's not a problem for you, you do not have the responsibility of judging me when all the while you are wrestling with something equally as incriminating.

Jesus' actions were massively different from ours. He focused on hurting people. Every time He saw a hurting person, He reached out and ministered to their need.

Once when He was preaching, He looked through the crowd and saw a man with a withered hand. He immediately healed him (Mark 3:1–5). He sat with the prostitutes and the winebibbers, not the upper echelon of His community. In fact, Jesus surrounded Himself with broken, bleeding, dirty people. He called a woman who was crippled and bent over (Luke 13:11–13). She had sat in the synagogue for years and years. Nobody had helped that woman until Jesus saw her. When He did, He called her to the forefront.

At first when I thought about His calling her, I thought, *How rude to call her.* Why didn't He speak the word and heal her in her seat? Perhaps God wants to see us moving toward Him. We need to invest in our own deliverance. We will bring a testimony out of a test. I also believe that someone else there who saw Jesus ministering had problems. When we can see someone else overcoming a handicap, it helps us to overcome.

HEALING THE WOUNDS OF THE PAST

We can't know how long it took the woman to get up to the front. Handicapped people don't move as fast as others do. As believers, we often don't grow as fast as other people grow because we've been suffering for a long time. We are incapacitated. Often what is simple for one person is extremely difficult for another. But Jesus challenged this woman's limitations. He called her anyway.

Thank God He calls women with a past. He reaches out and says, "Get up! You can come to Me." Regardless of what a person has done, or what kind of abuse one has suffered, He still calls. We may think our secret is worse than anyone else's. But rest assured that He knows all about it, and still draws us with an immutable call.

Jesus said, "Come unto me, all ye that labour and are heavy laden, and I will give you rest" (Matthew 11:28).

So no matter how difficult life seems, people with a past need to make their way to Jesus. Regardless of the obstacles within and without, they must reach out to Him. You may have a baby out of wedlock cradled in your arms, but keep pressing on. You may have been abused and molested and never able to talk to anyone about it, but don't cease reaching out for Him. You don't have to tell everyone your entire history. Just know that He calls, on purpose, women with a past. He knows your history and He called you anyway.

God will give you a miracle. He will do it powerfully in public. And many will say, "Is this the same woman who was bent over and wounded in the church?" Perhaps others will think, "Is this the same woman who had one foot in the church and the other in an affair?"

❧

JESUS WAS INTIMATE WITH "COLORFUL" PEOPLE

Many of the people who were a part of the ministry of Jesus' earthly life were people with colorful pasts. Some had indeed always looked for the Messiah to come. Others were involved in things that were immoral and inappropriate.

A good example is Matthew. He was a man who worked in an extremely distasteful profession. He was a tax collector. Few people today like tax collectors. Their reputation was even worse at that time in history. Matthew collected taxes for the Roman empire. He had to have been considered a traitor by those who were faithful Jews. The Romans were their oppressors. How could he have forsaken his heritage and joined the Romans?

And tax collectors did more than simply receive taxes for the benefit of the government. They were frequently little better than common extortioners. They had to collect a certain amount for Rome, but anything they could collect above that set figure was considered the collector's commission. Therefore, they frequently claimed excessive taxes. They often acted like common thieves.

But regardless of his past, Jesus called Matthew to be a disciple. He later served as a great apostle and wrote one of the books of the New Testament. Much of the history and greatness of Jesus would be lost to us were it not for Jesus calling Matthew, a man with a past. We must maintain a strong line of demarcation between a person's past and present.

PEOPLE WITH A PAST

These were the people Jesus wanted to reach. And He was criticized for being around such questionable characters. Everywhere He went the oppressed and the rejected followed Him because they knew that He offered mercy and forgiveness.

And it came to pass, as Jesus sat at meat in the house, behold, many publicans and sinners came and sat down with him and his disciples. And when the Pharisees saw it, they said unto his disciples, "Why eateth your Master with publicans and sinners?" But when Jesus heard that, he said unto them, "They that be whole need not a physician, but they that are sick."

MATTHEW 9:10-12

People with a past have always been able to come to Jesus. He makes them into something wonderful and marvelous. It is said that Mary Magdalene was a prostitute. Christ was moved with compassion for even this base kind of human existence. He never used a prostitute for sex, but He certainly loved them into God's kingdom.

When Christ was teaching in the temple courts, there were those who tried to trap Him in His words. They knew that His ministry appealed to the masses of lowly people. They thought that if they could get Him to say some condemning things, the people wouldn't follow Him anymore.

And the scribes and Pharisees brought unto him a woman taken in adultery; and when they had set her in the midst, they say unto him, "Master, this woman was taken in adultery, in the very act. Now Moses in the law commanded us, that such should be stoned: but what sayest thou?" This they said, tempting him, that they might have to accuse him. But Jesus stooped down, and with his finger wrote on the ground, as though he heard them not. So when they continued asking him, he lifted up himself, and said unto them, "he that is without sin among you, let him first cast a stone at her."

JOHN 8:3-7

41

Clearly Jesus saw the foolish religious pride in their hearts. He was not condoning the sin of adultery. He simply understood the need to meet people where they were and minister to their need. He also saw the pride in the Pharisees and ministered correction to that pride. He saw the wounded woman and ministered forgiveness. Justice demanded that she be stoned to death. But God's mercy threw the case out of court.

Have you ever wondered where the man was who had been committing adultery with this woman? She was caught in the very act. So surely they knew who the man was. There still seems to be a double standard today when it comes to sexual sin. Often we look down on a woman because of her past, but overlook who she is now. Jesus, however, knew the power of a second chance.

When Jesus had lifted up himself, and saw none but the woman, he said unto her, "Woman, where are those thine accusers? hath no man condemned thee?" She said, "No man, Lord." And Jesus said unto her, "Neither do I condemn thee: go, and sin no more."

JOHN 8:10-11

There are those today who are very much like this woman. They have come into the Church. Perhaps they have made strong commitments to Christ and have the very Spirit of God living within them. Yet they walk as cripples. They have been stoned and ridiculed. They may not be physically broken and bowed over, but they are wounded within. Somehow the Church must find room to throw off condemnation and give them life and healing.

The blood of Jesus is efficacious, cleansing the woman who feels unclean. So how can we reject what He has cleansed and made whole? Just as He said to the woman then, He proclaims today: "Neither do I condemn thee: go, and sin no more." How can the Church do any less?

THE CHAINS THAT BIND

The chains that bind are often from events that we have no control over. The woman who is abused is not responsible for the horrible events that happened in her past. Other times the chains are there because we have willfully lived lives that bring bondage and pain. But regardless of the source, Jesus comes to set us free. He is unleashing the women of His Church. He forgives, heals and restores. Women can find the potential of their future because of His wonderful power operating in their lives.

CHAPTER FOUR

The Victim Survives

Stand in a stream with waters
around your ankles. The
waters that pass by you at that
moment, you will never see
again. So it is with the misery
that has challenged your life:
Let it go, let it pass away.

Now I would like to share what is perhaps one of the most powerful stories in the Bible. It takes place in ancient Israel. The chosen people had become a great empire. Israel was at its zenith under the leadership of a godly king named David. There can be no argument that David frequently allowed his passions to lead him into moral failure. However, he was a man who recognized his failures and repented. He was a man who sought God's heart.

Although David longed to follow God, some of his passions and lusts were inherited by his children. Maybe they learned negative things from their father's failures. That is a tendency we must resist. We ought not repeat the failure of our fathers. We are most vulnerable, however, to our father's weaknesses.

And it came to pass after this, that Absalom the son of David had a fair sister, whose name was Tamar; and Amnon the son of David loved her. And Amnon was so vexed, that he fell sick for his sister Tamar; for she was a virgin; and Amnon thought it hard for him to do any thing to her. But Amnon had a friend, whose name was Jonadab, the son of Shimeah David's brother: and Jonadab was a very subtil man. And he said unto him, Why art thou, being the king's son, lean from day to day? wilt thou not tell me? And Amnon said unto him, I love Tamar, my brother Absalom's sister. And Jonadab said unto him, Lay thee down on thy bed, and make thyself sick: and when thy father cometh to see thee, say unto him, I pray thee, let my sister Tamar come, and give me meat, and dress the meat in my sight, that I may see it, and eat it at her hand. So Amnon lay down, and made himself sick: and when the king was come to see him, Amnon said unto the king, I pray thee, let Tamar my sister come, and make me a couple of cakes in my sight, that I may eat at her hand.

Then David sent home to Tamar saying, Go now to thy brother Amnon's house, and dress him meat. So Tamar went to her brother Amnon's house; and he was laid down. And she took flour, and kneaded it, and made cakes in his sight, and did bake the cakes. And she took a pan, and poured them out before him; but he refused to eat. And Amnon said, Have out all men from me. And they went out every man from him. And Amnon said unto Tamar, Bring the meat into the chamber, that I may eat of thine hand. And Tamar took the cakes which she had made, and brought them into the chamber to Amnon her brother. And when she had brought them unto him to eat, he took hold of her, and said unto her, Come lie with me, my sister. And she answered him, Nay, my brother, do not force me; for no such thing ought to be done in Israel: do not thou this folly. And I, whither shall I cause my shame to go? and as for thee, thou shalt be as one of the fools in Israel. Now therefore, I pray thee, speak unto the king; for he will not withhold me from thee.

Howbeit he would not hearken unto her voice: but, being stronger than she, forced her, and lay with her. Then Amnon hated her exceedingly; so that the hatred wherewith he hated her was greater than the love wherewith he had loved her. And Amnon said unto her, Arise, be gone. And she said unto him, There is no cause: this evil in sending me away is greater than the other that thou didst unto me. But he would not hearken unto her. Then he called his servant that ministered unto him, and said, Put now this woman out from me, and bolt the door after her. And she had a garment of divers colours upon her: for with such robes were the king's daughters that were virgins apparelled. Then his servant brought her out, and bolted the door after her. And Tamar put ashes on her head, and rent her garment of divers colours that was on her, and laid her hand on her head, and went on crying. And Absalom her brother said unto her, Hath Amnon thy brother been with thee? but hold now thy peace, my sister: he is thy brother; regard not this thing. So Tamar remained desolate in her brother Absalom's house. But when king David heard of all these things, he was very wroth.

2 SAMUEL 13:1–21

The name *Tamar* means "palm tree." Tamar is a survivor. She stands in summer and spring. She even faces fall with leaves when other trees lose theirs. She still stands. When the cold blight of winter stands up in her face, she withstands the chilly winds and remains green throughout the winter.

Tamar is a survivor. And like her, you are a survivor. Through hard times God has granted you the tenacity to endure stresses and strains.

ABUSE IS ABNORMAL USE

It's hard for me as a man to fully understand how horrible rape is for women. I can sympathize, but the violation is incomprehensible. I don't feel as vulnerable to being raped as a woman would. However, I have come to realize that rape is another creature inflicting his will on someone without her permission. It is more than just the act of sex. It is someone victimizing you. There are all kinds of rape: emotional, spiritual and physical. And there are many ways to be victimized. Abuse is abnormal use. It is terrible to misuse or abuse anyone.

GUILTY BY VICTIMIZATION

Many women feel guilty about things they had no control over. They feel guilty about being victimized. Often their original intention was to help another, but in the process they were damaged. Tamar must have been one of them.

Tamar was the king's daughter, and she was a virgin. She was a "good girl." She didn't do anything immoral. It is amazing that her own brother would be so filled with desire that he would go to such lengths to destroy his sister. He thought he was in love. But it wasn't love, it was lust. He craved her so intensely that he lost his appetite for food. He was visibly distorted with passion. Love is a giving force, while lust is a selfish compulsion centralized on gratification.

TWISTED AMNON

It is frightening to think about the nights that Amnon plotted and conjured Tamar's destruction. The intensity of his passion for her was awesome.

So much so, that even his father and cousin recognized something had altered his behavior. He was filled with lustful passion for her.

Amnon draws a picture for us of how badly the enemy wants to violate God's children. He is planning and plotting your destruction. He has watched you with wanton eyes. He has great passion and perseverance. That is why Jesus told Peter, ". . . Satan hath *desired* to have you, that he may sift you as wheat: but I have prayed for thee . . ." (Luke 22:31–32). Satan lusts after God's children. He wants you. He craves you with an animalistic passion. He awaits an opportunity for attack. In addition, he loves to use people to fulfill the same kinds of lust upon one another.

Desire is a motivating force. It can make you do things you never thought yourself capable of doing. Lust can make a man break his commitment to himself. It will cause people to reach after things they never thought they would reach for.

Like Peter, you may have gone through some horrible times, but Jesus intercedes on your behalf. No matter what struggles women have faced, confidence is found in the ministry of our High Priest. He prays for you. Faith comes when you recognize that you can't help yourself. Only trust in Christ can bring you through. Many have suffered mightily, but Christ gives the strength to overcome the attacks of Satan, and of human, selfish lust.

ALLOW CHRIST TO COME INTO THE DARK PLACES OF YOUR LIFE

Often, the residual effects of being abused linger for many years. Some never find deliverance because they never allow Christ to come into the dark places of their life. Jesus has promised to set you free from every curse of the past. If you have suffered abuse, please know that He will bring you complete healing. He wants the whole person well in body, emotions and spirit. He will deliver you from all the residue of your past. Perhaps your incident is over, but the crippling damage remains. Let Him deal with the crippling that's left in your life.

MANIPULATING THE MATERNAL

One of the things that makes many women particularly vulnerable to different types of abuse and manipulation is their maternal instinct. Wicked men frequently capitalize on this tendency in order to have their way with women. Mothers like to take care of little helpless babies. It seems that the more helpless a man acts, the more maternal a woman can become. Women instinctively are nurturers, reaching out to needy people in order to nurture, love and provide inner strength. But all too often, these healthy desires are taken advantage of by those who would fulfill their own lusts. The gift of discernment must operate in your life. There are many wonderful men. But I must warn you about Amnon. He is out there, and he is dangerous.

TWO KINDS OF RAPE

The number of cases of violence within relationships and marriages is growing at an alarming rate. The incidence of date rape is reaching epidemic proportions. And the fastest growing number of murders today is happening within relationships. Husbands and wives, and girlfriends and boyfriends are killing one another. Some women have taken to murder in order to escape the constant violence of an abusive husband. It is important that you do not allow loneliness to coerce you into Amnon's bed.

Another form of abuse is more subtle. There are those men who often coerce women into a sexual relationship by claiming that they love them. Deception is emotional rape! It is a terrible feeling to be used by someone. Looking for love in all the wrong places leads to a feeling of abuse.

A deceiver may continually promise that he will leave his wife for his lover. His lover holds on to that hope, but it never seems to come true. So he makes every kind of excuse possible for taking advantage of her. And she, because of her vulnerability, follows blindly along until the relationship has gone so far that she is trapped.

Men who have sex with women without being committed to them are just as guilty of abuse as a rapist. A woman may have given her body to such a man, but she did so because of certain expectations. When someone uses another person for sex by misleading them, it is the same as physical rape. The abuse is more subtle, but it amounts to the same thing. Both the abuser and the victim are riding into a blazing inferno. Anything can happen when the victim has had enough.

SUFFERING THE EXTREMES OF LOW SELF-ESTEEM

Some women suffer from low self-esteem. They are victims and they don't even know it. Perhaps that's you. Do you think it's your fault every time something goes wrong? It's not your fault if you are being abused in this way. However, it is your fault if you don't allow God's Word to arrest sin and weakness in your life. It is time to let go of every ungodly relationship. Do it now!

When Tamar came into that ancient Israeli bedroom, her brother took advantage of her maternal instincts. He told her that he needed help. He sought her sympathy. Then once she gave in to his requests for help, he violently raped her. Although the circumstances may be different, the same thing is happening today.

AMNON IS AMONG US

The kind of violent act that Amnon performed that night was more than an offense against a young lady. He offended God and society by committing incest. There are those who attend church who are incestuous. It still happens today, but God is saying enough is enough!

Some have been abused, misused and victimized. Some even played a part in their own demise. Then there are those who live in fear and pain because of the immoral relationships that took place in the home.

If you know this kind of pain, the Lord wants to heal you. Those who have a desperate need for male attention, usually come from a situation where there has been an absence of positive male role models in the home. Perhaps you didn't get enough nurturing as a girl. Therefore, it becomes easy to compromise and do anything to find male acceptance and love.

THE LORD IS CALLING!

The Lord is calling the hurting to Him. He will fill that void in your life. He wants to be the father you never had who will mend your heart with a positive role model. Through His Spirit, He wants to hold and nurture you. Millions have longed for a positive hug and nurturing embrace from fathers without ever receiving what they longed for. There is a way to fill that emptiness inside. It is through relationship with God.

Men, God is healing us so we can recognize that a woman who is not our wife is to be treated as our sister. Women must learn that they can have a platonic relationship with men. A brotherly and sisterly love does not include sexual intimacy. It does not include self-gratification.

There is a place in the heart of most women for an intimate, yet platonic relationship. Big brothers tend to protect their little sisters. They tend to watch for traps that may be placed in the sister's way. But abused women have confused ideas about relationships and may not understand a healthy platonic relationship with the opposite sex. This confusion comes from the past. One lady said she could never trust a man who didn't sleep with her. Actually, she had a long history of victimization that led to her poor view of relationships.

"MEN" ARE NOT THE ENEMY

Society often places a woman's worth on her sexual appeal. But nothing is further from the truth. Self-esteem cannot be earned by performance in bed. Society suggests that the only thing men want is sex. Although the male sex drive is very strong, all men are not like Amnon.

Men, in general, are not the enemy. We cannot use Amnon as a basis to evaluate all men. So don't allow an Amnon experience to taint your future. Draw a line of demarcation and say to yourself, "That was then—and this is now!"

THE CHURCH IS GOD'S CEDAR CHEST!

The Song of Solomon shows a progression of the relationship between the author and his wife. First she was his sister. Then she became his bride. He also wrote of protecting a little sister. There are many new converts in the Church who should be treated as little sisters. Solomon says, ". . . inclose her with boards of cedar" {Song of Solomon 8:9}. The Church is God's cedar chest!

God's people are to nurture and protect one another. It makes no difference how tempestuous our past life has been. Even in the face of abuse, God still cares. Allow Him the privilege of doing what Absalom did for Tamar. He took her in. He gave her a place of comfort, a place to abide.

He that dwelleth in the secret place of the most High shall abide under the shadow of the Almighty.

PSALM 91:1

Tamar laid outside Amnon's door a fragmented, bruised rose petal. Her dreams were shattered. Her confidence was violated. Her virginity was desecrated. But Absalom took her into his domain. Did you know that God has intensive care? He will take you in His arms. His love is flowing into broken lives all over the country. So don't believe for one moment that no one cares. God cares, and the Church is learning to become a conduit of His concern. At last, we are in His school of love. Jesus said, "By this shall all men know that ye are my disciples, if ye have love one to another" (John 13:35). Love embraces the totality of the other person.

SCARS FROM THE PAST

It is impossible to completely and effectively love someone without being included in that other person's history. Our history has made us who we are. The images, scars and victories that we live with have shaped us into the people we have become. We will never know who a person is until we understand where they have been.

The secret of being transformed from a vulnerable victim to a victorious, loving person is found in the ability to open your past to someone responsible enough to share your weaknesses and pains with. "Bear ye one another's burdens, and so fulfil the law of Christ," writes Paul in Galatians 6:2. You don't have to keep reliving it. You can release it.

TAKE THE FIRST STEP

There can be no better first step toward deliverance than to find a Christian counselor to share your past with. Then, come out of hiding. Of course, some care should be taken. No one is expected to air their personal life to everyone or everywhere. However, if you seek God's guidance and the help of confident leadership, you will find someone who can help you work through the pain and suffering of your victimized past.

The Church is a body. No one operates independent of another. We are all in this walk together and therefore can build one another up. Let's carry some of the load with which our sisters are burdened.

Tamar was victimized brutally, yet she survived. There is hope for the victim. If you are a victim, there is no need to feel weak if you have Jesus Christ. His power is enough to bring about the kinds of changes that will set you free. He is calling, through the work of the Holy Spirit, for you to be set free.

Walk Into the Newness

If you are a woman living today, and you're not learning spiritual warfare, you're in trouble. The enemy may be taking advantage of you.

Amnon was wicked. He brutally raped his sister Tamar. He destroyed her destiny and her future. He slashed her self-esteem. He spoiled her integrity. He broke her femininity like a twig under his feet. He assassinated her character. She went into his room a virgin with a future, but when it was over, she was a bleeding, trembling, crying mass of pain.

This is one of the saddest stories in the Bible. It reveals what people can do to one another if left alone without God. When Amnon and Tamar were left alone, he assassinated her. Tamar's body may have survived, but her femininity was destroyed. She felt she would never be the woman she should have been because it happened.

Have you ever had anything happen to you that changed you forever? Something you went through that somehow, like a palm tree, you survived? Something you knew would never let things be the same again?

Perhaps you have spent every day since then "bowed over," and you can in "no wise lift up yourself." You shout. You sing. You skip. But when no one is looking, when the crowd is gone and the lights are out, you are still that trembling, crying, bleeding mass of pain that is abused, bowed, bent backward, and crippled.

Maybe you are in the Church, but you are in trouble. People move all around you, and you laugh, even entertain them. You are fun to be around. But they don't know. You can't seem to talk about what happened in your life.

The Bible says Tamar was in trouble. The worst part about it was, after Amnon had abused her, he didn't even want her. He had messed up her life and spoiled what she was proud of. He assassinated her future and damaged her prospects. He destroyed her integrity and self-esteem. He had changed her countenance forever. And afterward, he didn't even want her. All Tamar could say was, "What you're doing to me now is worse than what you did to me at first." Or, "Raping me was horrible, but not wanting me is worse!" (2 Samuel 13:16).

When women feel unwanted, it destroys their sense of esteem and value. Some of you have gone through divorces, tragedies and adulterous relationships, and you've been left feeling unwanted. You just can't shout over that sort of thing. You can't leap over that kind of wall. It injures something about you that changes how you relate to everyone else for the rest of your life.

When Amnon rejected Tamar after he raped her, she also pleaded with him, "Don't throw me away." She was fighting for the last strands of her femininity. But Amnon called a servant and told him to, "Throw her out."

The Bible even says he hated her with a greater intensity than the love he felt for her before his violation (2 Samuel 13:15).

AMNON DOESN'T LOVE YOU

God knows that the Amnon in your life really does not love you. He's out to abuse you. His servant picked Tamar up, opened the door and threw the victimized woman out. Then as she laid on the ground outside the door—with nowhere to go—he told his servant to, "Lock the door."

What do you do when you are trapped in a transitory state, neither in nor out? When you're left lying at the door, torn up and disturbed, trembling and intimidated? The Bible says Tamar cried.

What do you do when you don't know what to do? When you're filled with regrets, pains, nightmare experiences, and are seemingly unable to find relief? Tamar stayed on the ground. And she cried.

Tamar had a coat, a cape of many colors. It was a sign of her virginity and of her future. She was going to give it to her husband one day. But she sat there and ripped it up. When she did, she was saying, "I have no future. It wasn't just that he took my body. He took my future. He took my esteem and value away."

Many of you have been physically or emotionally raped and robbed. And you have survived. But you left a substantial degree of self-esteem on Amnon's bed. Have you lost the road map that directs you back to where you were before?

A CALL OUT IN THE SPIRIT

There is a call out in the Spirit for hurting women. The Lord says, "I want you." No matter how many men like Amnon have told you, "I don't want you," God is saying, "I want you. I've seen you bent over. I've seen the aftereffects of what happened to you. I've seen you at your worst moment. And still, I want you." God hasn't changed His mind. He loves you with an everlasting love.

When Jesus encountered the infirm woman of Luke 13, He called out to her. There may have been many fine women present that day, but the Lord didn't call them forward. He reached around all of them and found that crippled woman in the back. And when He called forth that wounded, hurting woman with a past, He issued the Spirit's call to every other like her who has had their self-esteem destroyed by the intrusion of vicious circumstances.

The infirm woman must have thought, "He wants me. He wants me. I'm frayed and torn, but He wants me. I have been through trouble. I have been through this trauma, but still, He wants me." Perhaps she thought no one would ever want her again. But Jesus wanted her. He had a plan.

She may have known that it would take a while for her life to be put completely back together. She had many things to overcome. She was handicapped. She was probably filled with insecurities. Yet Jesus called her forth to give her His touch.

TURN YOURSELF TOWARD HOME

If you can identify with the feelings of this infirm woman, then know that Jesus is waiting on you and that He wants you. He sees your struggling and He knows all about your pain. He knows what happened to you eighteen years ago, ten years ago, or even last week. With patience He waits for you, as the father waited for the prodigal son. Jesus says to the hurting and crippled, "I want you enough to wait for you to hobble your way back home."

Now God says, "I'm going to deliver you and heal you. Now I'm going to renew you and release you. I'm going to tell you who you really are. Now I'm ready to reveal to you why you had to go through what you did to become what you shall become."

And God is saying, "Now I'm going to tell you a secret, something between you and Me that no one else knows. Something that Amnon didn't know, your boyfriend didn't know, and your first husband didn't know. Something that your father, uncle, brother or whoever abused you had no knowledge of. Come closer and let Me tell you. You are the daughter of a King. Your Father is the King."

YOU ARE A PRINCESS!

When the infirm woman came to Jesus, He proclaimed her freedom as she stood erect for the first time in eighteen years. When you come to Jesus, He will cause you to stand in His strength. You will know how important you are to Him. Part of your recovery will be to learn how to stand up and live in the "now" of His life, instead of the "then" of yours. That was then—but this is now.

I proclaim to the abused: There is healing going into your spirit right now. I speak life to you. I speak deliverance to you. I speak restoration to you. All in the mighty name of Jesus, in the invincible, all-powerful, ever-lasting name of Jesus. I proclaim victory to you. You will recover the loss you suffered at the hands of your abuser. You will get back every stolen item. Jesus will heal that broken twig. He will rebuild your self-esteem, your self-respect, and your integrity.

GIVE HIM ALL YOUR SECRETS

All you need to do is to allow His power and anointing to touch your hurting places. He will take care of the secrets. He touches the places where you've been assassinated. He knows the woman you would have been, the woman you should have been, the woman you could have been. God is healing and restoring her in you as you call out to Him.

The enemy wanted to change your destiny through a series of events, but God will restore you to wholeness as if the events had never happened. The triumphant woman locked inside shall come forth to where she belongs. He's delivering her. He's releasing her. He's restoring her. He's building her back. He's bringing her out. He's delivering by the power of His Spirit. ". . . Not by might, nor by power, but by my spirit, saith the Lord of hosts" (Zechariah 4:6).

GOD'S ANOINTING IS REACHING OUT TO YOU

The anointing of the living God is reaching out to you. He calls you forth to set you free. When you reach out to Him and allow the Holy Spirit to have His way, His anointing is present to deliver you. Demons will tremble. Satan wants to keep you at the door, but never let you enter. He wants to keep you down. Now his power is broken in your life.

Tamar knew the feeling of desertion. She understood that she was cast out. However, the Bible explains that Absalom came and said, "I'm going to take you in."

You too have been lying at the door. Perhaps you didn't have anywhere to go. You may have been half in and half out. You were broken and demented and disturbed. But God sent Absalom to restore his sister.

In this instance, Absalom depicts the purpose of real ministry. Thank God for the Church. It is the place where you can come broken and disgusted, and be healed, delivered and set free in the name of Jesus.

Jesus said, "The Spirit of the Lord is upon me, because he hath anointed me to preach the gospel to the poor; he hath sent me to heal the brokenhearted, to preach deliverance to the captives, and recovering of sight to the blind, to set at liberty them that are bruised" (Luke 4:18).

You may have thought that you would never rejoice again. But God declares that you can have freedom in Him now! The joy that He brings can be restored to your soul. He identifies with your pain and suffering. He knows what it is like to suffer abuse at the hands of others. Yet He proclaims joy and strength. He will give you the garment of praise instead of the spirit of heaviness (Isaiah 61:3).

HOLD UP YOUR HANDS AND HEAD

Once you have called out to Him, you can lift up your hands in praise. No matter what you have suffered, you can hold up your head. Regardless of who has hurt you, hold up your head! Forget how many times you've been married. Put aside those who mistreated you. You may have been a lesbian. You may have been a crack addict. It doesn't matter who you were. You may have even been molested. You can't change where you have been, but you can change where you are going.

Lift up your heads, O ye gates; even lift them up, ye everlasting doors; and the King of glory shall come in. Who is this King of glory? The Lord of hosts, he is the King of glory. Selah.

PSALM 24:9-10

He will restore to you that which the cankerworm and the locust ate up (Joel 2:25). He says, "I'm going to give it back to you." Maybe you wrestle with guilt. You've been hearing babies crying in your spirit. You feel so dirty. You've had abortions. You have been misused and abused. The devil keeps bringing up to you your failures of the past. But God is saying:

Come now, and let us reason together, saith the Lord: though your sins be as scarlet, they shall be as white as snow; though they be red like crimson, they shall be as wool.

ISAIAH 1:18

All my life I have had a tremendous compassion for hurting people. When other people would put their foot on them, I always tended to have

61

a ministry of mercy. Perhaps it is because I've had my own pain. When you have suffered, it makes you able to relate to other people's pain. So the Lord settled me in a ministry that just tends to cater to hurting people. Sometimes when I minister, I find myself fighting back tears. And sometimes I can hear the cries of anguished people in the crowd.

WALK INTO THE NEWNESS!

Like Tamar, you are a survivor. So you should celebrate it! Instead of agonizing over your tragedies, you should celebrate your victory and thank God you made it. I charge you to step over your adversity and walk into the newness. It is like stepping from a storm into the sunshine. Just step into it now.

God has blessed me with two little boys and two little daughters. As a father, I have found that I have a ministry of hugs. When something happens, and I really can't fix it, I just hug them. I can't change how other people treated them. I can't change what happened at school. I can't make the teacher like them. And I can't take away the insults. But I can hug them!

The Church needs to develop a ministry of hugs. I believe the best nurses are the ones who have been patients. They have compassion on the victim. If anyone understands the plight of women, it ought to be women. And if anyone understands the needs of the infirm, it ought to be the Church. The touch of the Master sets us free. The touch of a fellow pilgrim lets us know we are not alone in our plight.

RECEIVE YOUR FREEDOM NOW

The Holy Spirit is calling for the broken, infirm women to come to Jesus. He will restore and deliver. How do we come to Jesus? We come to His

Body, the Church. It is in the Church that we can hear the Word of God. The Church gives us strength and nourishment. The Church is to be the place where we share our burdens and allow others to help us with them. The Spirit calls; the burdened need only heed the call.

There are three tenses of faith! When Lazarus died, Martha, his sister, said, "Lord, if You would have been here, my brother would not have died." This is historical faith. Its view is digressive. Then when Jesus responded, "Lazarus will live again," Martha replied, "I know he will live in the resurrection." This is futuristic faith. It is progressive. But Martha also acknowledged God's working in the present when she said, "But *even now* You have the power to raise him up again" (John 11:21–27).

I feel like Martha. Even now, after all you've been through, I know that God has the power to raise you up again! This is the present tense of faith. Walk into the newness, even now.

CHAPTER SIX

Origins of Femininity

God will reward those who
perservere in seeking Him.
He may not come when you
want Him to, but He will be
right on time.

Nearly every home in America is wired for electricity. Walls are covered with receptacles that deliver the electric current. But in order to take advantage of the power, something must be plugged into the receptacle. The receptacle is the female, and the plug is the male.

Women were made like receptacles because they were made to be receivers in every area of life. Men were made to be givers. They were made to give physically, sexually and emotionally, and to provide for others in life.

The woman was made, or fashioned, out of the man, to be his helper. She was made to help him meet and accomplish his task. Through their union, men and women find wholeness in each other. In other words, a power saw has great potential for cutting, but it is ineffective until it is plugged in. The receptacle helps the power saw meet its purpose. Without that receptacle, the power saw, although mighty, remains limited.

A CERTAIN VULNERABILITY

However, there is a certain vulnerability built into the receptacle because of the different kinds of plugs it may be connected with. Receptacles, like women, are open. They are open by nature and design. Men are closed. Therefore, women must be careful what they allow to plug into them that will draw their strength. The wrong plugs may seek your help and drain your power.

Because God recognizes your vulnerability, He determined that those who would plug into the woman sexually would have to have a covenant. It was never God's intention for humanity to have casual sex. His design has always included the commitment of a covenant. So He purposed that a man who has sexual relations with a woman would be committed to her for life. And that nothing short of this commitment would meet His standards.

GOD WANTS YOU COVERED

God wants you covered like the electrical outlet is covered, so no one can tamper with your intended purpose. The married woman is covered by her husband. The single woman is covered by her chastity and morality. It is dangerous to be uncovered.

Originally, God created humanity perfect and good.

And God said, Let us make man in our image, after our likeness: and let them have dominion over the fish of the sea, and over the fowl of the air, and over the cattle, and over all the earth, and over every creeping thing that creepeth upon the earth.

GENESIS 1:26

God placed Adam in the garden He prepared for him with one simple rule: Man was not allowed to eat of the tree of the knowledge of good and evil. God wanted mankind to rely on Him for moral decisions. History records the consequences of man's attempts at making his own moral decisions after the fall. The history is bleak.

Although God had made a wonderful place for Adam to live, the man remained less than complete. He needed a woman. Keep in mind, though, that she was needed to complete his *purpose*, not his *person*. Therefore, if you are not complete as a person, marriage will not help you.

And the Lord God caused a deep sleep to fall upon Adam, and he slept: and he took one of his ribs, and closed up the flesh instead thereof; and the rib, which the Lord God had taken from man, made he a woman, and brought her unto the man.

GENESIS 2:21–22

In Genesis 3 we see that Eve allowed herself to be taken advantage of by Satan, who plugged into her the desire to see, taste, and be wise. The enemy took advantage of her weakness.

And the man said, "The woman whom thou gavest to be with me, she gave me of the tree, and I did eat."

GENESIS 3:12

Eve had given her attention over to someone else.

And the Lord God said unto the woman, "What is this that thou hast done?" And the woman said, "The serpent beguiled me, and I did eat."

GENESIS 3:13

Adam's anger is shown in his statement in Genesis 3:12, "You gave her to be with me!" to which the woman answered, "Well, I couldn't help it. He plugged into and beguiled me."

BE CAREFUL ABOUT WHO UNCOVERS YOU

You've got to be careful who you let uncover you, because, as with Eve, they can lead you to complete destruction. Notice what God did next:

> And the Lord God said unto the serpent, "Because thou hast done this, thou art cursed above all cattle, and above every beast of the field; upon thy belly shalt thou go, and dust shalt thou eat all the days of thy life: and I will put enmity between thee and the woman, and between thy seed and her seed; it shall bruise thy head, and thou shalt bruise his heel."
>
> GENESIS 3:14–15

A SPECIAL ENMITY

There is a special enmity that has been established between femininity and the enemy. There is a special conflict the enemy seeks with you. That's why you must do spiritual warfare. You must do so because of your vulnerability in certain areas, and the enmity that rages between Satan and you. So, be on your guard.

THIS IS WAR

Women do tend to be more prayerful than men once they get committed. But if you are a woman living today, and you are not learning spiritual warfare, you are in trouble. The enemy may be taking advantage of you. He is attracted to you because he knows you were designed as a receptacle to help meet someone's vision.

If the enemy can get you to help meet his vision, you will have great problems. Why? Because God said, "And I will put enmity between thee and the woman, and between thy seed and her seed . . ." (Genesis 3:15).

Now, God didn't say only "her seed and your seed." He said, "Between you and the woman." Stop and think about it. There is a special fight waged between you and the devil. Who are the victims of the most rapes in this country? Who are the victims of the most child abuse? Who are the victims of much of the sexual discrimination in the job market? And who has the most trouble getting together, unifying with each other, and collaborating? Satan has a special war with you.

Satan is continually attacking femininity. Mass populations of women have increased throughout the country. Isaiah 4:1 says the time will come when there will be seven women to every one man. According to recent statistics, we are living in those times right now. Where you have more need than supply, there is growing enmity between the woman and the enemy.

GET TRAINED FOR WAR!

If godly women do not learn how to start praying and doing effective spiritual warfare, they will not discern what is plugging into them. Perhaps you become completely vulnerable to moods and attitudes and dispositions. Perhaps you are doing things, and you don't know why. Look out, something's plugging into you. If you are tempted to rationalize, "I'm just in a bad mood. I don't know just what it is. I'm just evil. I'm tough," don't believe it, because something's plugging into you.

Unto the woman he said, "I will greatly multiply thy sorrow and thy conception; in sorrow thou shalt bring forth children; and thy desire shall be to thy husband, and he shall rule over thee."

GENESIS 3:16

God explained that birthing would come through sorrow. Everything you bring forth comes through pain. If it didn't come through pain, it probably wasn't worth much.

If you are going to *bring forth*, and I'm not merely talking about babies, I'm talking about birthing vision and purpose—you will do so with sorrow and pain. If you are going to bring forth anything in your career, in your marriage or your life, or if you are going to develop anything in your character through becoming a fruitful woman—it is going to come through sorrow. It will come through the things you suffer. And, you will enter into strength through sorrow.

SORROW IS NOT THE OBJECT: IT IS ONLY THE CANAL

Sorrow is not the object; it is simply the canal the object comes through. Many of you are mistaking sorrow for the baby, instead of the canal. In that case, all you have is pain. You ought to have a child for every sorrow. By that I mean, for every sorrow, for every intense groaning in your spirit, you ought to have something to show for it.

So don't let the devil give you sorrow without any seed. Be aware that any time you have sorrow, it is a sign that God is trying to get something through you and to you.

WOMEN GIVE LIFE LEGAL ENTRY

Women are the producers. You are the ones through whom life passes. Every child who enters into this world must come through you. Even Jesus Christ had to come through you to obtain legal entry into the world. It was required that He come through you. So you are a channel and an expression of God's blessings. If there is to be any virtue, any praise, any victory, any deliverance, it's got to come through you.

But Satan also wants to use you for legal entry into this world. He wants to use you to get into your family. That's how he destroyed the human race with the first family. He knows that you are the entrance of all things. And that you are the doors of life. So be careful what you let plug into and come through you. Close the doors to the enemy's planting. Then know that when travail comes into your spirit, it is because you are going to give birth.

And you will give birth! That is why you suffer pain. Your spirit is signaling you that something is trying to get through. So don't become so preoccupied with the pain that you forget to push the baby. Sometimes you are pushing the pain and not the baby, and you are so engrossed with what is hurting you that you are not doing what it takes to produce fruit in your life.

So when you see sorrow multiply, let it be a sign to you that God is getting ready to send something to you. Don't settle for the pain and not get the benefit. Hold out. Disregard the pain and get the promise. Understand that God has promised some things to you that He wants you to have. And know that you have got to stay there on the table until you get to the place where you ought to be in the Lord. After all, the pain is forgotten when the baby is born.

What is the pain when compared to the baby? Some may have dropped the baby. That happens when you become so engrossed with the pain that you leave the reward behind. Your attention gets focused on the wrong thing. You can be so preoccupied with how bad it hurts that you miss the joy of a vision giving birth.

A PAINFUL EXAMPLE

Wouldn't it be foolish for a woman to go into labor, go through all of its pain, stay on the delivery table for hours and hours, then simply get up and walk out of the hospital without her baby? Certainly it would. But this is exactly what happens when you become preoccupied with how bad the past hurts you. Maybe you have walked away and left your baby lying on the floor.

For every struggle in your life, God accomplished something in your character and in your spirit. So why hold the pain and drop the baby when you can hold the baby and drop the pain? Again, you are holding on to the wrong thing in life if all you do is concentrate on past pain. Release the pain. Pain doesn't release itself. It's got to be released. So *release* your pain. Allow God to loose you from the pain. He wants to separate you from what has afflicted you to be left with the baby, not the problem.

BRING FORTH

When God said, ". . . In sorrow thou shalt bring forth children . . ." (Genesis 3:16) it included every area of your life. It is in your character. It is true in your personality. And it is true in your spirit as well as in your finances. So bring forth, ladies! If it comes into this world, it has to come through you. If you are in a financial rut, bring forth! If you are in need of healing for your body, bring forth! Understand that it must be brought forth. It doesn't just happen by accident.

CRY IF YOU MUST, BUT PUSH

When the midwife tells a woman, "Push," the baby will not come forth if the woman doesn't push him. God will not allow you to become trapped in a situation without escape. But you have got to push while you are in pain if you intend to produce. I am told that when the pain is at its height, that is when they instruct you to push—not when the pain recedes. So when the pain is at its ultimate expression, that is the time you need to push.

As you begin to push in spite of the pain, the pain recedes into the background because you become preoccupied with the change rather than the problem. So push! You don't have time to cry. Push! You don't have time to be suicidal. Push! This is not the time to give up. Push! because God is about to birth a promise through you.

Cry if you must, and groan if you have to, but keep on pushing because God has promised that if it is to come into the world, it has got to pass through you.

Now let's talk about the conflict between past pain and future desire that remains. Here is the conflict. God said,

> ". . . in sorrow thou shalt bring forth children; and thy desire shall be to thy husband, and he shall rule over thee."
>
> GENESIS 3:16

In other words, woman, you will have so much pain in producing the child that if you don't have a balance between past pain and future desire, you will quit producing. So God says, "After the pain, your desire shall be to your husband." Pain is swallowed by desire.

IMPREGNATED WITH DESTINY

Impregnated with destiny, women of promise must bear down in the Spirit. The past may hurt and the pain may be genuine. But you must learn to get in touch with something other than your pain. If you do not have desire, you won't have the tenacity to resurrect. Desire will come back. After the pain is over, desire follows, because it takes desire to be productive again.

CHAPTER SEVEN

A Womb-Man

Until the desire to go forward becomes greater than the memories of past pain, you will never hold the power to create again.

I have been in the delivery room with my wife as she was giving birth. I have witnessed the pain and suffering that she has endured. I believe that there were times of such intense pain that she would have shot me if she only had the chance. But her desire made her continue. She didn't simply give up. She endured the pain so new life could be born. Then once the child was born, the pain was soon forgotten.

Until your desire to go forward becomes greater than the memories of past pain, you will never hold the power to create again. However, when desire comes back into your spirit and begins to live in you again, it will release you from the pain.

GO FORTH WITH GOD'S VISION

God wants to give us the strength to overcome past pain to move forward into new life. Solomon wrote, "Where there is no vision, the people perish . . ." (Proverbs 29:18). So vision is the desire to go ahead. Until you have a vision to go ahead, you will always live in yesterday's struggles.

God is calling you to *today*, but the devil wants you to live in *yesterday*. The devil is always telling you about what you cannot do. His method is to bring up your past. He wants to draw your attention backward.

God wants to put desire in the spirit of broken women. There wouldn't be any desire if there wasn't any relationship. You can't desire something that's not there. The very fact that you have a desire is in itself an indication that better days are coming. David said, "I had fainted, unless I had believed to see the goodness of the Lord in the land of the living" (Psalm 27:13). So expect something wonderful to happen.

When I was a boy, we had a dog named Pup. Don't let the name fool you, though. He was a mean and ferocious animal. He would eat anyone who came near him. We had him chained in the back of the house to a four-by-four post. The chain was huge. And we never imagined that he could possibly tear himself loose from that post. When he would chase something, the chain would snap him back. We often laughed at him, as we stood outside his reach.

One day, Pup saw something that he really wanted. It was out of his reach. However, the motivation before him became more important than what was behind him. So he pulled that chain to the limit. Then all at once, instead of drawing him back, the chain snapped and Pup was loose to chase his prey.

That's what God will do for you. The thing that used to pull you back, you will snap, and you will be liberated by a goal because God has put greatness before you. You can't receive what God wants for your life by looking back. He is mighty. He is powerful enough to destroy the yoke of the enemy in your life. And He is strong enough to bring you out and loose you, deliver you, and set you free.

PLANT GOD'S SEED OF TRUTH

What you need is a seed in the womb that you believe is enough to produce an embryo. And you must be willing to feed that embryo for it to grow and become visible. When it will not be hidden anymore, it will break forth in life as answered prayer. It will break forth. No matter how hard others try to hold it back, it will break forth.

So put the truth in your spirit and feed, nurture and allow it to grow. Quit telling yourself, "You're too fat, too old, too late, or too ignorant." Quit feeding yourself that garbage. That will not nourish the baby. Too often we starve the embryo of faith that is growing within us. It is unwise to speak against your own body. Women tend to speak against their bodies, opening the door for sickness and disease. Speak life to your own body and celebrate who you are. You are the image of God.

READ THE SCRIPTURES

Scriptures remind us of who we are.

I will praise thee; for I am fearfully and wonderfully made: marvellous are thy works; and that my soul knoweth right well.

PSALM 139:14

These are the words that will feed our souls. The truth will allow new life to swell up within us. Feed the embryo within with such words as these.

When I consider thy heavens, the work of thy fingers, the moon and the stars, which thou hast ordained; what is man, that thou art mindful of him? and the son of man, that thou visitest him?

PSALM 8:3–4

And the Lord shall make thee the head, and not the tail; and thou shalt be above only, and thou shalt not be beneath. . . .

DEUTERONOMY 28:13

I can do all things through Christ which strengtheneth me.

PHILIPPIANS 4:13

The Word of God will provide the nourishment that will feed the baby inside.

BECAUSE WE CAN'T SEE IT DOESN'T MEAN GOD WON'T DO IT

The book of Hebrews provides us with a tremendous lesson on faith. When we believe God, we are counted as righteous. Righteousness cannot be earned or merited. It comes only through faith. We can have a good report simply on the basis of our faith. Faith becomes the tender, like money is the legal tender in this world that we use for exchange of goods and services. Faith becomes the tender, or the substance, of things hoped for, and the evidence of things not seen. By it the elders obtained a good report {Hebrews 11:1–2}.

Through faith we understand that the worlds were framed by the word of God, so that things which are seen were not made of things which do appear.

HEBREWS 11:3

The invisible became visible and was manifested. God wants us to understand that just because we can't see it doesn't mean that He won't do it.

FAITH BEGINS WITH A WORD

What God wants to do in us begins as a word that gets into our spirit. Everything that is tangible started as an intangible. It was a dream, a thought, a word of God. In the same way, what man has invented began as a concept in someone's mind. So just because we don't see it doesn't mean we won't get it.

There is a progression in the characters mentioned in this chapter of Hebrews. Abel worshiped God by faith. Enoch walked with God by faith. You can't walk with God until you worship God. The first calling is to learn how to worship God. When you learn how to worship God, then you can develop a walk with God. So stop trying to get people to walk with God who won't worship. If you don't love God enough to worship Him, you will never be able to walk with Him. If you can worship like Abel, then you can walk like Enoch.

ENOCH AND NOAH

Enoch walked, and by faith, Noah worked with God. You can't work with God until you walk with God. And you can't walk with God until you worship God. So if you can worship like Abel, you can walk like Enoch. And if you walk like Enoch, you can work like Noah.

But without faith it is impossible to please him: for he that cometh to God must believe that he is, and that he is a rewarder of them that diligently seek him.

HEBREWS 11:6

God will reward those who persevere in seeking Him. He may not come when you want Him to, but He will always be right on time. If you will wait on the Lord, He will strengthen your heart. He will heal you and deliver you. He will lift you up and break those chains. God's power will loose the bands from around your neck. He will give you the garment of praise for the spirit of heaviness (Isaiah 61:3).

ABRAHAM

Abraham was a great man of faith. The writer of Hebrews mentions many areas of his faith. Abraham looked for a city whose builder and maker was God (Hebrews 11:10). However, he is not listed in the faith "hall of fame" as the one who produced Isaac. You would think if Abraham was famous for anything, it should have been for producing Isaac. However, he is not applauded for that.

SARAH

"Through faith also Sara herself received strength to conceive seed, and was delivered of a child when she was past age, because she judged him faithful who had promised" (Hebrews 11:11).

When it comes to bringing forth the baby, the Scriptures do not refer to a man; they refer to a womb-man.

Sarah needed strength to conceive seed when she was past childbearing age. So God met her need. She believed that He was capable of giving her a child regardless of what the circumstances looked like. From a natural perspective, it was impossible. The enemy certainly didn't want it to happen. God, however, performed His promise.

GO FORTH WITH A SARAH VISION

Why would you allow your vision to be incapacitated for the lack of a man? Many women have unbelieving husbands at home. Have faith for yourself. Be a womb-man. It doesn't matter whether someone else believes or not. Cling to the truth that He is doing a good work in you. Each of us needs our own walk with God. So stand back and thank God. Believe God and know that He is able to do it.

Sarah didn't stand on her husband's faith; she stood on her own.

YOU ARE GOD'S WOMAN

You are God's woman. You are not called to sit by the window waiting on God to send you a husband. So you had better have some faith yourself and believe God down in your own spirit. If you would believe God, He would perform His Word in your life. No matter the desire or the blessing that you seek, God has promised to give you the desires of your heart (Psalm 37:4).

GOD WILL TURN IT AROUND

Recognize that where life has seemed irrational and out of control, God will turn it around. When trouble was breaking loose in my life, and I thought I couldn't take it anymore, God intervened and broke every chain that held me back. He will do no less for you.

Abraham had many promises from God regarding his descendants. God told Abraham that his seed would be as the "sands of the sea and the stars of heaven" (Genesis 22:17). So there were two promises of seed given to Abraham.

First of all, God said his seed would be as the sands of the earth. That promise represents the natural, physical nation of Israel. These were the people of the Old Covenant. However, God didn't stop there. He also promised that Abraham's seed would be as the stars of heaven. These are the people of the New Covenant, the exalted people. The Church. We are exalted in Christ Jesus. So we too are seed of Abraham. We are the stars of heaven.

But God had more plans for Abraham's descendants than to simply start a new nation on earth. He planned a new spiritual kingdom that will last forever. The plan started as a seed, but it ended up as stars.

MULTIPLIED BLESSING

Now can you see why Sarah herself had to receive strength to conceive a seed when she was past childbearing age? The only thing that stood between the seed and the stars was her—the woman. The old man gave her a seed and she gave him the stars of heaven. In the same way, God wants whatever He gives you to be multiplied in the womb of your spirit. Then when you bring it forth, it shall be greater than the former.

The enemy wants to multiply fear in your life. In fact, he wants you to become so afraid that you won't be able to figure out what you fear. You may be afraid of living in your own home. Some are afraid to correct their children. Others fear standing up in front of others. Intimidated and afraid, many do not deliver a prophecy. So God wants to set you free from fear by filling you with faith.

SAY GOODBYE TO YESTERDAY

But in order to move forward, we must be willing to give up yesterday and go on toward tomorrow. We have to trust God enough to allow Him to come in and plow up our lives. Perhaps He needs to root out closet skeletons and replace them with new attitudes.

Sometimes women are so accustomed to being hurt that if anyone comes near them, they become defensive. Some may look tough and angry toward men, but God knows that behind that tough act, they are simply afraid. God deals directly with the issues of the heart. He lets you know you don't have to be afraid. And the plans of God are good. He is not like the people who have hurt and abused you. He wants only to help you be completely restored.

BREAK THE CHAINS OF THE PAST

However, the enemy tries to chain us to the circumstances of the past to keep us from reaching our potential. Satan has assigned fear to block up your womb. It blocks up your womb and causes you to be less productive than you like. He wants to destroy the spirit of creativity within you. But God wants you to know that you have nothing to fear. You can be creative. He will make you into the womb-man that He wants you to be.

Maybe you have been tormented and in pain. You have been upset. You have been frustrated and it is hindering your walk. But God is releasing you from fear.

For God hath not given us the spirit of fear; but of power, and of love, and of a sound mind.

2 TIMOTHY 1:7

You need to allow God an opportunity in your life. Then you will start seeing beauty at all different stages of your life. Maybe you have been afraid of aging. If you have, God will give you the strength to thank Him for every year.

Although we must be careful not to become trapped by the past, we should look back and thank God for how He has kept us through the struggles. If you're like me, you will want to say, "I would never have made it if You had not brought me through." So celebrate who you have become through His assistance. In every circumstance, rejoice that He was with you in it.

HEALTH INTO DRY BONES

I believe God is bringing health into dry bones. Bones that were bowed over, bones that were bent out of shape, bones that made you upset with yourself. All are giving way to the life of the Spirit. Perhaps you respond to your history with low self-esteem. God will heal the inner wound and teach you how important you are to Him. You do make a difference. The world would be a different place if it were not for you. You are a part of His divine plan.

When the angel came to Mary and told her what God was going to do in her life, Mary questioned how it could be possible (Luke 1:34). Perhaps God has been telling you things He wants to do in your life, but you have questioned Him. Perhaps your circumstances do not seem to allow you to accomplish much. And maybe you lack the strength to accomplish the task alone. Or perhaps, like Mary, you are thinking only in the natural and that you must have a man to do God's will.

And the angel answered and said unto her, "The Holy Ghost shall come upon thee, and the power of the Highest shall overshadow thee: therefore also that holy thing which shall be born of thee shall be called the Son of God."

LUKE 1:35

If you have been wondering how God will make things come to pass in your life, remember that He will accomplish the task. No man will get the credit for your deliverance. Just as He told Mary, "The Holy Ghost shall come upon thee," the same is true of godly women today. The Holy Spirit will fill you. He will impregnate you. He will give life to your spirit. He will put purpose back into you. He will renew you. And He will restore you.

God had a special plan for Mary. She brought forth Jesus. And He has a special plan for us. Unlike Mary, however, we aren't privileged to see the future. We don't know what kind of good things He has in store for us. But, He does have a plan. God's women are to be womb-men. They are to be creative and bring forth new life. That is exactly what God wants to do with those who are broken and discouraged.

SIMPLY BELIEVE

If great things came from those who never suffered, we might think that they accomplished those things of their own accord. When a broken person submits to God, God gets the glory for the wonderful things He accomplishes—no matter how far that person has fallen. The anointing of God will restore you and make you accomplish great and noble things. Believe it!

The hidden Christ that's been locked up behind your fears, your problems and your ministry, will come forth in your life. You will see the power of the Lord Jesus do a mighty thing.

After the angel told Mary those words, do you know what she said? "And Mary said, Behold the handmaid of the Lord; be it unto me according to thy word. And the angel departed from her" (Luke 1:38). Mary said, "Be it unto me according to thy word." Not according to my marital status. Not according to my job. Not according to what I deserve. But, "Be it unto me according to thy word."

Mary knew enough to believe God and to submit to Him. She was taking an extreme risk. To be pregnant and unmarried brought dire consequences in those days. Yet she willingly gave herself over to the Lord.

Mary had a cousin named Elizabeth who was already expecting a child. The child in Elizabeth's womb was to be the forerunner of the Messiah. When the two women came together to share their stories, the Bible says that the baby leaped in Elizabeth's womb and that she was filled with the Holy Ghost (Luke 1:41).

You need to know that the things you had stopped believing God for will start leaping in your spirit again. God will renew you! Often, women have been working against each other, but God will bring you together. You will come together like Mary and Elizabeth and cause your babies to leap in your womb. The power of the Lord Jesus will do a new thing in your life. Just let Him. The Holy Ghost will come upon you and restore you.

FOLLOW YOUR DREAM

If you are a woman who has had a dream and sensed a promise, reach out to Him. Every woman who knows they have another woman inside of them who is yet to come forth can reach their hearts toward God. When they do, He will meet those inner needs and cause them to live at their potential. He will restore what was stolen by your suffering and abuse. He will take back from the enemy what was swallowed up in your history.

He wants to bring you together, sisters. Every Mary needs an Elizabeth. He needs to bring you together. So stop your wars and fighting. Drop your guns. Throw down your swords. Put away your shields. God put something in your sister that you need. When you come together, powerful things will happen.

Satan attempts to keep us from our potential. He allows and causes horrible things to happen in lives so those lives will take on a different outlook. The fear of abuse can only be removed by the power of the Holy Spirit. There is great potential in women who believe. But that potential may be locked up at times because of ruined histories. Let God wipe the slate clean. He will likely use others to help in the process, but it is His anointing that will bring forth new life from deep within.

CHAPTER EIGHT

Anoint Me . . . I'm Single!

The Scripture calls unmarried women virgins because God is of the opinion that if you do not belong to a man, you belong strictly to Him.

Some of you do not understand the benefits of being single. In reality, while you are not married, you really ought to be involved with God. Because when you get married, you direct all of the training that you had while you were unmarried toward your spouse. The apostle Paul addressed this issue in his first letter to the church at Corinth.

> *But I would have you without carefulness. He that is unmarried careth for the things that belong to the Lord, how he may please the Lord: But he that is married careth for the things that are of the*

world, how he may please his wife. There is difference also between a
wife and a virgin. The unmarried woman careth for the things of the
Lord, that she may be holy both in body and in spirit: but she that is
married careth for the things of the world, how she may please her
husband.

I CORINTHIANS 7:32-34

Single women often forget some very important advantages they have. At five o'clock in the morning you can lie in bed and pray in the Spirit until half-past seven, and not have to answer to anyone. You can worship the Lord whenever and however you please. You can lie prostate on the floor in your house and worship, and no one will become annoyed about it. ". . . The unmarried woman careth for the things of the Lord. . . ."

Often, those who minister in churches hear unmarried women complain about their need for a husband. And rarely does a single woman boast about the kind of relationship she is free to build with the Lord. Are you complaining about how you need someone? If you are, quit complaining and start taking advantage of the time you don't have to worry about cooking meals and caring for a family. While a woman is single, she needs to recognize that she has the unique opportunity to build herself up in the Lord without the drains that can occur later.

BECOME FAITHFUL IN YOUR SINGLENESS

This time is in your life for you to charge up the battery cells. It's time to pamper; a time to take luxurious baths in milk and honey. You can lie there in the bath and worship the Lord. It's a ministry you have. So before you ask God for another man, take care of Him. If you are not ministering to His needs, and are always before Him asking Him to give you one of His princes to minister to, your prayers are not being heard because you are not being faithful to Him. When you become faithful in your singleness, then you will be better prepared to be faithful with a husband.

If you disregard the perfect husband, Jesus, you will certainly disregard the rest of us. If you ignore the one who provides oxygen, breath, bone tissue, strength, blood corpuscles, and life itself, you will certainly not be able to have regard for any earthly husband. The Lord wants to make sweet love to you. I'm not being carnal, I'm being real. He wants to hold you. He wants you to come in at the end of the day and say, "Oh, Lord, I could hardly make it today. Whew, I went through so much, I'm so glad I have You in my life. They tried to devour me, but I thank You for this we have together. I just couldn't wait to get alone to worship and praise and magnify You. You're the One who keeps me going. You're the lover of my soul, my mind, my emotions, my attitude, and my disposition. Hold me. Touch me. Strengthen me. Let me hold You. Let me bless You. I've set the night aside for us. Tonight is our night. I'm not so busy that I don't have time for You. For if I have no time for You, surely I will have no time for a husband. My body is Yours. Nobody touches me but You. I am holy in body and in spirit. I am not committing adultery in our relationship. My body is Yours."

❧

DON'T ASK FOR SAUL

The Scripture calls unmarried women virgins because God is of the opinion that if you do not belong to a man, you belong strictly to Him. God thinks you are His. God's heart was broken with the ancient nation of Israel. It was broken because Israel came to Him and said, ". . . Make us a king to judge us like all the nations" (1 Samuel 8:5). God had thought He was their King. But when they preferred a man over Him, He gave them Saul, and Israel went to the dogs.

TAKE THE TIME TO WORSHIP HIM

There is nothing wrong with wanting to be married. I am simply saying that you need to take care of the Lord while you are waiting. Minister to

Him. Let Him heal and loose you while you worship Him. Single women ought to be the most consecrated women in the Church.

Instead of singles being envious of married women, the married ought to be jealous of singles. You are the ones whose shadows ought to fall on people and they be healed. Why? Because you are in a position and posture of prayer. The Lord has become your necessary food. While some married women are dependent on their husbands, single women can learn to be dependent on the Lord. God has no limitations. A married woman may have a husband who can do some things, but God can do everything. What a privilege to be married to Him. He told Joel, ". . . and upon the handmaids . . . will I pour out my spirit" (Joel 2:29). God has a special anointing for the woman who is free to seek Him. Her prayer life should explode in miracles!

GOD IS YOUR EDGE

That does not mean it is wrong for you to want physical companionship. God ordained that need. While you are waiting, though, understand that God thinks He is your husband. So be careful how you treat Him. He thinks He is your man. That's why He does those special favors for you. It is God who made you into a beautiful woman. He has been taking care of you, even when you didn't notice His provision. He is the source of every good thing. He keeps things running, and provides for your daily care. It is He who opened those doors for you. He has been your edge, your friend, and your companion.

Those who are married seek to please their spouse, while unmarried people are much freer to seek and please the Lord. There is a special relationship of power between God and the single believer. Paul wrote, "Let every man abide in the same calling wherein he was called" (1 Corinthians 7:20). In other words, the person who is single should be abiding, not wrestling, in singleness. Rather than spending all of our effort trying to change our position, we need to learn to develop the position in which He has placed us. Isn't that what this means: ". . . I have learned, in whatsoever state I am, therewith to be content" (Philippians 4:11). I speak peace to you today.

SANCTIFY YOURSELF

Maybe you haven't been living like you should. Maybe your house hasn't been the house of prayer that it really could have been. I want you to take this opportunity to begin sanctifying your house and body. Maybe your body has been mauled and pawed by all sorts of people. That doesn't matter. I want you to sanctify your body unto the Lord, and give your body as a living sacrifice to God (Romans 12:1). If you can't keep your vow to God, you would never be able to keep your vow to a man. So give your body to God and sanctify yourself.

When God picks a wife for one of His royal sons, He will pick her from those who are faithful and holy unto Him. He may pass over those who didn't keep a vow to Him. If you are to marry a king, he will have claimed you to be a queen. So begin to sanctify yourself! Bring your body before God. Bring your nature before God. Bring your passion to Him and allow God to plug into your need.

Allow God to strengthen you until you can tell the devil, "My body belongs to God; my whole body belongs to God. I am God's. From the crown of my head to the soles of my feet, all that I am belongs to God. Early in the morning will I seek His face. I lie upon my bed at night and call on His name. I will touch Him and embrace Him. He is the God of my salvation."

THE MINISTRY OF MARRIAGE

Marriage is ministry. If you are single, your ministry is directly unto the Lord. But if you are married, your ministry is through your spouse. Those who are married are instructed in Scripture to learn godly devotion through relationship with their spouse.

Husbands, love your wives, even as Christ also loved the church, and gave himself for it; that he might sanctify and cleanse it with the washing of water by the word.

EPHESIANS 5:25-26

Marriage is the one place in human society where true love can be expressed in a great way. Marriage partners are to give self-sacrificially to one another. Just as Jesus gave Himself for the Church, husbands and wives are to give themselves to one another as selfless gifts of love. Marriage is not a place for seeking self-gratification. It is the place where we seek to gratify another.

The sacredness of marriage is found in the relationship between Christ and the Church. Jesus continues to intercede on behalf of the Church, even after He gave His all for us. He is the greatest advocate of believers. He stands before God to defend and proclaim our value.

YOU ARE YOUR HUSBAND'S GREATEST ADVOCATE

Similarly, husbands and wives are to be bonded together to the extent that they become the greatest advocate of the other. Not demanding one's own way, but always seeking to please the other.

There can be no doubt that God has special plans for each one of us. The woman who is single needs to recognize her position and seek to please God in every way. Single means to be "whole." So enjoy being a whole, single person. The greatest visitation of the Holy Ghost in history happened to an unmarried woman named Mary. Before Joseph could have relations, the Holy Ghost came upon her. And that same life-giving anointing wants to come upon you. So stop murmuring and complaining. His presence is in the room! Worship Him! He is waiting on you.

CHAPTER NINE

A Table for Two

A truly good relationship is a
spicy meal served on a shaky
table, filled with dreams and
pains and tender moments.
Moments that make you smile
secret smiles in the middle of
the day.

*So the Lord God caused the man to fall into a deep sleep; and
while he was sleeping, he took one of the man's ribs and closed up
the place with flesh. Then the Lord God made a woman from the
rib he had taken out of the man, and he brought her to the man.*

GENESIS 2:21–22 NIV

The first female mentioned in the Bible was created mature, without a
childhood or an example to define her role and relationship to her husband. She was created a woman while Adam was asleep. When the Lord
"brought her to the man" is the first hint of marriage. I believe life would be
better if we still allowed God to bring to us what He has for us.

The only evolution I can find in the Bible is the woman, who evolved out of man. She is God's gift to man. When God wanted to be praised, He created man in His own likeness and in His image. Then when God saw that it was not good for man to be alone, He gave man someone like himself. Adam said the woman was ". . . bone of my bones, and flesh of my flesh . . ." (Genesis 2:23). His attraction to her was her likeness of him. He called her "womb man" or woman. Like the Church of Christ, Eve was his body and his bride.

For no man ever yet hated his own flesh; but nourisheth and cher-isheth it, even as the Lord the church: for we are members of his body, of his flesh, and of his bones. For this cause shall a man leave his father and mother, and shall be joined unto his wife, and they two shall be one flesh. This is a great mystery: but I speak concerning Christ and the church.

EPHESIANS 5:29-32

SUPERFICIAL COMPONENTS

Man and woman were both made of the same material. Adam said, "She is bone of my bone." He said nothing of her size, body build, or hair color. These superficial components are like placing a product in an attractive container. The container may get the consumer to try it. But only the product will keep the consumer coming back. His attraction goes much deeper than externals. These outward attractions are certainly an advantage, but be assured that when it comes to marriage, no one ever stayed together simply because they were attractive.

FLESH IS JUST FLESH

I don't know whether I agree with those who say there is only one person in the world for you. I personally would be afraid that out of the billions of people on this planet, I wouldn't be able to find them. However, I do know that when you find a person with whom you are compatible, there is a bonding that consummates marriage that has nothing to do with sex. I also understand how you could feel this person to be the only choice in the world. Let's face it, everyone you meet isn't bone of your bone! It is so important that you do not allow anyone to manipulate you into choosing someone with whom you have no bond. When Ezekiel speaks about those dry bones in the valley, he says, ". . . the bones came together, bone to his bone" (Ezekiel 37:7). So every person must pray and discern if the other is someone they could cleave to the rest of their life.

The term *cleave* (joined) used in Genesis 2:24 from which Paul quoted in Ephesians 5:29–32 is translated from the Hebrew word, *debaq*. It means "to impinge, cling or adhere to; figuratively, to catch by pursuit or follow close after." [See Strong's Exhaustive Concordance of the Bible, #1692.] There is a great need in most of our lives to cleave, to feel that this is where we belong. But it is sad to realize our society has become so promiscuous that many have mistaken the thrill of a weekend fling for the cleaving of two thirsty souls in loving commitment.

BEFORE AND AFTER

If you are reading this book and are not married, I encourage you to consider these issues carefully as you pray and seek God for companionship. Find ten couples who have been married twelve years or longer. Then look at their wedding album to see how many of them have drastically changed. When you do you will realize that if those initial impressions were all that held a marriage together, they would probably have already come to an end.

Certainly, you owe it to your spouse and yourself to be all that you can. Still, there is much more involved in marriage than the superficial.

A HOLY BOND

Marriage is so personal that no one is able to stand outside of another relationship to see why they bond. If you are married, understand that your spouse isn't running for office. He shouldn't have to meet the approval of all your family and friends. And don't expect everyone to see what you see in each other that cleaves and sticks you together.

Have you made the commitment to stay together? The secret to cleaving is leaving. "For this cause shall a man *leave* his father and mother . . ." (Mark 10:7). If you enter into marriage and keep your former options open, whether mental, emotional or physical, your marriage will never work. When the tugging of adversity tries the bonds of your matrimony, you will fall apart. So you must leave and cleave to your spouse. It is very unhealthy to cleave to someone other than your spouse for support.

LEAVE AND CLEAVE

Now we all need wholesome friendships. However, none should have more influence over you than your spouse (that is, after God). Some of you could save your marriages right now if you would leave some of your extra-martial ties and cleave to your spouse!

It is not always a matter of feelings. The just shall live by faith. We use this verse for so many other things, so why not about marriage? Romans 1:17 says, "For therein is the righteousness of God revealed from faith to faith: as it is written, The just shall live by faith." Believe God for your marriage! It will not be your feelings that heal your relationship; it will be your faith. Did you know that you cannot trust your own feelings?

CLEAVE IN FAITH

I counsel people all the time who sit with tears streaming down their weary faces and say, "I just can't trust him." I've got news for you. You can't trust yourself either! Your feelings will swing in and out. But your faith will not move. Cleaving implies that you don't want to get away. A marriage erodes like the banks of a river do—a little each day.

BE YOURSELF

There is a certain way a woman treats a man when she is fulfilled. It takes faith to treat a frustrated marriage with the same kind of respect that you would treat a prosperous relationship. Many times you may feel yourself holding back from who you would like to be so you can maintain a strong exterior. All I am saying is, don't allow another person to cause you to play a role that isn't really who you are.

I realize that many of you may be in the middle of an awful relationship, but I can't counsel what I can't see. For specific needs, I recommend pastoral care and counseling. Nevertheless, I do want to warn you that suppressing the gentle side of you as a defense will not stop you from being hurt! If you suppress who you are, you will fall into depression! It is terrible to arrest who you are in an attempt to "fight fire with fire." The best way to fight fire is with water! The winning way of a woman is not in her words, it is in her character.

> *Wives, in the same way be submissive to your husbands so that, if any of them do not believe the word, they may be won over without words by the behavior of their wives, when they see the purity and reverence of your lives.*
>
> I PETER 3:1–2 NIV

> *For this is the way the holy women of the past who put their hope in God used to make themselves beautiful. They were submissive to their own husbands, like Sarah, who obeyed Abraham and called him her master. You are her daughters if you do what is right and do not give way to fear.*
>
> I PETER 3:5–6 NIV

A LESSON FROM PETER

Recently, while teaching a seminar, a lady raised her hand and said, "I am a widow. I lost my husband and he died unsaved." She continued, "I claimed 1 Peter 3:1, and at the end of his life he still was not saved."

She was obviously wrestling with grief, so I responded, "That scripture doesn't mean the responsibility of getting the husband saved rests on the wife. It just says that a submissive, quiet woman creates an atmosphere so he may be won." Then I rebuked the condemning spirit of guilt and she worshiped God under the anointing of the Holy Spirit.

This passage in Peter was not given to abuse women; it was given to instruct them about what works well in the home. Faith is not loud and fleshly. It is quiet and spiritual. Believe me when I say I know this to be effective. No one can do anything to make another person get saved. You can't make them come home. You can't make someone love you. But you can create an atmosphere where your conduct is not undermining your prayers! This is what Peter means.

LEARNING TO ACT AND TALK

Women tend to be vocal while men tend to be physical. Women feel that everything needs to be discussed. And communication is crucial to a healthy relationship, it is just that men don't always talk with words.

Men communicate through touch even in male to male relationships. A pat on the back, or a two-handed handshake, means "I like you." Some think that men always communicate through sex. But that isn't always the case. When a coach playfully slaps a basketball player on the rump, he is not being sexual. He is saying, "Good job!" We must learn each other's method of communication.

So instead of always feeling like you are neglected, ask your husband to share with you why he does what he does. Or better still, observe his method of communication and teach him yours.

TEACH YOUR LANGUAGE

Then in all your getting, get understanding! It is terrible to be misunderstood! I am a giver. So whenever I feel affection, the first thing I want to do is to buy a gift for my wife. I was shocked to find that although my wife will acknowledge the gifts, she will also go into orbit over cards! To me this is insane! She keeps cards that are so old they've turned yellow. I read cards and enjoy them, but I seldom keep them. So we spent the first few years of our marriage teaching each other our language.

BABBLING IN BABEL

Your husband may really think he's telling you something that you keep complaining about not getting. And he may feel like, "What more does she want? I told her that I loved her. I did this and that and the other." You may be living in the Tower of Babel. That was the place where families divided because they could not understand each other's language. So sit down and learn each other's language before frustration turns your house into the Tower of Babel. At Babel all work ceased and arguing began. If you are arguing, it is because frustration exists between you. People who don't care don't argue. No one argues over what they would rather leave!

But when you approach your husband, do not corner him. Catch him at a time when he won't feel interrogated. You would be surprised at how men tend to avoid open confrontation. I have seen big, burly, macho men intimidated about telling their 100-pound wives about how they were going to do something they feared she wouldn't like. Even men who are physically abusive still have moments when they feel anxiety about facing their wives. Solomon wrote, "It is better to dwell in the corner of the housetop, than with a brawling woman and in a wide house" (Proverbs 25:24). So unless you are trying to drive him away, remember you could win the argument and still lose the man.

LIVING IN PENTECOST

A man's communication is different. I am not suggesting that men can't learn the communication method of their wives. I am merely saying that spouses must learn to appreciate each other's language. Remember, I briefly discussed faith for your marriage. And faith calls those things that are not as though they were (Romans 4:17). So everything you plan to do for him *when* he changes, do it now. Do it by faith. Then God will turn your Tower of Babel into a Pentecost! At Pentecost each person heard the message in their own language (Acts 2:6). I pray that God would interpret the language of your spouse and that your love be fruitful and productive.

NAKED AND NOT ASHAMED

And the Lord God called unto Adam, and said unto him, "Where art thou?" And he said, "I heard thy voice in the garden, and I was afraid, because I was naked; and I hid myself."

GENESIS 3:9–10

Take it off—take it all off! No, not your clothes! It's the fig leaves that must go. Marriage is at its best when both parties can be naked and not be ashamed. It is important that your husband be able to take it off, to take it all off. There is no resting place for the man who hides in his own house. That's why the Lord asked Adam, "Where art thou?" When men are restored to their rightful place in the home, the family will come out of chaos. Listen as Adam exposes the tendency of most men to avoid open confrontation in these, the four points of his confession: (a) I heard thy voice. (b) I was afraid. (c) I was naked. (d) I hid myself. When women become confrontational, it's not that men don't hear you. But when men become afraid or exposed (naked), they have a tendency to hide.

BE TRANSPARENT

Marriage needs to be transparent. Fear will not heal, it will only hide. So both you and your spouse need to be able to expose your vulnerabilities without fear or condemnation. Woe to the man who has no place to lay his head.

> *And they were both naked, the man and his wife, and were not ashamed.*
>
> GENESIS 2:25

Now I want to share something with you that may sound unorthodox. But I pray it will bless someone. I want to stop by Delilah's house (Judges 16:4–20). Most women would not want to stop at her house; most men would! Most are not afraid of Delilah; most women would not like her. Her morals are inexcusable, but her methods are worth discussing. There are some very important things that every wife must learn from immoral Delilah.

All the colorful exegesis of our preachers have described her as some voluptuous love goddess. They say she walked like a swinging pendulum, smelled like the richest incense, and smiled like the glow of an exquisite candelabra. But, in actuality, the Bible says nothing about Delilah's appearance. Her clothing, makeup or hairdo are not even mentioned.

So what was it about this woman that was so powerful? What was it that attracted and captivated the attention of this mighty man, Samson?

What was it about this woman that kept drawing him back into her arms?

What was it about this woman that, when none of the warriors could get to Samson, the Philistine government put her on the payroll because of what she knew about men?

And what was it that made Samson keep going back to her bed even when he knew she was trying to kill him?

Samson could not leave her alone—he desperately needed her. What was it about this "fatal attraction" of the Old Testament?

WHERE CAN THE MIGHTY LAY HIS HEAD?

This discussion is for women married to men working in high-stress positions—men who are powerful and full of purpose—men who are the envy of everyone around them. Samson was one of them. Jesus described well the problem of such highly motivated men when He said, ". . . Foxes have holes, and birds of the air have nests; but the Son of man hath not where to lay his head" (Luke 9:58).

Where can the mighty man lay his head? Where can he become vulnerable? Where can he take off his armor and rest for a few hours? He doesn't want to quit; he merely needs to rest.

IS YOUR HOME A PLACE WHERE
THE MIGHTY CAN LAY HIS HEAD?

Is your home a restful place to be? Is it clean and neat? Is it warm and inviting? If it's not, Delilah's place is ready. And I am sure that she has problems, but he doesn't have to solve them as soon as he comes home from fighting the enemy. She knows he is tried, so she says, "Come, lay your head in my lap."

I know we have pictured Delilah as being as lust-ridden as a porno star. But remember, the Bible doesn't even mention Samson and Delilah's sex life. I am sure it was a factor. But Samson had had sex before. He had gotten up from the bed of the prostitute in Gaza and drove back the Philistines. He was not some high school boy whose mind was blown away by new sexual ideas. No, he was a mighty man.

HOW ARE THE MIGHTY FALLEN?

Wasn't it David who questioned at the demise of Saul, "How are the mighty fallen"? Well, tell David to ask Delilah, or if she is not at home, to ask his own Bathsheba!

Delilah knew that all men are little boys somewhere deep inside. They are little boys who started their lives being touched by women. You sang their first song. You gave their first bath. And when they were tired, they laid their weary heads against your warm breast and lapsed into sleep. They listened at your silky voice calling them, "Momma's little man." You talked to them. You touched them and they felt safe in your arms—not criticized, not ostracized, just safe. Delilah stroked Samson. She talked to him. She gave him a place to lay his head. Even God inhabits the room of a praiser and allows the murmurer to wander. Men, created in the likeness of God, respond to praise. Praise will make a weary man perform.

A woman who knows what to say to a man is difficult to withstand. This was the secret of Delilah. She knew all men had a little boy inside. And that for all men's tears and all their fears, they need a woman's arms. They need your words, and your song.

GIVE YOUR ARMS AND YOUR SONG

Again, marriage is a ministry. And there is much more involved in it than selfish fulfillment. So for the wearied husband, let him come home and relax. Give him your arms and your song. Let your love be centered around giving, not taking. When you marry someone, you marry everything he is, and everything he has been. You inherit his strengths, fears and weaknesses. It is impossible to pick the parts you want and to leave the parts you don't. It's a package deal. But God grants the grace to minister to him. So don't be discouraged if you don't see immediate change. Minister to that little child in him. And remember, it takes time even for a small cut to heal. Healing is a process and it takes time! God will give you the oil of compassion and the sweet wind of a sincere love to pour into your husband's workday wounds. Be there for him. Give him a place to rest his head.

But he that is married careth for the things that are of the world, how he may please his wife. There is difference also between a wife and a virgin. The unmarried woman careth for the things of the Lord, that she may be holy both in body and in spirit: but she that is married careth for the things of the world, how she may please her husband.

I CORINTHIANS 7:33–34

Marriage is so much of a ministry that the apostle Paul teaches the married woman she cannot afford to become so "spiritual" that she is unavailable for the ministry of marriage. The Greek word used for "careth" in this passage (*merimano*) means, "to be anxious about, or to have intense concern" [See Strong's Exhaustive Concordance of the Bible, #3309].

So God is saying through Paul, "I want the married woman to be concerned about pleasing her husband and vice versa."

HONOR GOD'S PRIORITIES

Many married women who spend a great deal of time fellowshipping with single women do not realize that their perspective and availability should be different. Your ministry, as a wife, begins not in the mall, not in the nursing home, but in your own home and to your own spouse. Now, I am certainly not implying that a woman should be locked in the kitchen and chained to the bed! I am simply sharing that priorities need to start in the home before spreading to careers, vocations and ministerial pursuits. For the woman who "careth for," God will anoint you to be successful in the ministry of marriage.

There will be no marriages in heaven (See Matthew 22:30). Marriage is for this world. And inasmuch as it is a worldly institution, married people cannot divorce themselves from the "things of the world." Returning to Paul's words in 1 Corinthians 7:34, notice this definition of the Greek word *kosmos* translated as "world" in our text:

> *. . . but she that is married careth for the things of the world, how she may please her husband. . . .*
>
> V. 34

Paul's use of the word *kosmos* implies that there should be a concern for harmonious order in a married couple's house. God gives the gift of marriage, but you must do your own decorating. Decorate your relationship or it will become bland for you and for your spouse. Decoration does not come where there is no concern. So God says, in effect, "I release the married woman from the level of consecration I expect from the single woman so she will be able to spend some time decorating her relationship."[1]

You have an important ministry to your companion. I can hear someone saying, "That is good, but I need to spend time with the Lord." I agree that this is true. The Scripture doesn't say married women are to be carnal. It just sets some priorities. Where there are no priorities, there is a sense of being overwhelmed by responsibility. You can still consecrate yourself as long as you understand you are called to be a companion to your spouse. However you choose to decorate your relationship is holy. So do not neglect each other in the name of being spiritual. God wants you to be together!

The husband should fulfill his marital duty to his wife, and likewise the wife to her husband. The wife's body does not belong to her

---

[1] Adorn, Adorning kosmos #2889 in Strong's, "a harmonious arrangement or order, then, adornment, decoration, hence came to denote the world, or the universe, as that which is Divinely arranged. The meaning 'adorning' is found in 1 Peter 3:3. Elsewhere it signifies the world. Cp. kosmos, decent, modest,1 Timothy 2:9; 3:2. See "World" (*Vine's Expository Dictionary of Biblical Words*, Thomas Nelson Publishers, 1985).

alone but also to her husband. In the same way, the husband's body does not belong to him alone but also to his wife. Do not deprive each other except by mutual consent and for a time, so that you may devote yourselves to prayer. Then come together again so that Satan will not tempt you because of your lack of self-control.

I CORINTHIANS 7:3-5 NIV

If you are looking for someone to be your everything, don't look around, look up! God is the only One who can be everything. By expecting perfection from the flesh, you ask more out of someone else than you can provide yourself.

TO BE MARRIED

To be married is to have a partner: someone who is not always there, or always on target, or always anything! On the other hand, should you ever get in trouble and you don't know who to look to for help, you can count on your partner! Marriage is having someone to curl up with when the world seems cold, and life uncertain. It is having someone who is as concerned as you are when your children are ill. It is having a hand that keeps checking your forehead when you aren't well. To be married is to have someone's shoulder to cry on as they lower your parent's body into the ground. It is wrapping wrinkled knees in warm blankets and giggling without teeth! To the person you marry you are saying, "When my time comes to leave this world and the chill of eternity blows away my birthdays and my future stands still in the night, it's your face that I want to kiss goodbye. It's your hand that I want to squeeze as I slip into eternity. And as the curtain closes on all I have attempted to do and be, I want to look into your eyes and see that I mattered. Not what I looked like. Not what I did or how much money I made. Not even how talented I was. I want to look into the teary eyes of someone who loved me and see that I mattered!"

A SPICY MEAL SERVED ON A SHAKY TABLE

As I close this chapter, I hope you can relate to what a blessing it is to be alive and what it means to be able to feel and taste life. Lift the glass to your mouth and drink deeply of life. It is a privilege to experience every drop of your marriage relationship. It is not perfect; like a suede jacket, the imperfection just adds to its uniqueness. I am sure that yours, like mine, is a mixing of good days, sad days, and all the challenges of life. But I hope you have learned with me how a truly good relationship is a spicy meal served on a shaky table, filled with dreams and pains and tender moments. Moments that, in those split-second flashbacks, made you smile secret smiles in the middle of the day. Moments so strong that they never die, yet are so fragile they disappear like bubbles in a glass.

It does not matter whether you have something to be envied or something to be developed. If you can look back and catch a few moments, or trace a smile back to a memory, you are blessed! You could have been anywhere doing anything, but instead the maitre d' has seated you at a table for two!

CHAPTER TEN

Daughter of Abraham

Whatever God gives you, He wants it to be multiplied in the womb of your spirit. When you bring it forth, it shall be greater than the former.

I believe it is important that women get healed and released in their spirits. I'm excited about what God is doing. And I believe that God will move freshly in the lives of women in an even greater way.

God knows how to take a mess and turn it into a miracle. If you're in a mess, don't be too upset about it because God specializes in fixing messes. God is saying some definite things about women being set free and delivered to fulfill their purpose in His kingdom.

Let's look once again at the infirm woman in the gospel of Luke, chapter 13:

And he was teaching in one of the synagogues on the sabbath. And, behold, there was a woman which had a spirit of infirmity eighteen years, and was bowed together, and could in no wise lift up herself. And when Jesus saw her, he called her to him, and said unto her, "Woman, thou art loosed from thine infirmity." And he laid his hands on her: and immediately she was made straight, and glorified God. And the ruler of the synagogue answered with indignation, because that Jesus had healed on the sabbath day, and said unto the people, "There are six days in which men ought to work: in them therefore come and be healed, and not on the sabbath day." The Lord then answered him, and said, "Thou hypocrite, doth not each one of you on the sabbath loose his ox or his ass from the stall, and lead him away to watering? And ought not this woman, being a daughter of Abraham, whom Satan hath bound, lo, these eighteen years, be loosed from this bond on the sabbath day?" And when he had said these things, all his adversaries were ashamed: and all people rejoiced for all the glorious things that were done by him.

LUKE 13:10-17

When the Lord gets through working on you, all your adversaries will be ashamed. All your accusers will be ashamed of themselves. All the people who contributed to your sense of low self-esteem will be ashamed when God gets through unleashing you. You won't have to prove anything. God will prove it. He will do it in your life. When He gets through showing that you've done the right thing and come to the right place, they will drop their heads and be ashamed.

We have already shown how this woman was so bound by Satan for eighteen years that she could not even straighten herself up. She had a past that tormented her, but Jesus set her free. He unleashed her potential that Satan had bound up.

YOUR DILEMMA

Many women in the Church have not really seen Christ as the answer to their dilemma. They go to church, they love the Lord, they want to go to Heaven when they die, but they still do not see Christ as the solution to their problem. Often, we try to separate our personal life from our spiritual life. Many see Jesus as a way to heaven and the solution to spiritual problems, but they fail to see that He is the solution to all of life's problems.

Can you imagine how hard life was for that woman who was bowed over? She had to struggle, because of her problem, to come to Jesus. Few of us are crippled in the same way. However, we all face crippling limitations. We can be bowed over financially. We can be bowed over emotionally. We can be bowed over where we have no self-esteem. Jesus wants to see us struggling toward Him. He could have walked to this woman, but He chose not to. He wants to see us struggle toward Him.

He wants you to want Him enough to overcome obstacles and to push in His direction. He doesn't want to just throw things at you that you don't have a real conviction to receive. When you see a humped-over person crawling through the crowd, know that that person really wants help. That kind of desire is what it takes to change your life. And Jesus is your answer.

JESUS IS THE ANSWER

I may seek help by going from one person to another, but only He is the answer. I may be sick in my body, but He is the answer. If my son is dead, or insane on drugs, and I need Him to resurrect my child, He is the answer. If I am having family problems with my brother who is in trouble, He's the answer. It doesn't matter what the problem is, Jesus is the answer.

Jesus touched this woman. There is a place in God where the Lord will touch you and provide intimacy in your life when you are not getting it from other places. But you must be open to His touch. If you can't receive from Him, you may find yourself like the woman at the well, who sought physical gratification (John 4:18). And if you seek only the physical when you really need intimacy, what you end up getting is simply sex. Sex is a poor substitute for intimacy. It's nice with intimacy, but when it's substituted for intimacy, it's frustrating.

Jesus knew this woman. He was the only one who truly knew her. He touched her and healed her. He unleashed her potential that had been bound for eighteen years. You can accomplish anything once you have been called to Jesus. From that moment on you become invincible.

HINDERING WORDS

However, most likely your words have hindered you. Often, we are snared by the words of our very own mouth. The enemy would love to destroy you with your own words. Satan wants to use *you* to fight against you. He will use your strength to fight against you. Many of you have beat yourself down with the power of your own words and have twisted your own back. The enemy worked you against yourself until you saw yourself as crippled. But now is the time to reverse his plan. If you had enough force to bend yourself, you've got enough force to straighten yourself back up.

TODAY IS YOUR DAY TO STRAIGHTEN UP

The Lord told this woman the truth about herself. He told her she was loosed and set her free. He saw the truth despite what everyone else saw. He saw that she was important.

The religious critics didn't like what Jesus had done. His power showed how powerless their religion was. So they accused Him of breaking the law by performing a miracle on the Sabbath day. But Christ acknowledged their hypocrisy by addressing a common occurrence in their day. They all valued their livestock, He said. Then He reminded them that they would loose their donkey on the Sabbath so that it could get a drink. Then He said surely this woman was more valuable than any animal. And that she could be loosed from her pain and sickness regardless of the day.

GOD IS YOUR LIBERATOR

Sometimes pain can become too familiar. Ungodly relationships often become familiar. Change doesn't come easily. Habits and patterns are hard to break. And sometimes we maintain these relationships because we fear change. However, when we see our value the way Jesus sees us, we muster the courage to break away.

He is your defense. He will defend you before your critics. Now is the time for you to focus on receiving the miraculous and getting the water you could not get before. He is loosing you to water. You haven't been drinking for eighteen years, but now you can get a drink. With Jesus, you can do it.

Have you been a beast of burden? Some of you have been a pack horse for many years. People have dumped on you and you have had to grit your teeth. You have never been allowed to develop without stress and weights, not just because of the circumstances, but because of how deeply things truly affect you. Our God, however, is a liberator.

The Lord is my light and my salvation; whom shall I fear? the Lord is the strength of my life; of whom shall I be afraid? When the wicked, even mine enemies and my foes, came upon me to eat up my flesh, they stumbled and fell. Though an host should encamp against me, my heart shall not fear: though war should rise against me, in this will I be confident. One thing have I desired of the Lord, that will

I seek after; that I may dwell in the house of the Lord all the days of my life, to behold the beauty of the Lord, and to inquire in his temple.

PSALM 27:1–4

You must reach the point where it is the Lord whom you desire. Singleness of heart will bring about deliverance. Perhaps you have spent all your time and effort trying to prove yourself to someone who is gone. Maybe an old lover left you with scars. The person may be dead and buried, but you are still trying to win his approval.

If this is the case, you may be dedicated to worthless tasks. You may be committed to things and unattainable goals that will not satisfy. Christ must be your ambition.

Luke 13:13b reads, "*. . . and immediately she was made straight, and glorified God.*" Christ dealt with eighteen years of this woman's torment in an instant. One moment with Jesus, and immediately she was well. For some things you don't have time to recover gradually. The moment you get the truth, you are loosed. When this woman got hold of the truth, immediately she was well.

Once you realize that you have been unleashed, you will feel a sudden change. When you come to Jesus, He will motivate you and get you to see that other woman in you. You need to blossom and bring her forth.

Notice the sixteenth verse of Luke 13:

"*And ought not this woman, being a daughter of Abraham, whom Satan hath bound, lo, these eighteen years, be loosed from this bond on the sabbath day?*"

Jesus called her "a daughter of Abraham." She may have been bent over, but she was still Abraham's daughter. So don't let your condition negate your position.

The woman was unleashed because of who her father was. It had little to do with who she was. The Bible doesn't even mention her name. We will never know who she was until we reach Heaven. But we do know *whose* she was. She was a daughter of Abraham.

FAITH IS AN EQUAL OPPORTUNITY EMPLOYER

Faith is an equal opportunity employer. There is no discrimination in it. Faith will work for you. When you approach God, never worry about the fact that you are a woman. Never become discouraged on that basis when it comes to seeking Him. You will only get as much from God as you can believe Him for.

You won't be able to convince Him, seduce Him, break Him down, or trick Him. God will not move because you cry and act melancholy. Now, you may move me like that. Certainly that works with men, but it doesn't work with God. God only accepts faith.

He wants you to believe Him. He wants you to personalize the truth that you can do all things through Him (Philippians 4:13). He is trying to teach you right now so when the time for a real miracle does come, you will have some faith to draw from. God wants you to understand that if you can believe Him, you can go from defeat to victory and from poverty to prosperity!

START BELIEVING AND BE SET FREE

Faith is more than a fact—faith is an action. So don't tell me you believe when your actions don't correspond with your conviction. If your actions don't change, you might still think you are bound. But when you finally understand that you are loose, you will start behaving as if you were free.

When you are loose, you can go anywhere. If I had one end of a rope around my neck, I would only be able to walk the length of the rope. But once I am unleashed from that rope, I can walk as far as I want. You are whole; you are loose. You can go anywhere.

Hebrews 11 is a faith "hall of fame." It lists great people of God who believed Him and accomplished great exploits. Abraham is given tremendous attention in this chapter. He is revered by millions as the father of faith. He is the first man in history to believe God to the point where it was counted as righteousness. He was saved by faith. Jesus said that the infirm woman was a daughter of Abraham. Because she was, she was worthy. She had merit because she was Abraham's descendant, the father of faith.

TWO HEROES OF FAITH

There are two contrasting women mentioned in the Hebrews 11 faith "hall of fame." Sarah, Abraham's wife, and Rahab, the Jericho prostitute. Isn't it interesting that a married woman and a prostitute both made it to God's hall of fame. A good, clean, godly woman and a prostitute made it into the book! I can understand how Sarah was included, but how in the world did this prostitute get honored? The answer is, faith. She was listed because God honors faith. That was the one thing Sarah and Rahab had in common; nothing else.

The Bible doesn't talk about Rahab having a husband. She had the whole city. Sarah stayed in the tent and knit socks. She moved wherever her husband went and took care of him. There was no similarity in their lifestyles, just in their faith. God saw the same thing in Sarah that He saw in Rahab. So don't accept the excuse that because you have lived like a Rahab you can't have the faith experience.

RAHAB AND SARAH

God wants you to believe Him. So make a decision and stand on it. Rahab decided to take a stand on the side of God's people. She hid the spies.

And she made the decision based on her faith. She took action. Faith is a fact and faith is an action. Rahab took action because she believed God would deliver her when Jericho fell to the Israelites.

Sarah received strength to carry and deliver a child when she was well past childbearing age. She took action because she judged Him faithful who had promised (Hebrews 11:11). She went through the birth process and delivered a child, not because of her circumstances, but because of her faith. Sarah believed God.

God wants your faith to be developed. Regardless of your position and your past, God raises people up equally. Faith is an equal opportunity business. No matter how many mistakes you have made, it is still faith that God will honor. You see, you may have blown it, but God is in the business of restoring broken lives. You may have been like Rahab, but if you can believe God, He will save your house. You know, He didn't save only Rahab. He saved her entire household. All the other homes in Jericho were destroyed. The only house God saved in the city was the house where this prostitute lived.

ONLY FAITH

You would have thought He would have saved some nice little lady's house. Perhaps He would have saved some cottage housing an old woman, or a little widow's house, with petunias growing next to the sidewalk. But God saved the prostitute's house. Was it because He wanted it? No, He wanted the faith. That is what moves God.

If you believe that your background will keep you from moving forward with God, then you don't understand the value of faith. The thing God is asking from you is faith. Some may live good, clean, separated lives. Maybe you are proud of how holy you are. But He still honors only faith.

If you want to grasp the things of God, you will not be able to because of your lifestyle. It will be because of your conviction. God gave healing to some folks who weren't even saved. They were sinners. Perhaps some of them never did get saved, but they got healed because they believed Him. The thing that moves God is faith. If you believe Him, He will move in your life according to your faith, not according to your experience. There was something in Rahab's house that God called valuable. Faith was there. So God protected her from the fire.

He also saved her things. When the fire was over, Rahab was the richest woman in the city. She was the only woman left in town who owned property. So God will also save your finances. Simply believe Him.

FIVE SISTERS

There was also a group of sisters in the Old Testament who proved that God is interested in what happens to women. Their names were, Mahlah, Noah, Hoglah, Milcah and Tirza.

> Then came the daughters of Zelophehad, the son of Hepher, the son of Gilead, the son of Machir, the son of Manasseh, of the families of Manasseh, the son of Joseph; and these are the names of his daughters; Mahlah, Noah, and Hoglah, and Milcah, and Tirzah. And they stood before Moses, and before Eleazar the priest, and before the princes and all the congregation, by the door of the tabernacle of the congregation, saying, "Our father died in the wilderness, and he was not in the company of them that gathered themselves together against the Lord in the company of Korah; but died in his own sin, and had no sons."
>
> NUMBERS 27:1–3

Mahlah, Noah, Hoglah, Milcah and Tizrah were five women who were left alone. There were no men left in their family. Their father had wealth and he had no sons. But prior to this time, women were not allowed to own property or to have an inheritance except through their husbands. Only men could own property.

But they appealed their situation to God through Moses.

"Why should the name of our father be done away from among his family, because he hath no son? Give unto us therefore a posses-sion among the brethren of our father."

NUMBERS 27:4

They appealed to Moses for help on the basis of who their father was. They stated their case and looked to him as God's authority. These women couldn't understand why they should not have some of their father's wealth simply because they were born female. If not for their boldness, their uncles would have received all their father's wealth while they would have been poor and homeless, receiving only leftovers from others.

DAUGHTERS OF ABRAHAM

But these women were daughters of Abraham. If you want the enemy to release you, remind him of whose daughter you are. No one would have listened to them if they had not initiated a meeting to plead their case. Per-haps you who have struggled need to call a meeting. Get in touch with people in power and demand what you want, or you will not get it. Speak for yourself. They could not understand why they were being discriminated against because of their gender.

DO YOU NEED TO CALL A MEETING?

One of the reasons Zelophehad's daughters could make a proper case for themselves was they were right. It was time to teach God's people that women have value. Abraham's daughters have worth. They didn't wait for a man to defend them; they took action in faith. And God saw it. He saw faith in those women.

> *And Moses brought their cause before the Lord. And the Lord spake unto Moses, saying, "The daughters of Zelophehad speak right: thou shalt surely give them a possession of an inheritance among their father's brethren; and thou shalt cause the inheritance of their father to pass unto them."*
>
> NUMBERS 27:5-7

When Moses heard the sisters' case, he didn't know what to do, so he asked God. And the women were vindicated. If they had failed, surely they would have been scorned by all the good people of Israel who would have never challenged Moses in such a way. But they succeeded instead and received the wealth of their father. God is no respecter of persons. Faith is based on equal opportunity.

YOU ARE A DAUGHTER OF ABRAHAM

Like the infirm woman, you are a daughter of Abraham if you have faith. You want the inheritance of your father to pass on to you. Why should you sit there and be in need when your heavenly Father has left you everything? Your Father is rich, and He left everything to you. However, you will not get your inheritance until you ask for it. Demand what your Father left you! That degree has your name on it. That promotion has your name on it. That financial breakthrough has your name on it.

There is no need to sit around waiting on someone else to get you what is yours. Nobody else is coming. The One who needed to come has already come. Jesus said, ". . . I am come that they might have life, and that they might have it more abundantly" (John 10:10). That is all you need.

LET YOUR FAITH SPEAK

The power to get wealth is in your tongue. You shall have whatever you say. So if you keep sitting around murmuring, groaning and complaining, you use your tongue against yourself. Your speech can keep you bent over and crippled. You may be destroying yourself with your words.

So open your mouth and speak something good about yourself and stand up on your feet. You used your mouth against yourself. Then you spoke against all the other women around you because you treated them just like you treated yourself. So open your mouth now and begin to speak deliverance and power. You are not defeated. You are Abraham's daughter.

ASK FOR YOUR INHERITANCE

When you start speaking correctly, God will give you what you say. But you must say you want it. Jesus said, "And all things, whatsoever ye shall ask in prayer, believing, ye shall receive" (Matthew 21:22). God willed you something. Your Father left you an inheritance. And if God would bless the sons of Abraham, surely He would bless the daughters of Abraham.

God will give you whatever you ask for (John 14:13). He will give you a business. He will give you a dream. He will make you the head and not the tail (Deuteronomy 28:13). God's power will bring all things up under your feet. So believe Him for your household. God will deliver. You don't need a sugar daddy. You have the Jehovah-jireh, the best provider this world has ever known.

For ye are all the children of God by faith in Christ Jesus.

GALATIANS 3:26

Women are just as much children of God as men are. Everything that God will do for a man, He will do for a woman. So you are not disadvantaged. You can get an inheritance like any man. Generally men don't cry about being single—they simply get on with life and stay busy. The same should be true for you. There is no reason a woman can't be complete in God without a husband.

But if you choose to get married, you should get married for the right reasons. Don't give in to a desperate spirit that forces you to put up with someone less than who you would really want. You could become stuck with someone immature and bear three little boys. Then you would have four boys. That is no way to live. You need someone who has some shoulders and backbone.

You need to marry someone who will hold you, help you, strengthen you, build you up, and be with you when the storms of life are raging. If you want a cute man, buy a photograph. But if you want some help, marry a godly man.

For as many of you as have been baptized into Christ have put on Christ. There is neither Jew nor Greek, there is neither bond nor free, there is neither male nor female: for ye are all one in Christ Jesus.

GALATIANS 3:27–28

Those ancient Israelite women, the daughters of Zelophehad, thought it was a disgrace for them to be starving when they considered who their father was. Rahab was a harlot until she found faith. But once she had faith, she no longer turned to her old profession. The infirm woman was bowed over until Jesus touched her. But once He touched her, she stood up.

WALK WITH RESPECT

You have put on Christ. So there is no reason to be bent over after you have received His touch. You can walk with respect even when you have past failures. It's not what people say about you that makes you different. It is what you say about yourself, and what your God has said about you, that really matters. Just because someone calls you a tramp doesn't mean you have to act like one. Rahab walked with respect. You will find her name mentioned in the lineage of Jesus Christ. She went from being a prostitute to being one of the great-grandmothers of our Lord and Savior Jesus Christ. You can't help where you've been, but you can help where you're going.

QUIT MAKING EXCUSES

God is not concerned about race. He is not concerned about your being black. You may think, "My people came over on a boat and picked cotton on a plantation." But it doesn't make any difference. The answer isn't in being white. Real spiritual advantage does not come from the color of your skin. It's not the color of your skin that will bring deliverance and help from God; it's the contents of your heart.

Some of us have particular problems based on where we came from, and we've got to deal with them. God says there is neither Greek nor Jew. There is no such thing as a black church. There is no such thing as a white church. There is only one Church, purchased by the blood of the Lamb. We are all one in Christ Jesus.

You may have been born with a silver spoon in your mouth too, but that doesn't make any difference. In the kingdom of God, social status doesn't mean anything. Rahab can be mentioned right next to Sarah because if you believe, God will bless. Faith is the only thing in this world where there is true equal opportunity. Everyone can come to Jesus.

". . . There is neither male nor female . . ." (Galatians 3:28). God doesn't look at your gender. He looks at your heart. He doesn't look at morality and good works. He looks at the faith that lives within. God is looking in your heart. You are spirit, and spirits are sexless. That's why angels don't have sexes; they simply are ministering spirits. Don't think of angels in terms of gender. They can manifest themselves as men, but angels are really ministering spirits. All people are one in Christ Jesus.

Christ saw the worth of the infirm woman because she was a daughter of Abraham. She had faith. He will unleash you also from the pain you have struggled with and the frustrations that have plagued you. Faith is truly equal opportunity. If you will but dare to believe that you are a daughter of Abraham, you will find the power to stand up straight and be unleashed. The potential that has been bound will be truly set free.

CHAPTER ELEVEN

A Woman Without Excuse

Many see Jesus as a way to heaven and the solution to spiritual problems, but they fail to see that He is the solution to all of life's problems.

꽃

Attitudes affect the way we live our lives. A good attitude can bring success. But a poor attitude can bring destruction. An attitude results from perspective. I'm sure you understand what perspective is. Everyone seems to have a different perspective. It comes from the way we look at life, and the way we look at life is often determined by our history.

The events of the past can cause us to have an outlook or perspective on life that is less than God's perspective. The little girl who was abused learns to defend herself by not trusting men. This attitude of defensiveness often stretches into adulthood. If we have protected ourselves a certain way in the past with some measure of success, then it is natural to continue that pattern throughout life. So we must learn how to look beyond our perspective to change old ways and attitudes.

The infirm woman whom Jesus healed was made completely well by His touch. She couldn't help herself no matter how hard she tried, but Jesus unleashed her. He lifted a heavy burden from her shoulders and set her free.

Today, many of us have things we need to be separated from, or burdens we need to have lifted. We will not function effectively until those things are lifted off of us. We can function to a certain point under a load, but we can't function as effectively as we would if the thing was lifted off of us. Perhaps some of you right now have things that are burdening you down.

You need to commend yourselves for having the strength to function under pressure. Unfortunately, we often bear the weight of our burdens alone, since we don't feel free to tell anyone about our struggles. So whatever strides you have made, be they large or small, you have made them against the current.

HAVE YOUR PROBLEMS
BECOME A SECURITY BLANKET?

It is God's intention that we be set free from the loads we carry. Many people live in co-dependent relationships. Others are anesthetized to their problems because they have had them so long. Perhaps you have become so accustomed to having a problem that even when you get a chance to be delivered, you find it hard to let it go. Problems can become like a security blanket.

But Jesus took away this woman's excuse. He said, ". . . Woman, thou art loosed from thine infirmity." And the moment He said that, it required something of her that she hadn't had to deal with before. For eighteen years she could excuse herself because she was handicapped. But the moment He told her the problem was gone, the woman had no excuse.

STRAIGHTEN OUT YOUR ATTITUDE

Before you get out of trouble, you need to straighten out your attitude. Until your attitude is corrected, you can't be corrected.

Why should we put up all the ramps and rails for the handicapped if we can heal them? You want everyone to make an allowance for your problem, but your problem needs to make an allowance for God and to humble itself to the point where you don't need special help. I'm not referring to physical handicaps; I'm addressing the emotional baggage that keeps us from total health. You cannot expect the whole human race to move over because you had a bad childhood. They will not do it. So you will end up in depression, frustration, and even confusion. You may even have trouble with relationships because people don't accommodate your hang-up.

One woman I pastored was extremely obnoxious. It troubled me deeply, so I took the matter to God in prayer. The Lord allowed me to meet her husband. And when I saw how nasty he talked to her, I understood why, when she reached down into her reservoir, all she had was hostility. That's all she had taken in. You cannot give out something that you haven't taken in.

A MATTER OF LIFE OR DEATH

Christ wants to separate you from the source of your bitterness until it no longer gives you the kind of attitude that makes you a carrier of pain. Your attitude affects your situation—your attitude, not other people's attitude about you. Your attitude will give you life or death.

One of the greatest deliverances people can ever experience in life is to have their attitude delivered. It doesn't do you any good to be delivered financially if your attitude doesn't change. I can give you $5,000, but if your attitude, your mental perspective, doesn't change, you will be broke in a week because you'll lose it again. The problem is not how much you have, it's what you do with what you have. If you can change your attitude, you might have only $50, but you can take that $50 and learn how to get $5 million.

When God comes to heal, He wants to heal your emotions also. Sometimes all we pray about is our situation. We bring God our shopping list of desires. Fixing circumstances is like applying a band-aid, though. Healing attitudes set people free to receive wholeness.

The woman who was crippled for eighteen years was delivered from her infirmity. The Bible says she was made straight and glorified God. She got a new attitude. However, the enemy still tried to defeat her by using the people around her. Satan doesn't want to let you find health and strength. And he may send another circumstance that will pull you down in the same way, if you don't change your attitude.

When you first read about this woman, you might have thought that the greatest deliverance was her physical deliverance. But I want to point out another deliverance that was even greater. The Bible says that when the Lord laid His hand on her, she was made straight. That's physical deliverance. Then her attitude also changed. How? She entered into praise and thanksgiving and worshiped the Lord. This woman began to leap and rejoice and magnify God and shout the victory like anybody who has been delivered from an eighteen-year infirmity should. But while she was glorifying God over here, the enemy was stirring up strife over there. That's how Satan operates. But she just kept on glorifying God. She didn't stop praising God to answer her accusers.

DEFENSIVE PRAISE

The Lord is your defense. You do not have to defend yourself. When God has delivered you, do not stop what you are doing to answer your accusers. Continue to bless His name, because you do not want your attitude to become defensive. When you have been through difficult times, you cannot afford to play around with moods and attitudes. Depression and defensiveness may make you vulnerable to the devil.

This woman had to protect herself by entering into defensive praise. This was not just praise of thanksgiving, it was defensive praise. Defensive praise is a strategy and a posture of war that says, "We will not allow our attitude to crumble and fall."

When you get to the point that you quit defending yourself or attacking others, you open up a door for the Lord to fight for you.

When this woman began to bless God, she built walls around her own deliverance. She decided to keep the kind of attitude that enabled the deliverance of God to be maintained in her life. When you have been through surgery, you cannot afford to fool around with band-aids.

GOD WILL PULL YOU OUT

When you're in trouble, God will reach into the mess and pull you out. However, you must be strong enough not to let people drag you back into it. Once God unleashes you, don't let anyone trap you into some religious fight. Keep praising Him. For this woman, the more they criticized her, the more she was justified because she just stood there and kept believing God. God is trying to get you to a place of faith. He is trying to deliver you from an attitude of negatives.

When you have had problems for many years, you tend to expect problems. God must have healed this woman's emotions too because she kept praising Him instead of paying attention to the quarrel of the religious folks around her. She could have easily fallen into negative thinking. But instead, she praised God.

Can you imagine what would have happened if she had stopped glorifying God and started arguing? If an argument could have gotten through her doors, this whole scene would have ended in a fight. But she was thankful and determined to express her gratitude.

LET THE WALLS COME DOWN

The Lord wants to speak a word of faith to you. He wants to set you free from every power that has kept you in bondage. But in order for that to be received in your spirit, you must allow Him to come in and instill faith. The emotional walls that surround us have to come down.

Love is eternal. It is not limited by time. When you commit yourself to loving someone, you make that commitment to all the person is. You are who you are because of your history. For me, that means I love my wife and who she has become. But in order for me to love her effectively, she must allow me into her history.

Many couples in a relationship argue over relatively insignificant things. Often, the reason these things are important is because one or the other is reminded of a past event. How can one person love another if he or she doesn't know the other person's history?

TOO NARROW AN APPROACH

The Church has become too narrow in its approach to attitude. We want to keep our attitudes to ourselves and simply take them to God. Although we certainly should take them to Him, we also need to learn to "bear ye one another's burdens . . ." (Galatians 6:2).

Thousands walk in fear. The Church could give strength to counter that fear. But thousands have built a wall around them because they do not trust anyone else. The Church can help its members learn to trust one another. Thousands are co-dependent and get their value from a relationship with

127

another person. The Church can point to God's love as the source for self-worth. We must help our members understand that we are not valuable because we love God; we are valuable because He loves us.

Jesus took away the ability of the infirm woman to make excuses for herself and gave her the strength to maintain an attitude of gratitude and praise. The Church today is to be the kind of safe haven that does the same thing. Those who are wounded should be able to come and find strength in our praise.

HAVE AN ATTITUDE OF GRATITUDE

Gratitude and defensive praise are contagious. Although the Bible doesn't specifically say so, I imagine that those who saw what was going on the day Jesus healed the infirm woman were caught up in praise as well. The Church must also find room to join in praise when the broken in our midst are healed. Those who missed the great blessing that day were those who decided to argue about religion.

The Bible describes heaven as a place where the angels rejoice over one sinner who comes into the faith (Luke 15:10). They rejoice because Jesus heals those who are broken. Likewise, God's people are to rejoice because the brokenhearted and emotionally wounded come to Him.

Christ unleashed power in the infirm woman that day. He healed her body and gave her the strength of character to keep a proper attitude. The woman who is broken and wounded today will find power unleashed within her too when she responds to the call and brings her wounds to the Great Physician.

CHAPTER TWELVE

The True Beauty of a Woman

It's not what people say about
you that makes you different.
It's what you say about
yourself, and what your God
has said about you, that
really matters.

W̶e are fascinated with beauty. There are contests of all kinds to determine who is the most beautiful of all. Advertisers spend millions of dollars to promote beauty pageants. The beauty industry is one of the largest in America. Women spend huge amounts of money on makeup, fashionable clothing, and jewelry. Plastic surgeons are kept busy cutting and tucking extra flesh and reshaping features to make people more attractive.

But in spite of all this attention, what is the true beauty of a woman? What is it that makes her genuinely attractive? Many feel unattractive because they don't meet a certain image to which they have aspired. Others are constantly frustrated in trying to get someone to notice how attractive they are.

No scientist has ever been able to make a woman. No doctor has been able to create a woman. And no engineer has been able to build a woman. But God has made some fine women. And according to Him, you don't have to look like a TV commercial to be beautiful. No one stays twenty-one forever.

START APPRECIATING YOURSELF

We must learn to thank God for who we are. Don't be a foolish woman watching television and crying because you don't look like the girl who opened up the window in the game show. You are not supposed to look like that. If God had wanted you to look like that, He would have made you like that. So be encouraged, God will send somebody along who will appreciate you the way you are.

And while you are waiting on that person, start appreciating yourself. Remind yourself, "I am valuable to God. I am somebody. And I won't let another use me or abuse me or treat me like I'm nothing. Yes, I've been through some bad times. I've been hurt and I've been bent out of shape. But the Lord touched me and loosed me, and now I am glorifying God and I'm not going back to where I came from."

As I mentioned earlier, there is an important lesson to learn from the account of Samson and Delilah in the Old Testament. (See Judges 16.) The Philistines were his enemies, but they could not kill Samson, until they found a door. The door was named Delilah. The Bible says Samson loved Delilah and that he became so infatuated with her that he made himself vulnerable.

It was not Delilah's beauty that captivated. It was not even her sexuality that destroyed Samson. Samson had known beautiful women before. He had slept with prostitutes. It was not just sexual exercise that caused her to get a grip on this man. What got Samson is what I call, *The Delilah Syndrome*. There is nothing in Scripture to prove that Delilah was beautiful. Maybe she was, but what got Samson was her understanding of the man.

LIFE IS NOT A FAIRY TALE

Beauty and sex appeal are not the areas to concentrate on. Because when you focus on the wrong areas, you don't get the right results. Society teaches you today that if you have the right hair, the right face, the right shape, the right clothes, and the right car, that you will get the right man. Then once you have this, you can expect you will buy the right house, have the right children, live the right life and live happily ever after. But this is simply not true. Life is not a fairy tale.

God put some things into the feminine spirit that a man needs more than anything God put on the feminine body. If a woman knows who she is on the inside, no matter what she looks like, she will have no problem being attractive to a man. If she knows her own self-worth, then when she comes before that man, he will receive her.

INWARDLY ADORNED

The enemy wants you to be so focused on your outer appearance that you won't recognize your inner beauty, your inner strength, your inner glory. Your real value cannot be bought, applied, added on, hung from your ears, or laid on your neck. Your real strength is in more than mere outward apparel and adornment for men. This real thing that causes a man to need you so desperately that he wants to be near you is not what is on the outside of you, but what is in you.

You need to recognize what God has put in you. When God made the woman, He didn't just decorate the outside. He decorated the inside of the woman. He put beauty in her spirit.

The Scriptures talk about not having the outward adornment of gold, silver, and costly array. And the Church took that passage and made a legal doctrine out of it. It was declared that there could be no jewelry, no makeup and no clothing of certain types. We are so negative at times. In fact, we were so busy dealing with the negative that we didn't hear the positive of what God said. God said that He had adorned the woman inwardly.

A WORD TO "BEAUTIFUL" WIVES

Likewise, ye wives, be in subjection to your own husbands. . . .

I PETER 3:1a

Notice that this verse in 1 Peter doesn't say women are to be in subjection to all men, just to their own husbands. God did not make you a servant to all men. You have the right to choose who you will be in subjection to—and please choose very carefully.

. . . that, if any obey not the word, they also may without the word be won by the conversation of the wives.

I PETER 3:1b

The word *conversation* here refers to lifestyle. You will not win your husband through lip-service; you will win him through the inward adornment of your beautiful lifestyle. He will see how you are—not what you say. He will watch how you act. He will watch your attitude. He will watch your disposition. A real problem with many women believers today is that with the same mouth they use to witness to their husbands, they are often cursing others. You cannot witness to and win a man while he sits up and listens to you gossip about others.

> *While they behold your chaste conversation [lifestyle] coupled with fear.*
>
> I Peter 3:2

This next verse of Peter doesn't say anything about your ruby red lips or your long $25 eyelashes. It says your husband should behold your lifestyle, your chaste (beautiful) lifestyle. *Chaste* is a word that means pure. Wives can win a husband by reverencing him.

> *Whose adorning let it not be that outward adorning of plaiting the hair, and of wearing of gold, or of putting on of apparel.*
>
> I PETER 3:3

Now if this verse means you cannot wear any of these things, then it means you must be naked. Apparel is clothing. The truth that Peter is telling us is that a woman's beauty and strength are not to be found on the outside. There is more to you than clothes. There's more to you than gold. There's more to you than hairdos.

Society promotes the notion that beauty is found in these outer things. However, if you keep working only on these outer things, you will find yourself looking in a mirror to find your value. You could go broke fixing up the outside and still be lonely and alone.

The *Delilah Syndrome* had to do with Delilah's ability to simply provide Samson with a place to rest. Samson felt comfortable around her. The man was tired, so he laid on her and slept. There is nothing in his story to say he loved her for sex. She simply gave him rest. He needed it so desperately that even when he knew she was trying to kill him, he couldn't stay away.

YOU ARE SARAH'S DAUGHTERS

If Satan can work Delilah's strengths against men, then God can use them for men. If you are married, you can enrich your marriage through inner beauty. If you're not married, when you do get married, you will understand that it's not the necklaces you wear that make you attractive. It's not the twists you put in your hair. It's something that God puts in your heart that actually affects the man.

> *But let it be the hidden man of the heart, in that which is not corruptible, even the ornament of a **meek and quiet spirit,** which is in the sight of God of great price.*
>
> I PETER 3:4

Ladies, God gave you the ornament of a meek and quiet spirit that is more valuable than any other outer form of jewelry. It is worth more than gold. It is more powerful than sexual ability.

When Samson hit Delilah's lap, she calmed him. Can you see what made Adam partake of the forbidden fruit, knowing it was evil? The Bible says Eve was deceived, but that he knew it. Do you see how powerful your influence is? The enemy wants to capitalize on what God put in you. That is why you must watch what goes through your doors.

> *For after this manner in the old time the holy women also, who trusted in God, adorned themselves. . . .*
>
> I PETER 3:5

This verse of Peter talks about how women decorated themselves in the times of the patriarchs. Sarah was beautiful because she exhibited inner beauty and lived in obedience to Abraham.

Even as Sara obeyed Abraham, calling him lord: whose daughters ye are, as long as ye do well, and are not afraid with any amazement.

I PETER 3:6

Here Peter says that you are Sarah's daughters when you are not afraid with any amazement. When you resist the temptation to react to circumstances and maintain a peaceful, meek and quiet spirit in times of frustration, then you are Sarah's daughters.

If you can stay calm in a storm, if you can praise God under pressure, if you can worship in the midst of critics and criticism, God says you are Sarah's daughter.

If you can keep a calm head when the bills are more than the income, and not lose control when Satan says you won't make it, if you can stand in the midst of the storm, you are Sarah's daughter.

If you can rebuke the fear that is knocking at the door of your heart, and tell that low self-esteem it cannot come in, and rebuke all the spirits that are waiting to attack you and take you captive, you are Sarah's daughter.

If you can stand calm in the midst of the storm and say, "I know God will deliver me," you are Sarah's daughter. If you can walk with God in the midst of the storm and trust Him to bring you through dry places, you are Sarah's daughter.

If you can judge God faithful, and know that God cannot lie, understanding that Satan is the father of lies, you are Sarah's daughter.

If you can stand there when fear is trying to get you to overreact and fall apart, you are Sarah's daughter. If you can stand there and push a tear from off the side of your face and smile in the middle of the rain, you are Sarah's daughter.

YOU ARE TRULY BEAUTIFUL

God is adorning you with glory, power and majesty. He will send people into your life to appreciate your real beauty, your real essence. It is the kind of beauty that lasts in a face full of wrinkles, gray hair, falling arches, crow's feet, and all the pitfalls that may come your way. There's a beauty that you can see in a ninety-year-old woman's face that causes an old man to smile. God is decorating you on the inside. He is putting a glory in you that will shine through your eyes. A man will come along and look in your eyes. He will not talk about whether they were blue or whether your eye-shadow was right or not. He will look in your eyes and see trust, peace, love and life.

YOU ARE A WONDERFUL PIECE OF ARTWORK

Appreciate the ornaments of God. Let God give you a new attitude. Let Him wash everything out of your spirit that is against Him. Let go of anger, hate, frustration and bitterness. God wants you unleashed. He repeats today, just as He did 2,000 years ago, "Woman, thou art loosed."

Beauty comes in many ways. However, true beauty is always on the inside. A faithful wife is more precious than words can express. The inner beauty that makes you valuable to God will also make you valuable to others. Some may just take longer to notice it. Regardless of how long it takes, know the attractiveness and beauty that is within.

Perhaps you feel scared by the past. Maybe you think you are unattractive and unworthy. Nothing could be more untrue. God painted a wonderful piece of artwork one day. That painting is you.

CHAPTER THIRTEEN

Every Woman Needs a Sabbath

You need the calmness of a
Sabbath rest because it is
through the resting of your
spirit that the restoration of
your life begins to occur.

W e have dealt with many aspects of the story of Jesus healing the infirm
woman. However, in this chapter I would like to look at an issue
underlying the miracle. It does not really concern either the woman or
Christ. It concerns the time of her healing: The Sabbath.

The Sabbath is a day of rest. It is a day of restoration. Following creation,
on the seventh day, God rested (Genesis 2:2). Rest is for the purpose of
restoration. It is not just because you're tired. It is during a time of rest that
you replenish or receive back those things that were expended or put out.

But it is also during the time of restoration that the enemy wants to break off your fellowship with the Lord.

I don't want you to think of rest just in terms of sleep. Please understand that rest and restoration are related concepts. You need the calmness of a Sabbath rest because it is through the resting of your spirit that the restoration of your life begins to occur. The enemy does not want you to have this rest.

It is not a mere coincidence that this woman was healed on the Sabbath day. The Bible goes to great pains to make us aware that it was during the Sabbath that this woman experienced her healing. The Sabbath was meant not only for God to rest, but also for God to enjoy His creation with man. So the issues here are rest and communion.

A SIGN OF THE COVENANT

In the nation of Israel, God used the Sabbath day as a sign of the covenant. It proved that they were His people. They spent time in worship and fellowship with the Lord on the Sabbath. That is what the Sabbath is truly all about. It is real communion between the heart of man and the heart of God.

When Jesus began to minister in a restful situation, needs began to be manifested. The infirm woman's need was revealed in the midst of the Sabbath. You can never get your needs met by losing your head. When you calm down, God speaks.

When you start murmuring and complaining, the only thing God can focus on is your unbelief. But when you start resting in Him, He can focus on your problems and on the areas of your life that need to be touched.

Also, when you begin to enter into real worship with God, that's the best time to have Him minister to your needs. That's the time when God gives restoration in your life. Satan, therefore, wants to break up your Sabbath rest.

THE "RELIGIOUS" AMONG US

Sometimes I would rather deal with rank sinners than with religious people. When Jesus healed this woman on the Sabbath, the religious folks got upset. Why? Because religious people esteem religiosity above God's creation. They are more concerned about keeping doctrine than about helping people. One thing you can't seem to deliver religious people from is their own *religiousness*. But man is God's concern above everything else.

The infirm woman was not sitting around complaining. She was not murmuring. She was not hysterical. She had a problem, but she was calm. She was just sitting there listening to the words of the Master. She had brought her problem with her, but her problem did not dominate her time of worship.

CHRIST IS OUR SABBATH REST

I want to zoom in on the Sabbath day, because what the Sabbath was physically, Christ is spiritually. Christ is our Sabbath rest. He is the end of our labors. We are saved by grace through faith and not by works, lest any man should be able to boast (Ephesians 2:8–9). Jesus said:

> *"Come unto me, all ye that labour and are heavy laden, and I will give you rest. Take my yoke upon you, and learn of me; for I am meek and lowly in heart: and ye shall find rest unto your souls. For my yoke is easy, and my burden is light."*
>
> MATTHEW 11:28–30

The *rest* of the Lord is so complete that when Jesus was dying on the cross, He said, ". . . It is finished . . ." (John 19:30). It was so powerful. For

139

the first time in history, a high priest sat down in the presence of God without having to run in and out bringing blood to atone for the sins of man. When Christ entered in once and for all, He offered up *Himself* for us that we might be delivered from sin.

YOU CAN REST IN HIM

So if you really want to be healed, you've got to be in Him. If you really want to be set free, and experience restoration, you've got to be in Him, because your healing comes in the Sabbath rest. Your healing comes in Christ Jesus. As you rest in Him, every infirmity, every area bent out of place will be restored.

But the devil knows this truth also. So he does not want you to rest in the Lord. Satan wants you to be anxious. He wants you to be upset. He wants you to be hysterical. He wants you to be suicidal, doubtful, fearful and neurotic.

There remaineth therefore a rest to the people of God. For he that is entered into his rest, he also hath ceased from his own works, as God did from his. Let us labour therefore to enter into that rest, lest any man fall after the same example of unbelief.

HEBREWS 4:9–11

Sometimes it takes work to find the place of rest and calm. Our hectic world does not lend itself to quiet and peace. It creates noise and uneasiness. Even though the infirm woman was bowed over and could not lift herself, she rested in the fact that she was in the presence of a mighty God. He is able to do exceedingly and abundantly above all that we may ask or think (Ephesians 3:20).

Jesus also confronted the woman at the well with some exciting truths.

Jesus answered and said unto her, "Whosoever drinketh of this water shall thirst again: but whosoever drinketh of the water that I shall give him shall never thirst; but the water that I shall give him shall be in him a well of water springing up into everlasting life."

JOHN 4:13-14

In this passage, Jesus was sitting at the well waiting for someone to return. He was relaxed. He was calm and resting. He knew who He was. God doesn't get excited about circumstances.

Another time the disciples and Jesus were on a ship. Then a storm arose that looked like it was about to sink the ship. However, Jesus didn't become concerned about circumstances. In fact, He was sleeping, resting in the middle of the crisis. While everyone else was running all over the boat trying to figure out how they would get into life jackets and into the lifeboats, Jesus was resting. Was Jesus resting because He was lazy? No, He was resting because He knew that He was greater than the storm. When the disciples ran frightened to Him not knowing what to do, Jesus rose up and spoke to the winds and waves and said, ". . . Peace, be still . . ." (Mark 4:39).

YOU DON'T HAVE TO STRUGGLE

When you know who you are, you don't have to struggle. You don't have to work Him up. That was Christ's attitude when the woman at the well met Him. When this woman came down with her waterpot on her shoulder, she was all upset and worried about the water she needed to draw. But when she met Jesus sitting by the well, He began to demonstrate calmness. He told her, "If you drink of the water that you have, you will thirst again, but if you drink of the water that I have, you will never thirst."

The woman saith unto him, "Sir, give me this water, that I thirst not, neither come hither to draw." Jesus saith unto her, "Go, call thy husband, and come hither."

JOHN 4:15-16

141

Jesus shifted the focus of the conversation to the real need.

The woman answered and said, "I have no husband." Jesus said unto her, "Thou hast well said, I have no husband: for thou hast had five husbands; and he whom thou now hast is not thy husband: in that saidst thou truly."

JOHN 4:17–18

Like this woman, you can get yourself into situations that wound and upset your spirit. These kinds of wounds can't be healed through human effort. You must get in the presence of God and let Him fill those voids in your life. You will not settle it up by going from friend to friend. This woman had already tried that. She had already gone through five men. So the answer is not getting another man. It's getting in touch with *the Man*, Jesus.

Once the woman at the well had been ministered to by Jesus, she threw down her waterpot and ran to tell others about the man she had met at the well. Her mind was no longer focused on her problems. They were focused on Jesus. We too need to get rid of the old, carnal man. Some of those old attachments and old ways of living need to be replaced with the calmness of the Spirit.

This woman could never have rid herself of the old man until she met the new man, Jesus. When you meet the new, you get the power to say good-bye to the old. You will never be able to break the grip on your life that those old ways have until you know Jesus Christ is the real way. You will never get it straight without Jesus. You must come to Him just as you are. Knowing Him will give you the power to break away from the old self and the ties that bind.

If you have something that has attached itself to you that is not of God, you won't be able to break it through your own strength. Submit yourself unto God, resist the enemy, and he will flee from you (James 4:7). As you submit to God, you receive the power to resist the enemy.

This woman didn't even go back home. She ran into the city telling everyone to come and see the Man who had told her about her life. You do yourself a disservice until you really come to know Jesus. He satisfies. Everyone else, well, they pacify, but Jesus satisfies. He can satisfy every need and every yearning. He heals every pain and every affliction. Then He lifts every burden and every trouble in your life.

YOU HAVE BEEN BENT OVER LONG ENOUGH

You have had enough tragedy. You have been bent over long enough. God will do something good in you. God kept you living through all those years of infirmity because He has something greater for you than what you've ever experienced. God kept you because He has something better for you.

You may have been abused and misused. Perhaps all those you trusted in turned on you and broke your heart. Still, God has sustained you. You didn't make it because you were strong. You didn't make it because you were smart. You didn't make it because you were wise. You made it because God's amazing grace kept you and sustained you. God has more for you today than what you went through yesterday. So don't give up. Don't give in. Hold on. The blessing is on the way.

I dare you to realize that you can do all things through Christ who strengthens you (Philippians 4:13). Once the infirm woman knew that, she didn't have to be bent over; she stood straight up. When Jesus told her to be loosed, she stood up and glorified God. He also told the woman at the well to get rid of the old. He wanted her to step away from that old pattern of selfishness. Then suddenly, she recognized that she didn't have what she thought she had.

GOD'S BEST GIVES US HIS REST

Just like the woman at the well, the sinful things that you have fought to maintain in your life are not worth what you thought they were. I'm referring to some to those things that have attached themselves to your life in which you find comfort. Some of those habits that you have come to enjoy, and some of those relationships you thought gave security. They just haven't been profitable. Often we settle for less because we didn't meet the best. But when you get the best, it gives you the power to let go of the rest.

LET GO NOW

The infirm woman didn't panic because of her crippling disease. She had been in torment and pain for eighteen years. But when she came into the presence of Jesus, she relaxed in Him. She expected that He would take care of her. And the result was a wonderful healing. What the woman at the well expected was regular water, but she left the well having found the Savior. She sought temporal satisfaction, but found eternal satisfaction!

That's what rest and Sabbath is. It is the ability to find eternal satisfaction in Jesus. The world can never give us peace and satisfaction. But Jesus offers both freely.

The woman who has struggled can find satisfaction. You can find hope for your soul. It is found in the Master of the universe. He will not deny you because of your past. He will not scrutinize your every action. He will take you as you are, and *give you rest*. He will provide a peace that will satisfy the very yearning of your soul.

And the peace of God, which passeth all understanding, shall keep your hearts and minds through Christ Jesus.

PHILIPPIANS 4:7

CHAPTER FOURTEEN

Winter Woman

Perhaps you feel scarred by the past. Maybe you think you are unattractive and unworthy. Nothing could be more untrue. God painted a wonderful piece of artwork one day. That painting is you.

And she said unto them, "Call me not Naomi, call me Mara: for the Almighty hath dealt very bitterly with me. I went out full, and the Lord hath brought me home again empty: why then call ye me Naomi, seeing the Lord hath testified against me, and the Almighty hath afflicted me?"

RUTH 1:20-21

This morning when I rose, the land was still asleep. I watched the miracle of beginnings from the verandah of my hotel. The waves of the sea wandered listlessly in and dashed themselves on empty beaches where the sand smiled at the peacefulness of the breaking day. Like the initial sounds of an orchestra warming up for a concerto, the sea gulls cried and screeched out their opening solos. The wind watched, occasionally brushing past the palm trees spreading their leaves like the fan of a distinguished lady. Far to the east the sun crept up on stage as if it was trying to arrive without disturbing anyone. It peeked up over the ocean like the eye of a child around a corner as he stealthily plays peek-a-boo.

If I had not stayed perched on my window's edge, I would have misjudged the day. I would have thought that the morning, or perhaps the bustling sun-drenched afternoon, was the most beautiful part of the day. I would have thought the sound of laughing, hysterically happy children running into or away from the ocean would have, without contention, won the award for the best part of the day.

But just before I turned in my ballot to cast my vote in the poll, the wisdom of the evening slipped up on the stage. The early morning entertainment and the bustling sounds of the afternoon had distracted me. Now I looked over in the distance as the sun began its descent. When I did, I noticed that the crescendo of the concert is always reserved for the closing.

How had I not noticed that the sun had changed her sundress to an evening gown, full of color and grandeur? The grace of a closing day is far greater than the uncertainty of morning. So too, the next time you get a chance to notice a sun burst into its neon rainbow and curtsy before setting in the west, you will scratch out your early scribbling and recast your vote. For the most beautiful part of the day, in fact the most beautiful part of a woman's life, is at the setting of the sun.

I write this with my mother in mind. Her hair has changed colors before my eyes. Like afterthoughts of an artist, lines have been etched upon her brow. Her arms are much weaker now, and her gait much slower; but she is somehow warmer at life's winter age than she was in her days of summer. All of life's tragedy has been wrestled to the mat, and still she stands to attest to the authenticity of her goals, dreams and ambitions.

THE WINTER OF LIFE

What is wrong with hanging around the stage to collect an encore from a grateful audience whose lives have been touched by the beauty of your song? Just because the glare of summer doesn't beat upon your face doesn't mean that there is nothing left for you to do. Whose presence will stand as a witness that God will see you through? Who will care to catch a glimpse of your children run their race or catch them when they fall beneath the weight of their day?

God never extends days beyond purpose. My daughters are in their springtime, my wife is in her middle of summer, and my mother is walking through autumn to step into the winter of her life. Together they form a chord of womanhood—three different notes creating a harmonious blend. To the reader I would suggest: Enjoy every note.

While the earth remaineth, seedtime and harvest, and cold and heat, and summer and winter, and day and night shall not cease.

GENESIS 8:22

Our culture has celebrated youth to such a degree that we have isolated the elderly. The Hollywood mentality accentuates the dynamics of youth as though each season of life didn't have its own beauty. But anyone who observes nature will tell you that all seasons have their own advantages and disadvantages. So it is important that we teach women to prepare for the winter.

I believe age can be stressful for women in a way that it isn't for men—only because we have not historically recognized women at other stages in their lives. Equally disturbing is the fact that statisticians tell us women tend to live longer, more productive lives than their male counterparts. And it is not their longevity of life that is disturbing; it is the fact that many times, because of the early death of their spouse, they have no sense of companionship.

HONOR WIDOWS WHO ARE WIDOWS INDEED

Although the Bible has very little to say in regard to the care of aged men, it does address ministry to widows. (See 1 Timothy 5:3–16.) So we need to invest some effort in encouraging older women. They have a need for more than just provision of natural substance. Many women spend their lives building their identity around their role, rather than around their own person. Then when their role changes, they feel somewhat displaced. Because being a good mother is a self-sacrificing job, when those demands have subsided, many women feel like Naomi. Her name meant "my joy." But after losing her children and her husband she said, "Change my name to *Mara*." *Mara* means "bitterness."

RESISTING THE "MARA MENTALITY"

Don't allow changing times to change who you are. It is dangerous to lose your identity in your circumstances. Circumstances can change and when they do, older women can feel empty and unfulfilled. This is what happened to Naomi. But in spite of her bout with depression, God still had much for her to contribute in life. So just because life's demands have changed doesn't mean your life is over. If yours has, you need to redefine your purpose, gather your assets and keep on living and giving. As long as you can maintain a sense of worth, you can resist the "Mara" mentality.

NO ONE HAS SEEN IT ALL

Naomi was a collection of tragedies. She had weathered many storms. Discouragement comes when people think they have seen it all and most of it was terrible! But no matter what age you are, you have never seen it all. There are no graduations from the school of life other than death. No one knows how God will end His book, but He does tend to save the best for last.

Israel didn't recognize Jesus because they were so used to seeing what they had already seen. God had sent dozens of prophets, but when He finally sent their King, they failed to recognize Him. So it is dangerous to assume that what you will see out of life will be similar to what you saw before.

God can have the strangest way of restoring purpose to one's life. For Naomi, it was through a relationship she had tried to dissuade. It is dangerous to keep sending people away. The very one you are trying to send away may have the key to restoring your purpose and fulfillment in life.

And Ruth said, "Intreat me not to leave thee, or to return from following after thee: for whither thou goest, I will go; and where thou lodgest, I will lodge: thy people shall be my people, and thy God my God."

RUTH 1:16

Ruth was Naomi's daughter-in-law. But Naomi thought their only connection was through her son, who was now dead. Many times we who have been very family-oriented do not understand friendships. When family circumstances change, we lapse into isolation because we know nothing of other relationships. There are bonds that are stronger than blood (Proverbs 18:24). They are God-bonds! When God brings someone like Ruth into our life, He is the bonding agent. When Ruth said, "Your God shall be my God," God wanted Naomi to see the splendor of winter relationships. He wanted her to experience the joy of passing the baton of her wisdom and strength to someone worthy of her attention. But we should let God choose such a person for us, because too often we choose on the basis of fleshly ties, not godly ties.

I have noticed in the Scriptures that the strongest female relationships tend to be exemplified between older and younger women. I am certainly not suggesting that such will always be the case. However, let me submit a few cases for your own edification.

NAOMI AND RUTH

1. Ruth would have died in Moab, probably marrying some heathen idolater if it were not for the wisdom of Naomi, an older, more seasoned woman. Naomi knew how to provide guidance without manipulation—a strength many women at that stage of life do not have. Ruth was, of course, one of the great-grandparents in the lineage of Jesus Christ. She had greatness in her that God used Naomi to cultivate. Perhaps Naomi would have been called Mara, and perhaps she would have ended up dying in bitterness without touching any lives, if it had not been for Ruth.

ELIZABETH AND MARY

2. Elizabeth, the wife of the priest Zacharias, is the biblical synonym for the modern pastor's wife. She was a winter woman with a summer experience. She was pregnant with a promise. And in spite of her declining years, she was fulfilling more destiny then than she ever had in her youth. Elizabeth is biblical proof that God blesses us in His own time, and on His own terms. But she was also in seclusion. Perhaps it was the attitude of the community. Many times when an older woman is still vibrant and productive it can cause jealousy and intimidation. Perhaps it was the silent stillness in her womb which some believe she experienced. Whatever the reason, she was a recluse for six months until she heard a knock at the door. If you have isolated yourself from others, regardless of the reason, I pray you will hear the knocking of the Lord. He will give you the garment of praise

to clothe the spirit of heaviness (Isaiah 61:3).

When Elizabeth lifted her still-creaking body, which seemed almost anchored down to the chair, and drug her enlarged torso to the door, she saw a young girl, a picture of herself in days gone by, standing there. Opening that door changed her life forever. As you open the door to new relationships and remove the chain from your own fears, God will overwhelm you with new splendor. Mary, the future mother of our Savior and Lord, Elizabeth's young cousin, was at the door! The splendor of this young girl's salutation, and the exposure to her experience, made the baby in Elizabeth's womb leap as Elizabeth was filled with the Holy Ghost. People probably wondered why these women who were so different, were so close. But it was a God-bond! God doesn't mean for you to go sit in a chair and die! *So in Jesus' name, get up—and answer the door!*

STRIPPING OFF THE OLD WAX

When I was in school, I worked at a local paint store, and of course had to acquaint myself with our products and procedures. As I became familiar with them, I became intrigued by a refinishing product that restored old furniture to its former luster. So I purchased the product to see if it was as effective as I had been told. I learned right away that the most difficult part of restoring furniture was stripping off the old wax. It takes patience to overcome the effects of years of use and abuse. And if you are not committed to getting back what you once had, you could easily decide that the process is impossible. Nevertheless, I assure you, it is not impossible.

RESTORATION IS A PROCESS

David, the psalmist, declares, "He restoreth my soul . . ." (Psalm 23:3). Restoration is a process. And only God knows what it takes to remove the build-up that may be existing in your life. But He specializes in restoring and renewing the human heart.

> *And the women said unto Naomi, "Blessed be the Lord, which hath not left thee this day without a kinsman, that his name may be famous in Israel. And he shall be unto thee a restorer of thy life, and a nourisher of thine old age: for thy daughter in law, which loveth thee, which is better to thee than seven sons, hath born him."*
>
> RUTH 4:14–15

Remember that Naomi had almost changed her name to Mara. She felt that God had dealt very bitterly with her. It is dangerous to be prejudiced against God. Prejudice means to pre-judge. Still, people, even believers, often prejudge God. Naomi did. However, God wasn't finished with her yet. Before it was over, everyone agreed that the hand of the Lord was upon her. Therefore, if you are being challenged with the silent struggles of winter, you can be encouraged that you're still on course. Trust God to see you through days that may be different from the ones you encountered earlier.

THE SILENT STRUGGLES OF WINTER

I believe the most painful experience is to have to look backward and stare into the cold face of regret. When doing so most people have thought, "I wonder how things would have been had I not made this decision . . . or that one. . . ." To realize that you have been both the victim and the assailant in your own life may be difficult to accept—especially since most of those dilemmas are birthed through the womb of your own decisions. Admittedly, there are those who inadvertently crashed into circumstances that stripped them, wounded them and left them feeling like the victim on the Jericho road! No matter which case best describes your current situation, first pause to thank God that, like Naomi, in spite of any tragedies of your youth, it is a miracle that you survived the solemn chill of former days. Your presence should be a praise. Look over your shoulder and see what could have been. Has God dealt with you bitterly? I think not. Anyone can recognize Him in the sunshine, but in the storm His disciples thought He was a ghost (Matthew 14:26).

TWO THINGS EVERY NAOMI CAN RELY UPON

There are two things every Naomi can rely upon as she gathers wood for winter days and wraps quilts around weak, willowy legs.

- First, God is a *restorer*. That is to say, as you sit by the fire sipping coffee, rehearsing your own thoughts, playing old reruns from the scenes in your life—some things He will explain, and others He will heal. Restoration doesn't mean all the lost people who left you will return. Neither Naomi's husband nor her sons were resurrected. It is just that God gives purpose back to the years that had question marks.

WAIT BY THE WINDOW

How many times have you been able to look back and say, "If I hadn't gone through that, I wouldn't have known or received this." Simply said, "He will make it up to you." He restores the effects of the years of turmoil. The people who heard Naomi running through the house with rollers in her hair complaining that God had dealt bitterly, should have waited with their noses pressed against the window pane as God masterfully brought His peace into her arms. If you wait by the window, you will hear the soft hum of an old woman nodding with her grandchild clutched in her arms. Perhaps she is too proud to tell you that she charged God foolishly, but the smile on her leathery face and the calmness of her rest says, ". . . He hath done all things well . . ." (Mark 7:37).

"And I will restore to you the years that the locust hath eaten, the cankerworm, and the caterpiller, and the palmerworm, my great army which I sent among you. And ye shall eat in plenty, and be satisfied, and praise the name of the Lord your God, that hath dealt wondrously with you: and my people shall never be ashamed."

JOEL 2:25-26

• Second, the Lord will be known as your *nourisher*. This may be a difficult role for you who have clutched babies and men alike to the warm breast of your sensitivity. You, who have been the source for others to be strengthened, may find it difficult to know what to do with this role reversal. The nourisher must learn to be nourished.

STRENGTH TO THE FEEBLE AND WARMTH TO THE COLD

Many women pray more earnestly as intercessors for others than for themselves. That is wonderful, but there ought to be a time that you desire certain things for yourself. Our God is El Shaddai, "the breasted one" (Genesis 17:1). He gives strength to the feeble and warmth to the cold. There is great comfort in His arms. Like children, even adults can snuggle into His everlasting arms and hear the heartbeat of a loving God who says, "And ye shall eat in plenty, and be satisfied, and praise the name of the Lord your God . . ." (Joel 2:26).

Expect God in all His varied forms. He is a master of disguise, a guiding star in the night, a lily left growing in the valley, or an answered prayer sent on the breath of an angel. Angels are the butlers of heaven; they open doors. He sends angels to minister to His own. Have you ever seen an angel? They aren't always dressed in white with dramatically arched wings. Sometimes they are so ordinary that they can be overlooked. Ruth was an angel that Naomi almost sent away. God can use anyone as a channel of nourishment. Regardless of the channel, He is still the source.

Do not forget to entertain strangers, for by so doing some people have entertained angels without knowing it.

HEBREWS 13:2 NIV

ANGELS IN YOUR PATH

When Hagar was lost in the wilderness of depression and wrestling exasperation, God sent an angel. When the labor-ridden mother of Samson was mundane and barren, God sent an angel. When young Mary was wandering listlessly through life, God sent an angel. When the grief-stricken Mary Magdalene came stumbling down to the tomb, God sent an angel. For every woman in crisis, there is an angel! For every lonely night and forgotten mother, there is an angel. For every lost young girl wandering the concrete jungle of an inner city, there is an angel.

My sister, set your coffee down, take the blanket off your legs, and stand up on your feet! Hast thou not known, hast thou not heard? For every woman facing winter, there is an angel!

Are not all angels ministering spirits sent to serve those who will inherit salvation?

HEBREWS 1:14 NIV

Through faith also Sara herself received strength to conceive seed, and was delivered of a child when she was past age, because she judged him faithful who had promised.

HEBREWS 11:11

THE MIRACLES OF WINTER

I think it would be remiss of me not to share, before moving on, the miracles of winter. In the summer, all was well with Sarah. At that time she knew little about Jehovah, her husband's God. She basically knew she was

155

in love with a wonderful man. She was the luckiest woman in Ur. An incredibly beautiful woman already, she wore her love like a striking woman wears a flattering dress. The air smelled like honeysuckle and the wind called her name. Then one day, her husband spoke to her about moving. Where . . . she didn't know. And crazy as it may sound to those who have forgotten the excitement of summer, Sarah really didn't care. She ran into the tent and began to pack. Sometimes it's good to get away from relatives and friends. Starting over would be fun!

But soon the giddy exuberance of summer started to ebb as she began wrestling with the harsh realities of following a dreamer. And Abraham had not completely done what God said. God said to ". . . Get thee out of thy country, and from *thy kindred* . . ." (Genesis 12:1). Still, Abraham took a few of their relatives with them.

"I am sure he had a good reason," Sarah thought. But what was really troubling her wasn't the strife between the relatives, or the fighting herdsmen. It was the absence of a child. By now she was sure she was barren. She felt like she had cheated Abraham out of an important part of life. Then when she was told she would have a baby, Sarah laughed. "If I am going to get a miracle," she said, "God had better hurry!"

DON'T SET YOUR OWN WATCH

I want to warn you against setting your own watch. God's time is not your time. He may not come when you want Him to, but He is always right on time. Twice it is mentioned that Sarah laughed. The first time she laughed *at* God. But in the winter time of her life, she laughed *with* God. The first time she laughed at the impossibility of God's promise. But after she had gone through life's experiences, she learned that God is faithful to perform His Word.

THE FIRST LAUGH

Abraham and Sarah were already old and well advanced in years, and Sarah was past the age of childbearing. So Sarah laughed to herself as she thought, "After I am worn out and my master is old, will I now have this pleasure?" Then the Lord said to Abraham, "Why did Sarah laugh and say, 'Will I really have a child, now that I am old?' Is anything too hard for the Lord? I will return to you at the appointed time next year and Sarah will have a son."

GENESIS 18:11–14   NIV

THE LAST LAUGH

Sarah became pregnant and bore a son to Abraham in his old age, at the very time God had promised him. Abraham gave the name Isaac to the son Sarah bore him. When his son Isaac was eight days old, Abraham circumcised him, as God commanded him. Abraham was a hundred years old when his son Isaac was born to him. Sarah said, "God has brought me laughter, and everyone who hears about this will laugh with me." And she added, "Who would have said to Abraham that Sarah would nurse children? Yet I have borne him a son in his old age."

GENESIS 21:2–7   NIV

Listen carefully at what I am about to say. It is relevant to you. I am not so much concerned with the eighteenth chapter of Genesis where Sarah laughs in unbelief. Nor am I focusing my attention on the twenty-first chapter where she laughs with "the joy of the Lord." I want to discuss with you the events that led to the miracles of her winter.

Often, we share our personal testimony by telling where we started and where we ultimately arrived without sharing the sequence of events that led to our deliverance. And because we leave out the process, our listeners feel defeated because they named it and claimed it and still didn't attain it! We don't tell them about the awful trying of our faith that preceded our coming forth as pure gold. Today, however, we will share the whole truth and nothing but the truth! Amen.

In between these powerful moments in the life of one of God's finest examples of wives, everything in her life was tested. I believe that her love for Abraham gave her the courage to leave home, but her love for God brought forth the promised seed. Careful now, I am not saying that her love for God replaced her love for her husband; I am merely saying that it complimented the other to the highest level. After all, what good is it to appreciate what God gave us, if we do not appreciate the God who gave it to us? If age should do nothing else, it should help us put things in proper perspective. There is nothing like time to show us that we have misplaced priorities.

SARAH'S TRAGIC BLESSING IN GERAR

In summer, Sarah followed Abraham out of their country and away from their kindred. But as the seasons of life changed, she took another pilgrimage into what could have been a great tragedy. Abraham, her beloved husband, led his wife into Gerar. As I am a man and a leader myself, I dare not be too hard on him. Anyone can make a poor decision. The decision to go to Gerar I could defend, even though Gerar means "halting place." I have made decisions that brought me to a halting place in my life. But what is reprehensible is that Abraham, Sarah's protector and covering, when afraid for his own safety, lied about her identity (Genesis 20). You never know who people are until you witness them under pressure. Now, I am not being sanctimonious about Abraham's flagrant disregard for truth. But it was a life-threatening lie.

MEN WILL FAIL YOU

Have you ever known someone upon whom you had cast the weight of your confidence, only to have your trust defrauded in a moment of self-gratification and indulgence? Someone who has a selfish need can jeopardize all that you have. Abraham's infamous lie jeopardized the safety of his wife. King Abimelech was a heathen king. He was used to getting whatever he wanted. And his reputation for debauchery preceded him to the degree that Abraham, the father of faith, feared for his life. So rather than risk himself, he told the king that his lovely wife was really his sister. Abraham knew that such a statement would cause Sarah to have to fulfill the torrid desires of a heathen. And Sarah now finds herself being bathed and perfumed as an offering of lust for the passions of the king.

GOD WILL SAVE YOU

Imagine the icy grip of fear that clutched this first lady of faith. Imagine her shock to realize that under real stress, a person can never be sure what another individual will do to secure his own well-being. Her Abraham had failed her. But God did not! Maybe there is someone in your life who selfishly threw you into a tempestuous situation. If so, take courage! Just because Satan set a snare for you doesn't mean you can't escape. The God we serve is able. His Word to you is "Woman, be loosed!"

Abraham's faith had always been the star of the Old Testament, but not that day. It's amazing how faith will come up in your heart at a crisis. Consider Sarah. She is facing the anxious footsteps of her rapist. She knows it will not be long until she will be abused. Like a frightened rabbit crouched in a corner, she realizes Abraham will not rescue her. I don't know what she prayed, but I know she cried out to the only One she had left!

Maybe she said, "God of Abraham, I need you to be my God too. Save me from this pending fate." Or maybe she just cried, "O God! Have mercy on me!" But whatever she said, God heard her, because God shut up all the wombs in the king's household, and He spoke up for Sarah when no one else would! He threatened the king and revealed the truth. "She is Abraham's wife!" declared the Lord. And He stopped Abimelech's footsteps of danger.

Very few men understand a woman's terror of being raped or sexually assaulted. I can only imagine the tears that ran down Sarah's face when she heard the door open. But when her would-be rapist comes in, he amazingly falls to the floor and cries out, "He touched me!" Did you know that the heart of the king is in His hand and He turneth it as He wills? (Proverbs 21:1) God delivered Sarah from the failure of her man.

THE GOD OF GERAR

When Sarah came out of Gerar, she knew something about life, about people, and most of all, about God. She didn't lose her relationship with Abraham, as we will soon see. But she did learn something that all of us must learn. She learned the faithfulness of God.

I am convinced that the things that worry us, would not, if we only knew the faithfulness of God. This proved true in Sarah's life, because right after her nightmare experience in Gerar, the Bible says in Genesis 21:1–2:

And the Lord visited Sarah as he had said, and the Lord did unto Sarah as he had spoken. For Sarah conceived, and bare Abraham a son in his old age, at the set time of which God had spoken to him.

You need to see that it wasn't Abraham who filled his woman with the supernatural promise of God. Without God Abraham could do nothing. Always remember that. Man may be the instrument, but God is the life source. It was God who visited Sarah, and did unto Sarah as He had spoken!

WINTER WOMAN

Because of Gerar, Sarah came to know God in a way that she had never known Him before. There are some things you can learn about God only in the winter. And Sarah won a spot in the hallmark hall of faith. When Hebrews 11 lists the patriarchs and their awesome faith, this winter woman's name is included. Abraham is mentioned for the kind of faith that would leave home and look for a city "whose builder and maker is God" (v. 10). But when the writer discusses the kind of faith that it took to cause an old woman's barren womb to conceive, he talks about Sarah's faith! It was Sarah's faith that did it.

Sarah didn't take "faith" classes. She just went through her winter clutching the warm hand of a loving God who could not fail. So when you hear Sarah laughing the last time, she is laughing with God. She is holding her baby to her now wrinkled breast. And she understands the miracles that come only to winter women.

Have you ever spent the night in Gerar? If you have, I'm sure you now know the Lord in a way you never could have otherwise. Like Sarah, you know that He cares for you. And like Sarah you know He will protect and will work through you. Look over your past and remember His faithfulness. Look at your future and trust Him.

CHAPTER FIFTEEN

Breaking the Chain

The past is paid for. The
wounds may leave scars, but
the scars are only there to
remind us that we are human.
Everyone has scars.

There is awesome power in women. God has chosen women to serve as the vehicles through which entry is made into this world. And He has shared His creativity with women. Women are strong and willing to nurture others.

But in spite of this, millions of women continually suffer emotional, physical, and spiritual strain. The enemy has attempted to destroy God's vehicle of creativity.

You may be one of those who suffer. Perhaps you sit and wonder whether life will ever be normal for you. Maybe you feel like your circumstance has made you different from other women. Possibly you feel like you are alone, with no one to help you find healing.

It could be that your emotional strain comes from having been abused. Others have taken advantage of you and used you in the most horrible and depraved ways. You feel used and dirty. And you think, *how could anyone want someone who has been abused?* Nevertheless, **you are wanted. God wants you, and God's people want you.**

Mistakes made early in life impact the rest of our lives. Some become involved sexually without the commitment of marriage. Maybe you believed him when he told you that he loved you. Perhaps you really did think that yielding would show your true love. Or, maybe, you simply wanted to have a good time without thinking about the consequences. And now you feel less than normal.

But God has already determined your need. He looked down from heaven long ago and saw your pain and guilt. He evaluated your situation and decided that you needed a Redeemer. He knew that you would need Someone to reach down and lift you up. He saw that you needed to recognize how important you are. It is impossible to know all that was in the mind of God when He looked down on broken humanity, but we can know that He looked past our broken hearts, wounded histories, and our tendency to sin, and saw our need.

God met that need through Jesus Christ. Jesus took your abuse on Himself on the cross of Calvary. He paid for your shame and made a way for you to be clean again. He took your indiscretions and sins upon Himself and died in your place. He saw your desire to please others and feel good. Thus, He took all your sinful desires and crucified them on the cross.

When you accept Jesus, you become clean and holy. You are made pure. And don't think you are alone—everyone struggles with the same kinds of sins as you, whether they show it on the outside or not.

YOUR PAST IS PAID FOR

The abused little girl with all her wounds was healed by the stripes of Jesus (Isaiah 53:5). The sins of the woman who wanted to fulfill her lusts were crucified on the cross with Him (Galatians 2:20). The past is paid for. The wounds may leave scars, but the scars are only there to remind us that we are human. Everyone has scars.

GOD SEES YOUR POTENTIAL

God recognizes the possibility of what you can become. He has a plan, and He sees your potential. But He also knows that your potential has been bound by your history. Your suffering has made you into a different woman from the one He originally intended you to be. The circumstances of life have shaped your way of thinking. And the responses you made to those circumstances have often kept you from living up to your potential.

But God knows that there is a Sarah, a Rahab, a woman at the well, a Ruth, or even a Mary in you. He knows that hidden inside of you is a great woman who can do great exploits in His name. And He wants that woman to be set free. He wants the potential within you to be unleashed so you can become the person you were created to be.

GOD IS CALLING

There is only one way to reach that potential. He is calling you. He will spiritually stir your heart and let you know that He is moving in your life, if you will only respond to His call.

The power to unleash you is in your faith. Dare to believe that He will do what He said He would do. Shift your confidence from your own weaknesses to His power. Trust in Him rather than in yourself. Anyone who comes to Christ will find deliverance and healing. He will soothe your wounds. He will comfort you in your desperate moments. He will raise you up.

Believe that He paid the price for your sin and guilt. Believe that He has washed you and made you clean. Believe that He will satisfy every need created by your history. Have faith that He will reward you when you call on Him and it shall be done.

You have nothing to lose, and everything to gain. Jesus will straighten the crooked places in your heart and make you completely whole. When you allow Him access to every area of your life, you will never be the same broken person again.

Therefore, if anyone is in Christ he is a new creation; the old has gone, the new has come!

2 CORINTHIANS 5:17 NIV

And, behold, there was a woman which had a spirit of infirmity eighteen years, and was bowed together, and could in no wise lift up herself. And when Jesus saw her, he called her to him, and said unto her, "Woman, thou art loosed from thine infirmity."

LUKE 13:11–12

And he laid his hands on her: and immediately she was made straight, and glorified God. And the ruler of the synagogue answered with indignation, because that Jesus had healed on the sabbath day, and said unto the people, "There are six days in which men ought to work: in them therefore come and be healed, and not on the sabbath day."

LUKE 13:13–14

The Lord then answered him, and said, "Thou hypocrite, doth not each one of you on the sabbath loose his ox or his ass from the stall, and lead him away to watering? And ought not this woman, being a daughter of Abraham, whom Satan hath bound, lo, these eighteen years, be loosed from this bond on the sabbath day?"

LUKE 13:15–16

The **Princess** Within

RESTORING THE SOUL OF A WOMAN

by
Serita Ann Jakes

CONTENTS

Therefore if any woman be in Christ,
she is a new creature:
old things are passed away;
behold, all things are become new.

2 CORINTHIANS 5:17

(AUTHOR'S PARAPHRASE)

Foreword

Way back in a hollow in the back woods of West Virginia, somewhere over a rope bridge traversing a mountain creek, lived my Serita. A young diamond set among mountains of coal, she was a girl whose life would grow and become multifaceted through pressures without and godly influences within. Then one day, when she reached the full flower of womanhood, she became the one I sought for: flesh of my flesh and bone of my bone, my Nubian princess, my lover, my friend, a jewel by my side to reflect the radiance of the Master. Her confidence now strengthens me and moves me on when I am tired. Her joy brings a smile to my face when I am low. Her playfulness keeps my child's heart alive. She is my glory! When she is flourishing, I prosper; and God looks good. Ever since the day we became one flesh, I have entrusted my heart in Serita's hands. Now, in commending her to you, I entrust you to her also.

As a pastor, it means a lot to me to know that the women of my church are finding out who they are in Christ. It is important for them to be strengthened in their faith as they represent over half the number of those who attend our church, The Potter's House in Dallas, Texas, and an even larger percentage of the global church. I have watched and listened as my wife has ministered to women at home and around the country. Her heart, like mine, is to see women healed, strengthened, and renewed. Her message is that, as a woman of God, there is a place for you beyond feelings of helplessness, aimlessness, or hopelessness. Strength and confidence can be your life foundation as you discover the Father's presence in the pressures and influences of your daily routine.

If you are finding it hard to forget the woman you used to be before you gave your life to Jesus, then please read this book. If the woman you were behaved in unthinkable ways and is now blocking your view of God's love for you, then let Serita, as a sister in the faith, show you how God sees you through Christ. As she shows you how He has worked so faithfully in her walk, I trust you will reflect on how He has shown His power and grace in your life. Or, where your life is like a scratched or marred diamond, or is missing the full-faceted splendor that God intends for you, let her words and testimony impart to you both the future and the hope that are yours in Christ.

I thank God that my wife felt it was important to write this timely message. There is a rich deposit within her heart that she has exposed for your benefit. The fine lace and satin that clothes her frame, her silk purse, and her regal coiffure are but a well-tooled cover to a book that holds many chapters of brokenness and loss, love and laughter, abundance and lack. It is because she has allowed God to pour oil, spikenard, and myrrh through the chapters of her life that He has turned her ashes into beauty, her mourning into joy, and now has allowed her to aromatize the lives of others.

God bless you as you read, ponder, and pray; and may your life, like a precious stone, reflect the fullness of His faithfulness, grace, mercy, and love in your life.

T. D. Jakes

And he that sat upon the throne said,
Behold, I make all things new.
And he said unto me,
Write: for these words are
true and faithful.

REVELATION 21:5 KJV

Is This Book for You?

Every woman was born to be a princess. Our Father, God in heaven, is the ruler over all the earth. As His children, adopted into His family through our faith in Jesus Christ, the King of Kings, we are royal heirs to all of God's promises. Our Creator designed His daughters to be the glory of men and the mothers of all living things. We were the final touch of creation and the solution to loneliness in mankind. Why have so many women fallen from that place of honor and esteem?

It grieves me to see women hiding in the shadows of a busy church, shamed and saddened by sacred secrets from their past they wish to conceal. Christian women should be restored to their place of wholeness before God so their testimony will draw all women back to the Lord. Yet many beautiful Christian women are still trying to keep their secrets instead of giving them to the Lord, their Secret Keeper.

The dirt of their old lives clings to them as if they bathe in liquid silt each morning. They go about their daily routine covered with fresh mud, concealing their true identity, pretending not to even notice their filthy condition. Their light is not shining, and no one can see the princess within whom their Father created them to be. All signs of their royal inheritance have been covered with the degradation of mistakes that were made at some point in their lives.

These women are like Cinderella. Even after giving their lives to Jesus, being fully aware of their rightful inheritance, they continue to retreat to the corners and dust themselves with the cinders of the ash heap. Are you like her?

Wicked oppressors tried to make Cinderella ashamed of her humble position, convincing her that she was not worthy to participate in the celebrations of the kingdom. When the truth came that she could indeed go to the ball, she had to lift her chin, regain her dignity, and dress herself with attire more befitting a woman ready to offer her hand to a prince.

Have you put on wedding clothes since you were adopted into the family of God?

Are you waiting for someone to give you a ride to the celebration, or will you find your own way to the dance as Cinderella did?

Are you willing to be obedient to the One who redeemed you to your rightful place, even to the point of leaving behind your beautiful shoe?

Once Cinderella became joint-heir with her prince, she used her good fortune to help others. How did this all come about for her? Her humility and willingness to serve positioned her for blessing, and once she understood who she really was, her passion to serve others was empowered by the king.

A prince waited to find Cinderella.

A Prince of Peace awaits you.

There are critics who say that life is not like fairy tales with happy endings. I write this book to prove otherwise. I have been like Cinderella, and I am convinced through a working of the Holy Spirit, who is whispering within me, that you are like her too. Each chapter will examine the phases of our growth from shame to spiritual maturity. We will see how to move from the cinders of our past to the celebration of our future.

Will you be free of your past and enjoy all that God has for you?

Will you let His truth cleanse you from the secrets to which you remain in bondage?

Will you learn to give your secrets to your precious Secret Keeper?

When I gave my secrets to the Secret Keeper, He replied with words that made the secrets lose their power over me. He released the woman within me to walk with dignity, not because of who I was, but because of who my Father is. If we are not condemned before God, where is the shame?

It is time for all women to be restored to this place of honor that God first intended for them to have. He gave women the power to help men enjoy His presence. We must be restored to that relationship with God if we are to be an influence on mankind to do the same.

My husband, Bishop T. D. Jakes, author of *Woman, Thou Art Loosed,* teaches in his recent *New York Times* bestselling title *The Lady, Her Lover, and Her Lord,* that it is crucial for every woman to find balance in her life and fulfillment in her heart. He says it is "the duty of every man to help his lady achieve her greatness."

I believe that God has gifted women with the power to influence the men in their lives to action. I also believe it is the opportunity of every woman to give her husband the courage to believe for impossible things through Jesus Christ. However, she can take this gift that was meant to be a positive reinforcement to a man's faith and misuse it to pull him down. When Christian women are no longer deceived, when we fully understand who we are in Christ, our gift of influence will lead our men and children back to God's promise. But we must first find the truth ourselves, before we can light the way for others.

My prayer for writing this book is to demonstrate God's power to remove the shame of our deception and to restore the joy of our royal inheritance. When we find this balance and fulfillment that my husband speaks of in his books, we will lead our families to an intimate encounter with the Father.

It is time to forget the woman you used to be. God has forgotten her. It is time to prepare for the great celebration that our King of Kings is planning for us. Come away from the cinders, and please stay with me through the end of the book. Spend this time with me as I tell you my own story of discovering *The Princess Within.*

Love,

Serita Ann

If we confess our sins, he is faithful
and just and will forgive us our sins
and purify us from all
unrighteousness.

1 JOHN 1:9

CHAPTER ONE

Princess, Why Are You Hiding?

LIFE IS LIKE A FAIRY TALE!

Cinderella forgot that she was the rightful heir to her father's fortune.

Shamed into servanthood, she allowed her inheritance to be squandered by unworthy benefactors.

Have you forfeited what your Father in heaven has written in His will for you?

Once upon a time, not so very long ago, a beautiful daughter was born to the King of all kings, and the Lord of all lords. Her father loved her and attended to her needs as if she were his only child. His greatest hope was that she would grow to understand how very much he loved her.

The King was a good king and used his wealth to provide for all the people in his kingdom. He hoped that one day his beautiful daughter would help him to demonstrate his love for his people.

This powerful king had an evil enemy who hated the King and all that was his. Those who encountered the King's enemy referred to him as the Evil One. The Evil One wanted to hurt the King, but knowing he was invincible, the Evil One tried to hurt the King's daughter instead. Disguised as a prince, the Evil One came to the daughter to court her and win her trust away from the King.

This Evil Prince used cunning flattery to draw her away from the protection of the King's castle by promising to give her all the things for which her father had asked her to wait. She followed the Evil Prince, and once he had her in his clutches, he robbed her of her most precious gift—her dignity.

The Evil Prince dressed her in rags, smeared her face with ashes, and stood her before his evil followers, who mocked her and called her names. Shamed before the contemptuous crowd, the beautiful princess retreated to the dungeon, where the Evil Prince had told her she belonged. She forgot the words of her father, and only remembered the humiliation of standing in public view and feeling naked and ashamed. She vowed to herself that if she ever went outside of her dungeon, she would disguise her true identity so the crowd would never mock her again.

From that day on she covered her beautiful face whenever she ventured out of her secluded hiding place. The Evil Prince had convinced her that she was unworthy, unloved, and unwanted. He had separated her from her father and gloated in his apparent victory to hurt the King by making the princess ashamed of who she was. Her secret humiliation kept her imprisoned by the evil enemy who had tricked her with his lies.

SECRETS CREATE INVISIBLE STRONGHOLDS

Perhaps you know how the princess in this story feels. Perhaps her story sounds just like yours. I know it sounds like my story. The devil's only weapons against God's children are his lies, but he fires them against us with relentless force. If we know to hide behind God's shield of truth, we will not fall subject to these lies. But if we listen to the devil's lies, we will become afraid of God and want to hide from Him.

It is difficult to love God or anyone else when we are looking for a hiding place. Shameful secrets cause us to withdraw in fear that someone will bring our experience to the knowledge of others. Intimidation is a dark and dreary place in which to live. Even when light penetrates our room, we look for dark corners in which to retreat so we can keep our secrets from exposure.

Hiding feels comfortable at the time, but it is a lonely lifestyle to maintain. If secrets are allowed to run the course of their destruction, finding new ways to keep these secrets can become more sacred than our search for freedom from them. There is hope, however, for people who find a trustworthy friend to whom they can tell their secrets. Many people have found healing by revealing their secrets to a person who can demonstrate forgiveness to them. Secrets lose their power if there is no longer a reason to hide their truths. The right secret keeper can make the person feel acceptable again. •

This need for the acceptance of others drives us to great measures because we tend to agree with the opinions that others have of us. If our peers want to imitate us, we are flattered. If they make fun of us, we are defeated. We must be careful whom we choose to be our secret keeper. If we tell our secret to the wrong person, they might use it against us and inflict more shame on us than we previously carried. But it is also true that if we share a secret with someone who accepts us for the new person in Christ that we are becoming, we find liberation from our guilt and enjoy new beginnings.

LOVE COVERS A MULTITUDE OF SINS

I am careful with secrets that others give to me. It is my way of showing them that I accept them as they are. My confidence in them helps to relieve their sense of shame as they accept my love in spite of what has happened to them or what they have done. I am not concerned about the choices they made in their past, but in the choices they will make in the future. I have learned this art of secret keeping from God, who has been faithful to keep my own secrets, secrets that intimidated me and kept me from enjoying the new life He gave to me.

We have nearly 10,000 women enrolled in our Dallas church, The Potter's House. I see many who are reluctant to participate in the move of God because they have secrets that they feel are worse than those of any other woman. It is in my heart to reveal how the Lord has been my Secret Keeper in hopes that all women who read my story will also learn to trust their secrets to Him.

I know that secrets rob us of the freedom we have to enjoy our royal inheritance through Jesus Christ. I too have hidden behind appropriate smiles when inappropriate pain robbed me of my right to be content. I was afraid of my future because of my past until I met my Lord, my Secret Keeper. I am proof that the Lord can be trusted to keep secrets. Once I gave to Him the secrets that kept me from being totally His, I found that those same secrets were now totally His to keep. He removed the shame that I felt and covered me with His truth and love again. His love made me transparent, with nothing to hide.

I have found healing by writing letters to the Lord, my Secret Keeper. The act of explaining my fears and waiting on God to respond has taken me to a place of solitude with Him where He can speak to me and direct my thoughts to His Word. When I felt troubled about the loss of my brother, and a subsequent encounter I had with a young man that I dated shortly after my brother's death, I wrote the following letter to my Secret Keeper. I was honest before God and He was faithful to show me truths that set me free from the pain of those memories.

As I began to write this letter to Him, I remembered the passage of Scripture from Genesis 32:24:

So Jacob was left alone, and a man wrestled with him till daybreak.

Jacob was afraid that his own brother, Esau, was going to kill him because he had tricked him out of his birthright. By going before God, Jacob laid his fears before his Lord and requested deliverance from the things that kept him from receiving God's promises. In answer to his prayers, an angel came and wrestled with Jacob until daybreak. Once Jacob realized that he was strong enough to wrestle all night with an angel, who in the end blessed him, he realized that it was foolish to fear his brother who was merely a man.

Through that midnight struggle, God put strength into Jacob that he could not have developed without that encounter. Even though Jacob left limping, he was no longer afraid of the challenges a new day brought to him. Like Jacob, when it was time for me to let God heal my infirmities, I laid my grief before God to see what His healing power could do.

You are not alone if you have sacred secrets that shame you from participating in the great things God has planned for you, but it is time for you to confess to God the truth of your secret so that He can free you from your past.

I had wanted to hide as a teenager because of the shame I felt when a violent boyfriend rejected me. His actions toward me made me feel unlovely, unwanted, and jilted. I hid this sense of rejection for many years, not realizing how much it affected me until I took time to be honest before God and admit my secret pain to Him. I was free from the secret after writing a letter to my Lord. Once I told Him how I felt and saw how much He loved me, the event lost its power to hurt me. It even seems odd now that I ever felt it was a secret worth keeping. I wrote,

Dear Secret Keeper,

I think that being young and naïve often creates a canvas for You to show us how You paint Your master plan for our lives. All I can say is that I believed him. He had been so nice. He picked me up from school every day. Even the gifts he brought to me were such a surprise. What went wrong? At first I didn't notice his weaknesses, because he seemed to be such a strong man.

It was right after my brother had died. No, let me correct that statement. It was right after my brother was murdered. My whole world seemed to come to a screeching halt. How could his life be ended so abruptly, just when he was trying to get it all together? He had given his life to You. For the first time in his life, my brother seemed to have found true happiness—the kind of happiness that I knew (even then) only came from having You as the center of his life.

One evening he went out with his daughters to one of the local hangouts. The girls were raising money for a trip to an amusement park, and their daddy was taking them where all of his friends would be. Everybody liked my brother, I thought. But something went wrong. There was an argument. Then there were gunshots, and my brother tumbled to the bottom of the stairs.

His knees were drawn to his chest in the fetal position, but this

was not his entrance into life. It was his tragic exit. When they took our mother to him, she went into shock. Her firstborn was gone, and she was left alone.

Oh, Secret Keeper, I was looking for my brother! I was looking for someone who enjoyed having fun like my brother. But instead, I found him. He liked to have fun, but sometimes he seemed so angry. I began to notice bouts of anger that soon became hostility toward me. The hostility turned into verbal outbursts that I could not believe my ears were hearing. As suddenly as it happened, he would return to being the person I had grown so fond of.

He visited every day. I even recognized the sound of his car when he drove up. But the visits became shorter; there was always something else he had to do. As the visits grew briefer, the atmosphere became more intense and often resulted in senseless arguments. I felt like something wasn't right. I could almost sense danger every time he came.

In my heart, I felt warned that the relationship was taking a turn for the worse. I heard his car, but he didn't stop one day. Then I heard his car as he passed without stopping a second day. When he finally decided to stop and come in, he accused me as if I had done something wrong. I was so amazed that I had sat there for several days waiting for someone who I thought really cared for me. The accusations turned into rage. The rage turned into threats of violence. What game was this we played?

My Secret Keeper stopped me from continuing by pouring into my soul the memory of His promise from Psalm 121:1–8. I looked up the Scripture and read it to myself as though the Lord were speaking it directly to me. Such a paraphrase reads like this:

Dear Serita Ann,

You will lift up your eyes to the hills—where does your help come from? Your help comes from Me, the Lord, the Maker of heaven and earth.

I will not let your foot slip—I who watch over you will not slumber; indeed, I who watch over Israel will neither slumber nor sleep. I, the Lord, watch over you—I am your shade at your right hand; the sun will not harm you by day, nor the moon by night.

I, the Lord, will keep you from all harm—I will watch over your life; I, the Lord, will watch over your coming and going both now and forevermore.

My Lord had wrestled with me just as He had done with Jacob. Though I had been weakened by the young man who pulled down my countenance, my Lord strengthened me with the memory that He was always there with me. I returned to my writing and finished telling my Lord the secret that had haunted me.

I don't know why I didn't heed the warning that You gave to me. I knew that things were about to come to a boil. Whenever I heard his car, I became nervous. It had been nearly a week. There had been neither phone calls nor visits. If history was to be repeated, I knew that when he did return he would be very hateful.

The day he finally came again, he left his opinion of me written on my heart. He destroyed my sense of value that day. He made me feel ashamed for being me. I relived the day in my letter to my Secret Keeper:

It sounds like the car has stopped. Why is he walking so fast? Oh please, no arguing again. "But I haven't been anywhere!" I remember saying.

It hurts when he shoves like this.

Why is he pushing me?

Is that a gun in his hand?

What is he doing?

I've never seen such a face; it's like looking at the devil himself. Is he going to kill me, Secret Keeper? He's got his gun to my head, and I'm lying on the floor. God, help me!!!

This poor man called, and the Lord heard him; he saved him out of all his troubles. The angel of the Lord encamps around those who fear him, and he delivers them.

PSALM 34:6-7

I looked up and he was gone. I crawled to the window and peeked under the shade. He stood there beneath the full moon, cocked the gun and fired it into the air five times. I sat on the floor trembling; tears would not come. Everything that I thought he was had turned to lies. When I met him, I felt so lonely. When he drove off, again I felt left alone.

But then I realized that I had not been left alone. I had called out to You, and You had sent an angel to rescue me from death! I'm never alone because I always have You, Secret Keeper.

Love,

Serita Ann

In this last event, I was merely the victim, but I felt exposed. Over a course of time I began to believe that I must have deserved this treatment. I believed the lie and was tormented by his opinion of me. He had stripped me of my sense of self-worth and had robbed me of my dignity. But now, after laying my secret before the Lord, after wrestling with the truth that God was there protecting me and saving me from further harm, I am no longer ashamed. I no longer limp from the wounds the enemy of God inflicted upon me. I no longer believe that lie . . . and I am free to love again.

The Lord is the best Secret Keeper of all. I confessed my secret shame to

Him: I had fallen for the wrong person. I had ignored His warnings, but He took my honesty and my fears and cleansed me, sending my secret away as though it had never happened. What is this power He offers?

What is this power that comes from Jesus' death and makes us live? He paid a price in that death for every secret that we hide so that we can stand justified before God. Evangelists explain "justified" as "Just as if I'd never done it—just as if it had never happened to me."

Why keep our secrets to ourselves instead of giving them to the Lord, our Secret Keeper and trusted friend? With Jesus we can come out of hiding.

WHAT SECRETS ARE YOU HIDING?

What secrets are keeping you from enjoying new opportunities that lie ahead? You are not alone if you have sacred secrets that shame you from participating in the great things God has planned for you, but it is time for you to confess to God the truth of your secret so that He can free you from your past. It is time for you to enjoy your inheritance, which is to be purified from all unrighteousness.

> **If we confess our sins, he is faithful and just and will forgive us our sins and purify us from all unrighteousness.**
>
> 1 JOHN 1:9

For us, "purify" means "to make pure again." God offers more than forgiveness to us. He offers the power to make us free from what *Webster's New World Dictionary* defines as "adulterating matter." When lies and mistakes enter our otherwise pure lives, we become a mixture of good and evil, we are *adulterated* by the adding of the bad to the good that God made in the beginning. Reversing this, God takes our secrets and restores our innocence, freeing us from the evil of sin and its corrupting elements. Through our confession, we allow God to cleanse us from anything that is not right in our lives.

There is no secret that can separate you from God's love.

There is no secret that can separate you from His blessings.

There is no secret that is worth keeping from His grace.

God has already provided deliverance for all that you have done and all that has been done to you. He has demonstrated His love from the beginning of time, and He continues faithfully to reach out to you even this very second in time as you read this book.

Confess your secrets to the Lord, your Secret Keeper. Let Him make right the things in your life that cause you to retreat. You are no longer a lady-in-waiting or a lady-in-hiding. You are a princess!

WRITE YOUR OWN STORY

Before we continue, I would like to make a suggestion. Writing out your feelings will help you to see what the Lord already knows about you. So why not write a letter to the Lord, your Secret Keeper, in your journal. Each time you write, tell Him what secret makes you want to hide.

When you finish each letter, ask Him what He thinks about your secret. Then listen to His still, small voice within your heart and record His response in your journal.

But as many as received him, to them gave he power to become the sons [daughters] of God, even to them that believe on his name.

JOHN 1:12 KJV

CHAPTER TWO

But Everyone Is Invited to the Party!

LIFE IS LIKE A FAIRY TALE!

Cinderella believed that everyone in the entire kingdom was entitled to go to the ball except her.
Without an argument she agreed to stay home, even though she had a great desire to see the Prince.
What or who is keeping you at home?

Cinderella's mean stepsisters told her that she wasn't invited to the ball. At first, she believed them and planned to stay at home. *After all,* she thought, *who would want to dance with a servant girl?* If she had continued to listen to the lies, what were Cinderella's chances of living happily ever?

Have you ever heard of a party that a friend was having, but you didn't know for sure if you were invited? Perhaps a general announcement was made at work or at church, but you didn't hear it. When an associate asked if you were going, you were too embarrassed to admit that you didn't think you were on the guest list, so you just said, "No, I'm not going." Perhaps you were too proud to find out for sure if you were to be included, so you said that you had plans for that day. What makes us so willing to be left out?

It hurts me to see women hiding in the shadows because they feel left out. In a church as large as ours, it is difficult to personally reach each woman and invite her to participate in what we have planned. How I long to see the day when women are restored to the place God esteemed for them, when they boldly come to the forefront to celebrate their position in His kingdom!

God looks at each of us as if we were His only daughter. And of course, He wants us to be included in all He is doing. He doesn't want us to lie to ourselves about that. But people are not always like God, and they often do things which make us feel left out.

Feeling left out can fill us with a sense of shame. It's difficult to admit that we feel hurt when our peers do not include us, so we keep our pain of being excluded a secret. But what would happen if we told our Secret Keeper how we felt? What would He say to us if we would quiet ourselves before Him after admitting our shame to Him?

I have felt left out before, so I wrote to my Lord, and my Secret Keeper:

Dear Secret Keeper,

Why are we so cruel to one another? I've always been a somewhat sensitive person. Whatever I felt, I would feel to the third power. I tried desperately not to say or do anything that would make anyone feel less than me. I wanted to get along with everyone and could never understand why two people could not share the same friend. I didn't want to say words to others that I would not want said to me. I never believed the old saying, "Sticks and stones may break my bones, but words will never harm me." I knew how vicious the mouths of insensitive people could be.

Even as a child, I learned that insensitive remarks inflicted pain. I often felt that I was the target of most of the darts of humiliation. I can still feel some of the pain from those who would chant, "Fatty, fatty, two-by-four!" These were the children that I wanted most to impress. I wasn't athletic, but was forever trying to be selected for the neighborhood sporting events. My dresses often looked like they were designed for someone much older because the chubby selections of the mail order catalogues were very limited.

*In my eyes, everyone looked like they could model for **Seventeen Magazine**. They all were tall with long legs, unlike me, who was the runt of the litter and as wide as I was tall. No one would accept me but my mama, who indulged me with her sweet potato pies and chocolate cakes. She understood that I was a growing girl.*

I thought the other girls who had called me names were so

beautiful. Somehow they were the epitome of all I ever hoped to be—thin. I set out to become just like them. I ran extra laps during physical education class and made sure I did twice as many sit-ups. I did so many jumping jacks that for minutes later I felt as though I were a windmill. I even said no to all of Mama's goodies. All of this was to no avail.

After losing a few pounds, all I became was sore and hungry. I still wasn't one of "them." I wasn't like them. It wasn't only the outside that I couldn't match; it was something emanating from the inside. It was their spirit. They were beautiful outwardly, but there was something very rotten inside of them. Suddenly I realized that I didn't want to be like them after all. Physically, they were all I aspired to be, but the lost condition of their souls overwhelmed that outward beauty.

Yes, I was fat on the outside, but they were ugly on the inside. I could go on a diet; they would need far more than a charm course.

Realizing this truth, I began to take inventory of myself, and an invaluable transformation took place in my self-esteem. I suddenly realized that beauty is not just expressed outwardly. Beauty is more than how you look. Beauty is in how you accept others for who they are. It comes from inside no matter what the image in the mirror suggests or what society dictates.

Beauty is You, Secret Keeper. You continually look beyond my flaws and meet my needs. Now when I look for a role model or someone to imitate, I look into the mirror of Your Word. I behold palely the image that You are creating, and I shed secret tears because I can hardly believe that this is how You see me.

Love,

Serita Ann

I remembered the words of my Lord in Matthew 23:27–28 when He said,

> **Woe to you, teachers of the law and Pharisees, you hypocrites! You are like whitewashed tombs, which look beautiful on the outside but on the inside are full of dead men's bones and everything unclean.**
>
> **In the same way, on the outside you appear to people as righteous but on the inside you are full of hypocrisy and wickedness.**

Obviously, the Lord is also grieved by insensitive people who act piously while making others feel worthless and insignificant. He too longs for His truth to be made known to us. He is planning a party to celebrate the union of His Son, Jesus, and His bride, the Church. Everyone is invited, but an RSVP is necessary.

A general announcement has been made throughout the Scriptures, but many people still have not heard about the party He has planned. Many of those who have heard don't understand that this party is very real. In fact, that day of celebration is closer to us with each new day.

PLEASE RSVP!

When John the disciple had a revelation of Jesus Christ, the angel who was with him said, **Blessed are they which are called unto the marriage supper of the Lamb.** The angel continued, **These are the true sayings of God** (Revelation 19:9 KJV). The revelation recorded in the last book of the Bible was a record of the things that would come to pass in the future. We know that God wants everyone to come to the party. He is not willing that any should perish, but that all should respond to His invitation.

In the Bible, Peter explains how the RSVP works.

The Lord is not slow in keeping his promise, as some under-stand slowness. He is patient with you, not wanting anyone to perish, but everyone to come to repentance.

2 PETER 3:9

God wants all of us to come to repentance. By grace, He is delaying the beginning of the dance in order to give us all time to come forth and accept His invitation to be a part of that great reunion.

There is room at God's house for everyone who is willing to come. John confirms this in his gospel:

But as many as received him, to them gave he power to become the sons [daughters] of God, even to them that believe on his name.

JOHN 1:12 KJV

We only have to acknowledge receipt of the invitation, and all that God has to offer becomes ours.

Many people look at the coming of Jesus Christ as something far in the future. While writing this book, a hurricane swept across Central America, causing floods and mud slides throughout the countryside. The death toll in Honduras may be impossible to accurately assess, but so far, we know that Jesus came for at least seven thousand people in just one day. I hope the people in Honduras had responded favorably to the wedding invitation. An entire community now knows the reality of the party that Jesus has planned for those who have received Him.

God's faithfulness is so dependable, it will fill you with awe to discover how much He loves you. His love is unconditional, meaning He *always* loves you, not just when you do something right. No matter what you do, no matter who you do it with, God still loves you. Does that sound like a love that only happens in fairy tales?

Well, Cinderella's story doesn't compare to the happiness God has planned for you. Daily He invites you to come to His garden party and visit with Him in the cool of the evening, just as He first did with Adam and Eve. He's waiting for you now.

What keeps us from going to our Lord and sharing our secrets with Him? The self-punitive tendency to hide from God when we feel ashamed is inherited from our parents, Adam and Eve. From the beginning, God enjoyed meeting His children for an evening talk. God extended a standing invitation to meet in the garden where Adam and Eve could walk with Him and enjoy the fellowship of His wonderful presence. This daily garden party would have continued for their children and eventually for us, but Adam and Eve stopped going to the party because they were ashamed of what they had done and of what had been done to them.

Eve had believed a lie, and when it came time to meet with God for her evening embrace, she wanted to hide from Him instead. But God continues to invite us into His presence and has made a way for us to escape the penalty of our fallen nature. We can be restored to the relationship with Him that He originally planned for all women. We can learn of God's original plan for us through Eve's story.

The life God had planned for Eve was what we would now call a fairy tale. Her husband adored her and he listened to her every whim and fancy. She was a perfect "ten" in his eyes. They were in such agreement that they were known by the same name, Mr. and Mrs. Adam. Because they were one with each other, there was no need to identify him independently from her. What she wanted, he wanted. Their union was a picture of the communion they had with God.

Cinderella's story doesn't compare to the happiness God has planned for you. Daily He invites you to come to His garden party and visit with Him in the cool of the evening, just as He first did with Adam and Eve. He's waiting for you now.

Their wealth surpassed their need, and every desire they had was satisfied as the land they owned was filled with gold, pearls, and onyx. They lived in the garden called Eden, which meant "pleasure and delight," and it was filled with every imaginable fruit for their enjoyment. There were no weeds in their fields nor blight on their fruit trees and roses. Mrs. Adam was heralded as the woman who had everything.

Every evening she and her husband attended this continual party with God in the garden. They loved listening to His words, and they ran to Him with shameless abandonment whenever they heard the sound of His arrival. The Lord loved her and her husband and enjoyed His time with them. He gave them everything He had created because He so greatly cherished them. He even told them to eat from the tree of life, which gave them immortality.

Only one tree did God ask them not to eat from, the tree of knowledge of good and evil, because with that knowledge came the painful understanding of the difference between blessing and calamity. Only this one thing was withheld from them, but even that was because of His great desire to protect them from pain. But Mrs. Adam became curious.

Imagine with me how it might have happened:

One morning, Mrs. Adam asked, "Why is this tree of knowledge of good and evil bad for us?"

"I don't know why it's not good for us, but we are to simply trust Him," Mr. Adam explained.

"I don't even understand what it means not to trust Him. Help me to understand, lest I accidentally do the very thing I shouldn't do," she pleaded.

"Just stay away from the tree. To trust God means to obey Him. He has given us unlimited freedom to enjoy all that our eyes can see. The only thing He has asked of us is that we don't eat fruit from that one tree. Once we eat of it, we will understand what evil is. I do know that evil is everything that God is not."

"That's it?" Mrs. Adam responded with surprise. "All that my eyes behold is ours? Everything is ours except that one tree? What more could we possibly want than what we see here in our own home?" So Mrs. Adam was content with all that the Lord had given to her—at least for a while longer.

Life or death, blessings or calamity had been laid before her. The power of choice was hers. She could choose to enjoy all that pleased her loving God, or she could choose to experience everything that He cast away from His presence. She could choose to taste of fruit that nourished her life, or to swallow garbage that would drain the very essence of her womanhood.

WHAT WOULD YOU HAVE DONE?

What if we had been the first woman to be tempted to do the wrong thing? How long would we have resisted the fruit of the tree of knowledge of good and evil? How long would we have lasted in the Garden of Eden? Perhaps the more important question for us would be: *How long did we last before we forfeited the innocence of our childhood for the knowledge of evil?*

It doesn't matter if we were the first woman on earth or the one-billionth woman to face the choice of blessing or calamity. Adam failed the test, and every man who was born after him failed to choose life. Following him, we have all failed the test. We have all used the liberty of our free will to choose curses instead of God's blessing in our lives.

All have sinned and are falling short of the honor and glory which God bestows and receives.

ROMANS 3:23 AMP

Yes, Mrs. Adam, the woman who had everything that was good, wanted more. But if all we have had is good, the only thing we haven't had is the experiential grief of having nothing. That is what our enemy, Satan, the devil, wants for all of mankind. He wants to take away our blessings because he knows that the only way he can hurt God is to hurt God's children. He's in a war against God, and the battle is over our souls. His only weapon against us is his ability to deceive us through twisting the truth.

Satan, this vile serpent, came to Mrs. Adam and planted doubt in her heart against her Creator saying,

> "Isn't it true that God said you could not eat of every tree in the garden?"
>
> "We may eat of all the trees except the one called 'The Knowledge of Good and Evil.' We aren't to touch that one or we will die." But God had not told them not to touch it. He told them not to *eat* of it.
>
> Satan used her own misunderstanding against her. "You won't die," he said confidently, knowing that touching it would not destroy her, but that eating it would. He continued, "Go ahead, touch it and see if what I say is true. Not only that," he added, "if you eat of it, you will be like God, who knows the difference between good and evil."
>
> So Mrs. Adam touched the fruit that had tempted her and discovered that she did not die. She then doubted the instruction the Lord had given her. Holding the fruit in her hand, she examined this forbidden mystery. She concluded it would be good to be like God, whose friendship she enjoyed each evening. So she took the fruit to Mr. Adam, and they explored together the one thing God said they should not have.

Some philosophers defend Eve's fall into sin as a sincere drive to know God better. The Word teaches clearly that she was *deceived* by Satan. Perhaps she believed she would think more like the Father whom they loved if she knew the difference between good and evil.

God's Word does not say that Adam was deceived. It says that he heeded the voice of his wife, implying that with full knowledge of the consequences, he made a decision to do something against God's instruction. Here we see an illustration of the great influence a wife has over her husband. He listened to her and knowingly chose disobedience to God in order to be with her.

Can you see the great war that the enemy has waged over the woman? He could not have worked through the woman in this way unless a high value had been placed on her both by her lover and her Lord. He knew the influence she had over her husband. He knew the passion that both her lover and her Lord felt for her. But he did not foresee the great lengths to which her Lord would go to win her back.

As the bitterness of the fruit dripped onto their lips, both Adam and Eve were filled with panic. In that millisecond of deception and disobedience they instantly knew the horror of regret, the despair of remorse, and the loneliness of feeling separated from all the goodness of God. That one act of tasting forbidden fruit caused them to be suddenly alienated from one another, from the one who had moments before been so much a part of their own flesh that they were known by the same name.

They wanted to hide, and so they did.

WHY ARE YOU HIDING?

After they had eaten the fruit of the tree that God had told them to resist, they heard God walking in the garden and hid in the trees. It was time for the party, but the guests of honor refused to come.

God called to Adam, which is what He called both of them in those days, and He said, "Where are you?"

But they would not answer Him.

Have you ever been shopping with a small child in a department store who hid herself in the racks of clothes and would not reveal herself to you?

There is nothing more heartrending than seeing a mother who cannot find her child in a large public place. She knows the possibilities are endless as to where her child may have gone.

An unbearable grief instantly grips the mother's heart as she considers that something may have happened that will keep her from ever seeing her child again. She calls with compassion and panic, "Where are you? Please come to me from wherever you are!" Everyone in the store rallies to help her find the lost child and restore her to her loving mother. And everyone cheers when the child is once again in her mother's arms.

God cried out to Adam and Eve with the same compassion that a mother has for her lost child. Yes, He knew where they were, and He knew that they had done something that would make them want to keep hiding from Him for the rest of their lives. That must have grieved Him more than we can comprehend. He knew that if Adam and Eve couldn't stand before Him without shame, they would never enjoy the true delight of His love which He intended for them to receive.

Please follow my paraphrased version of Genesis, chapter 3:8–24, recalling the painful conversation they had, and consider if this is a conversation that you might have had with God if you had done the one thing He had told you not to do.

> God called out to His children, "Where are you, Adam?"
>
> Adam responded, "I am afraid of You because I am ashamed."
>
> God asked him, "Who told you to be ashamed?"
>
> But Adam dropped his eyes and looked away from his Father.
>
> "Have you done the one thing which I commanded you not to do?" God asked him, hoping that he would admit his mistake.
>
> But Adam couldn't confess the truth, so he said, "The woman You gave to me gave me the fruit that I ate."

And Eve couldn't confess her mistake, for she said, "The serpent tricked me into eating the fruit."

I wonder what would have happened if they had admitted their wrongdoing? What if they had confessed their secret sin? Would the horrid consequences of their wrongdoing have been changed? What if Adam and Eve had known to trust God's unconditional love for them and had honestly admitted they had been disobedient?

God knew that if they could see how much He loved them, they would not be afraid to tell Him the truth, so He initiated His great plan of redemptive love for Adam, for Eve, and for us all.

DO YOU KNOW HOW MUCH GOD LOVES YOU?

After telling Adam and Eve what the consequences of their choice to do evil would bring into their lives, God demonstrated His love for them by making garments to cover their nakedness so they would come out of their hiding places. He covered their shame with the skins of an animal, thus illustrating the first death and sacrifice of life to pay for the wages of sin. This was a foreshadowing of Jesus' death, the final Lamb who was sacrificed for our sins.

For the wages of sin is death, but the gift of God is eternal life in Jesus Christ our Lord.

ROMANS 6:23

Knowing that underneath their new clothes, they still felt ashamed of themselves, God sent them away from the Tree of Life, lest they would eat of it and live forever in their broken relationship with Him (Genesis 3:22–23). God put them out of Eden because He loved them. It is difficult to comprehend, but keeping them from the Tree of Life was an act of grace. He didn't want them to live forever with this guilt and shame on them. He separated them from the Tree of Life and immediately began His plan to win His children back.

WHO TOLD YOU TO BE ASHAMED?

God wasn't the one who told Adam and Eve to be ashamed. He didn't tell them not to come to the garden party. He was faithfully waiting for them. The invitation was still standing, even though He knew what they had done. It was their loss of innocence, their failure to trust Him, and their knowledge of evil that robbed them of their confidence to approach Him. Their secret sin, their rebellion against His instructions, had caused them to be ashamed of themselves. He wanted to restore them to the place where they would run with open arms to Him again.

It didn't matter to God who was first to sin. The one who was seduced and the one who knowingly submitted to seduction both suffered the shame of a secret that they didn't want to confess before God. Adam and Eve were both ashamed. It doesn't matter to God if you were the offender or the victim, the despair of sin is still the same, and God simply doesn't want you to live forever with that sense of shame separating you from His love.

God doesn't care about your secrets, He cares about your freedom to be honest with Him. He invites you to come out of hiding and into His arms, where He can restore the relationship of love and trust that He has always planned for you.

If you have secrets that make you want to hide from God, He wants you to confess those things to Him. In exchange for your confession, in exchange for believing that Jesus died so that you could live, in exchange for receiving His Holy Spirit to dwell inside of you, He will give you the power to be His child.

But to as many as did receive and welcome Him, He gave the authority (power, privilege, right) to become the children of God, that is, to those who believe in (adhere to, trust in, and rely on) His name.

JOHN 1:12 AMP

God invites us to accept His power to overcome the secrets in our lives. He will give us His overcoming power to fight off temptation. He invites us to draw near to Him when we are weak and afraid. Then He will fill us with His magnificent strength so we can triumphantly walk away from the bondage of our past and begin a new life in Him.

For if anyone is a hearer of the word
and not a doer, he is like a man
observing his natural face in a mirror;
for he observes himself, goes away,
and immediately forgets
what kind of man he was.

JAMES 1:23–24   NKJV

CHAPTER THREE

Is That Any Way for a Princess to Act?

LIFE IS LIKE A FAIRY TALE!

Cinderella looked at the circumstances and believed that she was not worthy to receive what everyone else enjoyed.

She couldn't imagine looking into the eyes of the Prince and feeling His admiration for her.

Do you look forward to seeing the face of the Lord?

In the story of Snow White, the evil queen wanted to be the most beautiful woman in the kingdom. But the lovely princess Snow White, who did not desire to be counted as the fairest one in all the land, was given the honor because of her pure heart and gentle ways.

A princess doesn't need to go to the mirror and ask, "Who's the fairest of us all?" She understands that her worth is defended by all the soldiers in her father's kingdom. She doesn't need to feel like she is the most beautiful or the most talented in all the land. She knows her value is not based on her own performance but is based on who her father is. Her value is inherited and is unconditional. Although she can change what she does, nothing can change who she is—the precious daughter of the King.

A princess doesn't pretend to be greater than those who defend her, but she humbly uses her protected freedom to serve others who are less fortunate than herself. Beautiful is the princess whose eyes are on the needs of her subjects and not upon herself.

ARE YOU LOOKING INTO MIRRORS
OR OUT OF WINDOWS?

When we are given the opportunity to start our lives over through salvation in Jesus Christ, we should take full advantage of what it means to be born again. Our new position in the kingdom of God is not conditional. It does not depend upon what we have done in the past or what we will do in the future. Our title is based on who we are in Christ. Second Corinthians 5:17 explains,

Therefore, if anyone is in Christ, he is a new creation; the old has gone, the new has come!

As a new creation, we are no longer subject to the evil prince of this world, but to the King of Kings. This means we can ignore the degradation of the devil's lies and enjoy the uprightness of our royal inheritance. This means we can forget about how others see us and focus on how we see others. We exchange our self-gratifying mirrors for windows that allow us to see the needs of others the way Jesus did.

We know that Jesus did not look into mirrors and submit to anxiety over His appearance. No, He looked out through the windows of compassion and saw each new day as an opportunity to lift someone, to heal someone, to lead someone back to a closer relationship with God, the Father.

Sometimes we forget that we are no longer paupers. We are God's servants who bring the Gospel, the Good News of Jesus Christ, to those around us. I remember a most significant day when I met a young woman who needed encouragement. I could not have encouraged her if I had never been where she had been, if I had never felt alone or had forgotten the way she was feeling that day. But it is also true that I could not have helped her if I had not learned to enjoy my position in the kingdom of the living God.

I realized how far the Lord had brought me by seeing myself in her eyes. Her need to know Him was great. I was blessed to be the one to introduce her to her Father, to her inheritance in Him, and to her new title of princess.

My Secret Keeper reminded me that there is only one mirror we should look into every day, and sometimes many times a day. That mirror is the Word of God:

> **For if anyone is a hearer of the word and not a doer, he is like a man observing his natural face in a mirror;**
> **For he observes himself, goes away, and immediately forgets what kind of man he was.**
>
> JAMES 1:23-24 NKJV

There is a blessing that comes from being a doer of the Word. When we administer grace to others, we can see ourselves in their hungry faces. We remember what kind of woman we used to be. To be whole enough to minister to the needs of others is the goal of our Christian walk. Then we see that God has taken us from grace to grace and from glory to glory. I wrote a letter to my Lord, about the joy I felt while looking into a young woman's eyes and seeing the reflection of God's love for me by seeing His love for her.

Dear Secret Keeper,

This has got to be the most memorable altar call that I have ever experienced. There were souls kneeling, lying prostrate, and standing. But they were all crying out to You for deliverance, forgiveness, and direction. And You were walking in and out of them, weaving a new pattern for their lives.

It was very difficult for me to maintain my composure, for I kept thinking about all that You had done for me. I thought about how You had called me holy when I had felt most undeserving. The sound of their lamentations was superseded only by the whisper of Your voice in my ear, rehearsing Your love for us.

Through swollen, tear-filled eyes I surveyed the crowd. There were as many men as there were women. Even teens and children raised their hands in surrender and submission to Your presence. For each individual there seemed to be an assigned angel of comfort. It was so awesome to see lives transformed by Your loving forgiveness.

Suddenly, I remembered when I had been at this place with You before. I didn't know You personally, but even then I knew that I could not live without You. I was desperate to know the power of Your forgiveness. I had felt that my life was in complete disarray. But I wondered how I could ask someone that I didn't have a relationship with to help me? I certainly did not want to use You to get out of my mess so that as soon as it was convenient I could return to the way things had been before. I wanted change, not as a temporary solution, but as a continued lifestyle. I was just like these people for whom You were now leading me to pray. I too had had to make You my Lord of all.

Now, through Your leading, I began to surge through the crowd, exhorting the broken to rush into Your waiting arms. I whispered in their ears, "You'll never be the same!" "I've sat where you've sat!" Faces too numerable to commit to my memory passed before me, each crying for a closer walk with You.

I felt weightless as I forged through the worshipers. Some were being slain in the spirit and fell as I gently touched them. There seemed to be a fog of glory; it was almost dreamlike. Then the fog lifted and through the eyes of my heart, I could see only one person.

There was a young lady standing in front of me. Surely, she had not been there all along. How could I have laid hands on everyone around her and not seen her? She stood there silently with her head bowed, tears streaming down her face. Her arms were folded just below her breast, resting on what I soon realized was a promised birth.

Dressed neatly outwardly, I could discern that inwardly she was in great turmoil. I approached her ever so tenderly, noticing everything about her. Somehow I knew this was her first attempt to approach You. I wanted to make the introduction. I took her left hand away from the precious shelf it rested upon. Her hand was ringless. You prompted me, and I knew that the bowed head was not only a result of the guilt of sin but the shame of it as well.

"This is a wonderful day to give your life to the Lord," I whispered in her ears. "He doesn't care what you've done; if you ask Him to forgive you, He will. He loves you, and He will never change His mind about you. You can depend on Him to always be there for you. Won't you give your heart to Him? He will mold you into the mother that you need to be."

With these words she raised very sorrowful eyes to mine, and we immediately traded places. In her eyes I saw myself. Through her eyes I saw You, Secret Keeper.

There are some failures and tragedies that we experience in life from which we feel we can never recover. It seems as if all of the exit ramps are closed and the detours endless. But when I get a glimpse of You, as I did in that moment of exchange with this young woman, I know that there is still help for the helpless.

I wanted with all of my strength to usher her into Your arms so that You could restore her fallen soul. I had felt Your arms before when I had despaired of life itself and had wondered if there was hope for me at all.

Somehow I wanted her to fully understand the words of my Secret

Keeper from 2 Corinthians 5:17. If she is in Christ, she is a new creation! Her old life is gone, and her new life has come! This was not a temporary bandage for her pain. God was performing a miraculous change in her heart. *He* was making the changes; the work was not for her to do. She simply was to receive His grace and take a new look at the blessings He was putting into her new life.

I could not bring myself to look into her eyes and walk out of her heart without depositing hope in her spirit. Her new responsibility of motherhood did not mean that life was over for her. She still had years and years ahead of her if she allowed You to patch her together and heal her brokenness. I wanted to convince her to put not only her life but also her unborn child's life into Your hands. As she exchanged places with me, she saw how You could turn her shame to glory through Your simple plan of salvation. In an instant, You unraveled the complexities of the issues in her life.

As I held her in my arms, You held us both and rocked away the pain. We both repeated after You the sinner's prayer. We both received forgiveness. We both felt shameless. Our past was behind us with the promise of a bright future. Through grateful eyes we stared at one another and only You knew the depth of the secret we shared.

The Lord reaffirmed what we felt in our hearts that day by bringing this Scripture to my mind as I wrote to Him.

For with the heart man believeth unto righteousness; and with the mouth confession is made unto salvation.

For the scripture saith, Whosoever believeth on him shall not be ashamed.

ROMANS 10:10–11 KJV

We believed on the Lord and our shame was lifted. I continued:

> *All we really need is You, Secret Keeper. You know all of our tormented secrets and the shame that tries to consume us. Yet You teach us to share each testimony for Your glory. Thank You for not allowing us to be swallowed up in guilt. I know Your power and will tell of it to others. It is because of Your mercies that we are not consumed, because Your compassions fail not (Lamentations 3:22).*

> *Love,*

> *Serita Ann*

To be whole enough to minister to the needs of others is the goal of our Christian walk. Then we see that God has taken us from grace to grace and from glory to glory.

I have looked into mirrors and out through windows, and I have found that it is better to look for windows of opportunity to help others than to grasp for glimpses of my own reflection. I have been on both sides of an altar. I have knelt there because I needed help, and I have knelt beside those who have needed encouragement. I understand now why it is better to give than to receive, just as it is better to be a princess for God instead of His pauper.

To be in a position to give, we must keep our hearts full of encouragement. The apostle Paul taught us in Ephesians 5:18–20 to be filled with the Holy Spirit. He says we can do that by speaking to one another with psalms, hymns, and spiritual songs. We should sing and make music in our heart to the Lord, always giving thanks to God the Father for everything, in the name of our Lord Jesus Christ.

Praying in tongues, as taught in 1 Corinthians 14:4, also keeps us built up. If we take responsibility to keep ourselves edified, we will not face the day like a pauper in search of provision. Our heart will be filled with intercession, ready to meet the demands of our Father's kingdom, and we will act like princesses ready to distribute good news of our Father's provision.

If our hearts are continually full of praise to God, we will be prepared to serve in a moment's notice. We will be ready to say yes when our Master calls us. Our knees will already be bent on the side of the altar which gives instead of being there to receive.

Esther was a wonderful example of a woman who looked through windows of opportunity to help others. When the Lord summoned her to service, she was ready to respond to the work her Lord had prepared for her. We've all been summoned into the presence of the Lord. Will we be ready to say, "I will do as You ask, Lord," as Esther did? We will look more fully at the impact of Esther's willingness to submit to God's call in the next chapter, but first we will study together the illustration of a woman whose beauty soured when her focus was on herself instead of on the needs of her lord.

The story begins in the first chapter of Esther, verse 10. It's a long passsage, but I want you to see the whole story.

On the seventh day, when King Xerxes was in high spirits from wine, he commanded the seven eunuchs who served him—Mehuman, Biztha, Harbona, Bigtha, Abagtha, Zethar and Carcas—to bring before him Queen Vashti, wearing her royal crown, in order to display her beauty to the people and nobles, for she was lovely to look at.

But when the attendants delivered the king's command, Queen Vashti refused to come. Then the king became furious and burned with anger.

Since it was customary for the king to consult experts in matters of law and justice, he spoke with the wise men who understood the times and were closest to the king—Carshena, Shethar, Admatha, Tarshish, Meres, Marsena and Memucan, the seven nobles of Persia and Media who had special access to the king and were highest in the kingdom.

"According to law, what must be done to Queen Vashti?" he asked. "She has not obeyed the command of King Xerxes that the eunuchs have taken to her."

Then Memucan replied in the presence of the king and the nobles, "Queen Vashti has done wrong, not only against the king but also against all the nobles and the peoples of all the provinces of King Xerxes.

"For the queen's conduct will become known to all the women, and so they will despise their husbands and say, 'King Xerxes commanded Queen Vashti to be brought before him, but she would not come.'

"This very day the Persian and Median women of the nobility who have heard about the queen's conduct will respond to all the king's nobles in the same way. There will be no end of disrespect and discord.

"Therefore, if it pleases the king, let him issue a royal decree and let it be written in the laws of Persia and Media, which cannot be repealed, that Vashti is never again to enter the presence of King Xerxes. Also let the king give her royal position to someone else who is better than she.

"Then when the king's edict is proclaimed throughout all his vast realm, all the women will respect their husbands, from the least to the greatest."

The king and his nobles were pleased with this advice, so the king did as Memucan proposed.

He sent dispatches to all parts of the kingdom, to each province in its own script and to each people in its own language, proclaiming in each people's tongue that every man should be ruler over his own household.

ESTHER 1:10–22

This is a fascinating account of two women. One spent much time looking into mirrors and was so taken by her own beauty that she forgot the benefits that come from bringing pleasure to others. The other was more beautiful than the first, but she was more interested in the needs of her people than in her own prosperity. The first had the title of queen, but the latter acted like one. Which one do you suppose held the title the longest?

The king had asked Vashti, the queen, to show the people and the princes her beauty, for she was fair to look on. But when Queen Vashti refused to come at his command, the king's anger burned in him. Imagine the event. Vashti was invited to a royal banquet where everybody who was anybody was there. Everybody whom the king wanted to impress was there. Everybody who was impressed by the king was there. They were having a wonderful, political celebration.

The king was upon his throne and servants were all around him. They were eating and making merry, and the queen, Vashti, was in another part of the palace entertaining her feminine court. Everybody knew Xerxes and Vashti. They were the crème de la crème of the kingdom. Everybody wanted to be like them when they grew up. And right in the middle of the celebration the king stood up and sent his servants scurrying, saying to them, "I command Vashti to come into the presence of her king." He probably sat down with great expectancy.

When the servants went into Vashti's chambers, they most likely found the women giggling, acting silly, and talking about their children and their husbands. They were celebrating being the queen's guests. The servants said, "Queen Vashti, King Xerxes commands your presence."

Queen Vashti looked into the eyes of the servant in the midst of her court royal, and said, "No."

The queen told the king no?

The wife told her husband who had commanded her to come, no?

Now, I'm a little confused here. I know this is not a book about marriage, but if my "king" called me right now, I would be "outta here"! I would turn off the computer and put my ministry of writing aside. I don't understand what Vashti was thinking, but since I'm not teaching on marriage right now, maybe I'll address that in my next book.

We're looking at the spiritual parallel in this story. But she did not act like a princess that day. She acted like a spoiled, vain woman who thought only of herself. The king called the queen and she refused to appear before him. Now, theologically, I'm not here to debate what the king's motives were, because it doesn't matter what he wanted. What matters is that he called her.

He called her just as the Lord has called us. Have we ever refused the King of Kings when He has summoned us into the presence of God? The Lord has called us over and over and over and yet haven't we told Him no?

Vashti's downfall is only a small part of this story:

Later when the anger of King Xerxes had subsided, he remembered Vashti and what she had done and what he had decreed about her.

Then the king's personal attendants proposed, "Let a search be made for beautiful young virgins for the king.

"Let the king appoint commissioners in every province of his realm to bring all these beautiful girls into the harem at the citadel of Susa. Let them be placed under the care of Hegai, the king's eunuch, who is in charge of the women; and let beauty treatments be given to them.

"Then let the girl who pleases the king be queen instead of Vashti." This advice appealed to the king, and he followed it.

Now there was in the citadel of Susa a Jew of the tribe of Benjamin, named Mordecai son of Jair, the son of Shimei, the son of Kish,

Who had been carried into exile from Jerusalem by Nebuchadnezzar king of Babylon, among those taken captive with Jehoiachin king of Judah.

Mordecai had a cousin named Hadassah, whom he had brought up because she had neither father nor mother. This girl, who was also known as Esther, was lovely in form and features, and Mordecai had taken her as his own daughter when her father and mother died.

When the king's order and edict had been proclaimed, many girls were brought to the citadel of Susa and put under the care of Hegai. Esther also was taken to the king's palace and entrusted to Hegai, who had charge of the harem.

The girl pleased him and won his favor. Immediately he provided her with her beauty treatments and special food. He assigned to her seven maids selected from the king's palace and moved her and her maids into the best place in the harem.

ESTHER 2:1-9

When Vashti said no, the king found someone who would say yes. Like King Xerxes, God always has somebody else He can call. God will not be left without a witness. If we won't allow Him to bless us so that our testimony can win multitudes of people, then He will find someone else upon whom to bestow His kindness. God can always find somebody who would like a chance to move from rags to riches, who needs a miracle to become a princess. He will find her even if she is under a bridge or in a homeless shelter. God will find somebody who will say, "I will, I will! I will let You make me into a princess, and I will respond to Your call!"

Oh, but the Father wants all of us to reflect His glory. He wants all of us to dress in the wedding garment He has designed for us. Does it matter that He only wants to stand us before His enemy and say, "Look at my beautiful daughter"? Does it matter that He wants so little from us? Will we respond to the task He wants us to do? Oh, that we might respond like Esther did. She said, "Here am I, Lord. Send me. I'll go."

Conditions might not be right when He calls us. We might be dirty. We might be lost in sin, not knowing the way out. But He will call, and all we need to say is yes for Him to restore our souls.

Oh my Lord, my Secret Keeper, I pray that You ask my sister who is reading this book to come into Your presence, now that she knows all she needs to do is say, "Yes, Lord, I will come."

We were therefore buried with him
through baptism into death in order
that, just as Christ was raised from the
dead through the glory of the Father,
we too may live a new life.

ROMANS 6:4

CHAPTER FOUR

Wash Off Those Cinders!

LIFE IS LIKE A FAIRY TALE!

When Cinderella's fairy godmother told her the good news that she could go to the ball, Cindy washed off the ashes of her despair and left her own little corner in her own little room.
Haven't you heard the Good News?
Your Father God has rescued you.

God does not expect us to be in perfect condition before we say yes to His offer to rescue us. He simply wants His daughters to come forward, to step out of the shadows and into His light, where He can stand us before all those who look toward Him and say, "Look at My daughter. Look how beautiful she is. Behold her countenance of peace and her fine garments that I have put upon her. Surely, whoever looks at her can see that she has a Father who loves and cares for her."

In our willingness to let God's grace rest upon us and stand as a testimony to His good works, we become the testimony of His power. He did not ask for workers, He asked for witnesses. He did not ask us to perform, but to tell of His wondrous performance, the loving things we have seen Him do for us and for others.

God offers to each of us what was offered to Esther. The king's servants looked everywhere for a replacement for Vashti, the woman who had said no. They looked in the top parts of the city, where the upper echelon of the community lived. They gathered women from the homeless shelters. They went into the colleges and universities.

They invited the women who had been appointed as the least likely to succeed and gave them an opportunity to apply for the role of queen. Where did God's servants have to look to find us? Do we remember? Where were we when the Holy Ghost arrested us? Did He walk right into the club, right into that business meeting, and say, "The king has need of thee"?

It doesn't matter where we were. It matters that we were ready to say, "Yes, Lord. I will be the princess who offers testimony of Your grace. Choose me." It only matters that we were willing to come out of our corner to see what the Lord had ready for us.

The Scriptures are full of people like you and me. Abraham, the pagan Gentile, became the father of many nations. Joseph, the boy who was sold into bondage by his brothers, became the prime minister of Egypt. David, the shepherd boy, became the king of Israel. And our queen today, Esther the orphan, became the queen of King Xerxes. Just like a fairy tale, these people were taken from low and humble beginnings and lifted up to places of honor where they could serve and protect multitudes of God's people.

Each of them, however, had to leave behind their old lifestyles in order to accept the new blessings God had for them. Esther was ready to say yes to God's call on her life. He was only asking her to be a wife. But in that simple act of loving submission, she saved God's remnant and the precursors to the line of Jesus Christ from mass murder. Dreams do come true, and real people have lives that are better than fairy tales when they trust their decisions to God.

Something quite wonderful happened to Esther when she went to the king's palace. But first let's review the results of Queen Vashti's selfish reign. After Vashti said no to the king, he enforced a law for all women to respect and honor their husbands.

Reverence that was once motivated by love had become a requirement by law. The heart was no longer invited to be a part of the act. Husbands could no longer discern if their wives truly loved and respected them or if they were simply subject to a law in the land. Their wives did everything they were told, but were they acting out of love? To disobey their husbands was now punishable by a decree of the king. Could Vashti have ever dreamed that her own selfish actions would destroy the intimate partnerships of every couple in their kingdom?

When the wrath of King Xerxes was appeased, his servants ministered to him, "Let there be fair young virgins sought for the king. And let the maiden which pleaseth the king be queen instead of Vashti" (Esther 2:1–2).

So when the king's commandment was heard, many maidens were gathered together unto the custody of Hegai, keeper of the women. Esther was also brought to the king's house and put in the custody of Hegai. Esther pleased him and obtained his favor and kindness, so he speedily gave her things for purification (Esther 2:3–4, 8–9).

HIS WAYS ARE BETTER THAN FAIRY TALES

I find this fascinating. Esther only needed to respond with a yes, and once she was in the king's palace, everything she needed for purification was given to her. She didn't have to shop first or buy fine dresses and perfumes in order to make herself beautiful for the king. He provided all she needed to look radiant, just as Jesus provides what we need to be purified. Hebrews 1:3 confirms this for us,

> **The Son is the radiance of God's glory and the exact representation of his being, sustaining all things by his powerful word. After *he had provided purification for sins,* he sat down at the right hand of the Majesty in heaven.**

If you have not understood this before, I hope that you comprehend what Good News this is for all of us. By believing in Jesus Christ, all the cinders of our past are washed away and we are purified, just as new babies are pure.

We celebrate this cleansing through water baptism as an outward testimony of what we know God has done to our secret soul. Jesus' blood redeems us from the penalty of our sins. The water of baptism celebrates the washing away of our habit of sin. Although we are saved by Jesus' blood, and not by being baptized, we are commanded by the Lord to submit to the act of baptism in the name of the Lord Jesus Christ.

If you have not followed the Lord in this act of obedience, I implore you to submit yourself to this wonderful ceremony He has prepared for you. Peter taught in Acts 2:38 that we are to repent and be baptized in the name of Jesus Christ for the remission of sins. He promised that we would receive the gift of the Holy Spirit. In Acts 10:47–48 we see that even those who had already received the Holy Spirit were commanded to be baptized in the name of the Lord.

There is a power that comes upon those who submit themselves to this public testimony that they accept God's gift of salvation. Through baptism we identify our past with His death, proclaiming that we are released from the bondage of sin.

Romans 6:1–8 explains what happens to us through baptism.

What shall we say, then? Shall we go on sinning so that grace may increase?

By no means! We died to sin; how can we live in it any longer?

Or don't you know that all of us who were baptized into Christ Jesus were baptized into his death?

We were therefore buried with him through baptism into death in order that, just as Christ was raised from the dead through the glory of the Father, we too may live a new life.

If we have been united with him like this in his death, we will certainly also be united with him in his resurrection.

For we know that our old self was crucified with him so that

the body of sin might be done away with, that we should no longer be slaves to sin—

Because anyone who has died has been freed from sin.

Now if we died with Christ, we believe that we will also live with him.

Water baptism marks the fact that we are separated from our past sins. Clean! Free from our indebtedness to the memory of wrongdoing! Water baptism is not simply a ritual that God asks us to do as a test of obedience. There is an authority with baptism that declares our independence from the powers that held us in bondage to our old nature.

When Jesus submitted to baptism, we know He did it to fulfill all righteousness. We also know that the Holy Spirit came upon Him in a visible way after He submitted Himself to baptism. His public ministry began after this testimony of His submission to God. We know that God announced His Sonship before the crowd during that public immersion. He was baptized so that His followers would do as He did. Matthew records that Jesus said,

Whosoever therefore shall confess me before men, him will I confess also before my Father which is in heaven.

MATTHEW 10:32 KJV

I have a friend who was baptized three times. Knowing I was working on this chapter, she shared her experience with me through the following letter,

Dear Lady Jakes,

I was first baptized when I was eight years old. I remember that my pastor asked me if I wanted to repent of my sins, and I

said yes. I had loved God since I was four years old.

No one had yet told me about Jesus. No one in the church had explained to me that Jesus paid the price for my sins and the baptism was to celebrate the truth of this cleansing from my old nature. No one told me that Jesus was God, or that He wanted to be my personal friend.

Then we changed churches to another denomination, and I had to be baptized again in order to become a member of the church. So at eleven years old I was baptized a second time.

Finally, when I was twelve someone explained to me salvation through Jesus Christ. It was then that I finally understood that I would not go to heaven because I went to church, but because He had paid the price through the shedding of His blood for all the sins that separated me from God.

When I was seventeen a zealous young minister asked me if I had been baptized since I believed in the Lord Jesus. I couldn't believe that God would ask me to be baptized a third time. "Doesn't He know I love Him by now?" I questioned.

But one night I read the account of believers in Acts 19 who had been baptized by John unto repentance and were told to be baptized again now that they had received Jesus. Their story was just like mine.

The third time I was baptized, only the minister was present beside me, but I felt like all of heaven and hell were watching me. It took great humility to do it again, but I didn't want to miss any blessing that my Father might have for me. When I came up out of the water that third time, the minister told me to expect to receive the gift of tongues just as believers in Acts 19 had experienced. He told me to say whatever words came to mind and not to worry if they sounded strange.

I could only whisper "Abba," not knowing at that young age

that it meant Father and was the same word Jesus used to cry unto His Father.

Needless to say, that day of my third baptism marked the beginning of my ministry. There was no turning back for me after that powerful day of testimony before my cloud of witnesses. I have remained in full-time ministry now for thirty years. It truly was the day that the Holy Spirit came upon me with the power to be a witness for Him.

I hope my letter will encourage your readers to find the cleansing power of His baptismal waters, now that they believe in Christ alone.

Love,

Your Sister in the Lord

Dreams do come true, and real people have lives that are better than fairy tales when they trust their decisions to God.

This sister's experience well illustrates the power of water baptism. There are many Scriptures that explain the grace that comes upon us during this important event with God. The apostle Paul wrote,

> **For you did not receive a spirit that makes you a slave again to fear, but you received the Spirit of sonship. And by him we cry, "Abba, Father."**
>
> ROMANS 8:15

For this precious woman, it was as though baptism confirmed her adoption. She was given His name to call upon before anyone ever told her that her Daddy's name was Abba. Galatians 4:6 shows that the Spirit of Jesus, the Holy Spirit, is the one who told her who sealed her adoption by giving her the name that she was now to use. The Scripture reads,

> **Because you are sons, God sent the Spirit of his Son into our hearts, the Spirit who calls out, "Abba, Father."**
>
> GALATIANS 4:6

Read the rest of this passage to see the good news that is in store for us.

> **So you are no longer a slave, but a son; and since you are a son, God has made you also an heir.**
>
> **Formerly, when you did not know God, you were slaves to those who by nature are not gods.**
>
> **But now that you know God—or rather are known by God— how is it that you are turning back to those weak and miserable principles? Do you wish to be enslaved by them all over again?**
>
> GALATIANS 4:7–9

No, God does not leave us to fend for ourselves against our old ways. He gives us the power to be His daughters. Acts 1:8 declares,

But you will receive power when the Holy Spirit comes on you; and you will be my witnesses in Jerusalem, and in all Judea and Samaria, and to the ends of the earth.

What a wonderful God we serve! Not only does He do all the work to save us, He does all the work to cleanse us. All we need to do is walk into His water and let Him wash away the cinders of our past life. Our old nature remains buried as we rise up to walk in newness of life.

Queen Esther enjoyed her new life as first lady in the king's house. She served with such humility that the king favored her above all others. She didn't go before the king with excuses as to why she couldn't be his queen. She didn't use the excuses we hear in the church like, "Well, you don't know my mamma, and my daddy, and then my children, and I've got a husband in jail and. . . ."

Nor did Esther do what I did to the Bishop when he asked me to be his lady. I told him, "I don't play, I don't sing, and I can't preach." All he said to me was, "But what *can* you do?"

Don't go to God telling Him who you're not! He knows us. He knows everything about us and He called us anyway. Don't give God a negative résumé. Instead, tell Him, "I can do all things through Christ who strengthens me" (Philippians 4:13).

The Bible says that Esther obtained kindness and favor. She still had to go through the same thing everybody else went through, but it was easier for her because she already had favor. We have favor through the grace of God. Grace is the unmerited favor and power of God on our lives as taught in 2 Corinthians 12:9:

But he said to me, "My grace is sufficient for you, for my power is made perfect in weakness." Therefore I will boast all the more gladly about my weaknesses, so that Christ's power may rest on me.

Now just because we have favor with God does not mean we are going to escape going through our "go-throughs." We're not exempt from difficulty. He loves us, and He will walk us through it, but through it we all must go. Some of us will go through the water, some of us will go through the flood, and some of us through the fire.

I have favor, but it doesn't keep me from going through things. The one sustaining force that has never changed is the knowledge that the King has called me. Moreover, because I found favor with the King, He's with me every step of the way, just as He is with you.

Favor. You must remember that it is undeserved. You can't earn God's grace so you can't lose it. His unmerited favor is a free gift that comes to us with our salvation. Simply enjoy His provision and prepare yourself to please and serve Him.

FAVOR CHANGES THE WAY THINGS ARE GOING

Esther's turn came after all the women were paraded before the king, both the haves and the have-nots. Everybody came before the king for him to find a suitable queen. Then his eyes saw Esther. The king favored her above every other woman who was in the room.

Aren't those secret moments with God, when we feel like we are His favorite, wonderful? It is okay to admit that we have felt that way, because He makes us all feel singled out and loved. Sometimes, don't we feel like we are above all the other people in the world, because He chose us? Out of all the people that He could have selected, somehow in His infinite wisdom,

He saw what we would become, not what we used to be, but what we are going to be, and He favored us. He did us a favor. Esther must have felt that way the day she stood before the king.

Customarily, after all of the virgins had paraded before the king, there were three places to which they could be assigned. The first chamber was reserved for all whom the king had basically sent on their way because he didn't want to become further involved with them.

The second chamber was where those women whom he liked a little bit were sent. The Bible calls them concubines. He entered into a pseudo relationship with them, without a covenant. Today we call them "live-ins."

The third chamber was reserved for the queen. Those three places reveal three ways that we can approach God. We can be satisfied just to have a mundane Sunday morning experience with Him, which would be the first chamber. Everybody can do that, and most of us do only that.

Then there is the second chamber, where we get just close enough to the glory to brush up against it and know that it's real. The problem is, we go no further and we want to be on a live-in basis so we can leave if things get inconvenient. To be a live-in with God is to say we don't trust Him to be "a rewarder of those who diligently seek Him" (Hebrews 11:6).

But there is a place reserved for intimacy, for those who have entered into a covenant relationship with God. This place is reserved for the queen, where we become intimate with Him, where we become wrapped up, tied up, and tangled up with Him, and we can't let Him go. It's a place where, once we have been there, we will never be satisfied to be anywhere else because we have been in the awesome presence of God.

That's where they put Esther—right into the queen's chamber. They didn't even bother to return her to those other superficial, inner courts or outer courts. They took her right into the place where she could approach the king as her husband. This is where God wants us, the Holy of Holies where we can worship Him.

That's where I want to be—right in the presence of God! So day and night I can praise Him in the third chamber reserved for the queen. We are all to aspire to go into that third chamber, whether we are babes in Christ or mature, seasoned Christians. We've got ready access to the King of Kings. In the time of need, when nobody else is around, you know that your King is always present to carry you through whatever you have to go through. That's trust!

When the king saw Esther, he extended his scepter and said, "Whatever you want will be done, and I will give you up to half of my kingdom." Her story continues in Esther 7:2–10:

> And as they were drinking wine on that second day, the king again asked, "Queen Esther, what is your petition? It will be given you. What is your request? Even up to half the kingdom, it will be granted."
>
> Then Queen Esther answered, "If I have found favor with you, O king, and if it pleases your majesty, grant me my life—this is my petition. And spare my people—this is my request.
>
> For I and my people have been sold for destruction and slaughter and annihilation. If we had merely been sold as male and female slaves, I would have kept quiet, because no such distress would justify disturbing the king."
>
> King Xerxes asked Queen Esther, "Who is he? Where is the man who has dared to do such a thing?"
>
> Esther said, "The adversary and enemy is this vile Haman." Then Haman was terrified before the king and queen.
>
> The king got up in a rage, left his wine and went out into the palace garden. But Haman, realizing that the king had already decided his fate, stayed behind to beg Queen Esther for his life.
>
> Just as the king returned from the palace garden to the banquet hall, Haman was falling on the couch where Esther was reclining. The king exclaimed, "Will he even molest the queen

while she is with me in the house?" As soon as the word left the king's mouth, they covered Haman's face.

Then Harbona, one of the eunuchs attending the king, said, "A gallows seventy-five feet high stands by Haman's house. He had it made for Mordecai, who spoke up to help the king." The king said, "Hang him on it!"

So they hanged Haman on the gallows he had prepared for Mordecai. Then the king's fury subsided.

Esther said yes to God's invitation to be a queen. Her willingness won His favor and in so doing she saved her people from genocide.

THE SCEPTER IS IN YOUR HANDS

God is calling us something that we think we're not, but He knows us, who we really are. The scepter is now extended to us and He is saying, "Whatever you want, whatever you will, ask what you will and it shall be done unto you."

The scepter is extended toward you, so ask Him what you will. Let Him show you His love for you. Let Him prove His grace so that He might be glorified in the earth through the testimony of your praise. So reach out and grab hold of God's scepter, which is all that He has for you.

God just wants you to know that whatever you need from Him, He's able to provide. He has chosen you to be His daughter. He has provided the waters to make you pure. He has a plan to lift you up. All He wants is to hear you say to Him unequivocally, "Yes! Absolutely yes!"

Now Joshua was dressed in filthy
clothes as he stood before the angel.
The angel said to those who
were standing before him,
"Take off his filthy clothes."
Then he said to Joshua, "See, I have
taken away your sin, and I will put
rich garments on you."

ZECHARIAH 3:3–4

CHAPTER FIVE

Put On a More Revealing Dress

LIFE IS LIKE A FAIRY TALE!

Cinderella knew that if she wanted to
dance with a prince,
she must dress like a princess.
She willingly traded her rags for
the beautiful gown that had been
made just for her.
Isn't it time you put on the garment of
praise to dance with the Lord?

Cinderella was transformed simply by putting on the new dress that had been prepared for her. A new outfit can give us a sense of confidence over who we are, or at least over who we appear to be. Afternoon talk shows draw large audiences with promises of makeovers that change hard looking women to beautiful covergirls. The ones who feel the makeover expresses who they really are inside smile radiantly as they come from behind the screens.

We all use clothes to cover our insecurities and boost our self-worth. Things haven't changed much since Adam and Eve first tried to hide behind fig leaves! God made clothes for them because the ones they made weren't very functional.

Many people will admit that even when they meet someone for the first time, they enjoy having on a new outfit to make that memorable first impression. They know that the person they are meeting wouldn't know whether their clothes were new or ten years old, but they still feel better through the nervousness of that first handshake when they are dressed in something fresh and stylish.

Most of us notice when a friend is wearing a new outfit that we have never seen on her before and agree that there is something satisfying to our own souls in seeing another woman look her best. Don't we all enjoy watching a well-dressed man or woman energetically enter a room with confidence? I'm not referring to the well-dressed people who enter a room and tacitly express, "Look at me." But we are charmed by immaculately groomed people who stand before us and imply, "Ah, there you are." What is this difference?

As wonderful as new clothes are, they do not make up for the grace of a humbled heart. First Peter 5:5–7 says,

> **All of you, clothe yourselves with humility toward one another, because, "God opposes the proud but gives grace to the humble."**
> **Humble yourselves, therefore, under God's mighty hand, that he may lift you up in due time.**
> **Cast all your anxiety on him because he cares for you.**

It's not easy to clothe ourselves in humility, but I have learned that the more we understand how very much God loves us, and the more we comprehend the grace He has demonstrated toward us, the more humble we become.

There is a false humility that cripples us, telling us we are not worthy of any good thing. This is humiliation and it is not from God. But godly humility affirms that all good things are ours only because of God's goodness and not our own. When we understand that God's love is unconditional, when we become aware that we can neither earn His love nor lose it, we are filled with awe toward Him, and it humbles us in His presence.

Applying this difference between humiliation and humility to our lives will clothe us more beautifully than the world's most fashionable clothiers and designers. A humbled heart does not ask for attention from others; it gives attention to others. Even this gift of humility comes to us from the Lord.

SECOND-HAND ROSE

We are all affected by seeing someone who needs a clean shirt, a mended hem, or a new pair of shoes, especially if they hang their head with embarrassment or humiliation. I well remember being the woman who needed something to wear to "the dance." I remember the insecurity of wondering whether or not others would feel I was acceptable. It wasn't so very long ago, though it now seems a lifetime away from where the Lord has carried me.

I pen these words as a testimony of what God can do. I want the words to encourage those who have given up on their future because of obstacles that seem to be immovable. Before I even began to write the following admission to my Secret Keeper, He reminded me of His desire to clothe me more beautifully than the lilies of the field, in garments of praise to His glory.

I remembered Zechariah's account of seeing Joshua, the high priest, standing before the angel of the Lord. Satan stood at his right side accusing him before God. Then the Lord said to Satan,

> "The Lord rebuke you, Satan! The Lord, who has chosen Jerusalem, rebuke you! Is not this man a burning stick snatched from the fire?"
>
> Now Joshua was dressed in filthy clothes as he stood before the angel.
>
> The angel said to those who were standing before him, "Take off his filthy clothes."
>
> Then he said to Joshua, "See, I have taken away your sin, and I will put rich garments on you."
>
> ZECHARIAH 3:2-4

I wrote,

Dear Secret Keeper,

I was so excited as we prepared to attend our first National Convention as husband and wife. It was my first national appearance as my husband's new bride. I was so honored to be his helpmeet, and I wanted to represent him well.

As Pastor's wife, it seemed important to me that I looked the part of his "First Lady." I had such a hard time trying to pack my clothes. I certainly wanted to look my best; after all, I am the First Lady. I couldn't afford anything new, but I was so pleased with the suits, dresses, and shoes that the sisters from the church gave me out of their closets. They all fit almost perfectly. I didn't have enough things to change twice a day, but I knew I could wear the outfits from the beginning of the week again at the end of the week. I hoped no one would remember them.

I would be meeting so many prominent people. I prayed that I had selected my best pieces. When it was finally time to pack up the car and get on the road, I packed a lunch since it was a long drive to the conference. I felt the trip would be simply unforgettable.

But the Lord said to Samuel, "Do not consider his appearance or his height, for I have rejected him. The Lord does not look at the things man looks at. Man looks at the outward appearance, but the Lord looks at the heart."

I SAMUEL 16:7

It was so embarrassing. Upon my arrival, everyone seemed to be staring, first at me, and then right through me. It was as though they were as embarrassed by me as I was for me. I tried so very hard to be appropriate.

I knew that this was a very special occasion for us. Everyone we thought was anybody had flown in for the occasion. But I didn't know that it was going to be so fashionable.

Suddenly, all of the things that the sisters from the church had given me seemed so dingy. The shoes turned over on my feet. And how could it be that the hem was always falling out of the dress I had chosen? If I could have found a corner in which to hide, I could have made it easier for them to ignore me; then I would have been just fine.

I wondered if You were as concerned about my appearance as I was. And You answered my question as I entered the service. The anointing was so strong that many lay prostrate before You. The Word was so powerful that I soon forgot what I had on and who was around me. I began to think of all the wonderful things that You had done in my life and I began to weep.

I sensed Your presence reassuring me that You didn't care about what I had on, that Your mind was full of who I would become. I urgently rushed into Your presence and worshipped You. You changed my garments. Surely, I must have felt like Joshua when he stood in Your presence dressed in filthy garments. You must have instructed the angels to remove the filthy garments from me while You clothed me in righteousness.

To console those who mourn in Zion, to give them beauty for ashes, the oil of joy for mourning, the garment of praise for the spirit of heaviness; that they may be called trees of righteousness, the planting of the Lord, that He may be glorified.

ISAIAH 61:3 NKJV

That day seems so long ago and far away from me now. I can go into any store in any city or country and select the best, often without regard to price. The outward adornment is no longer from consignment stores, yet the inward self remembers how You attired me when I felt most naked.

You accepted me for who I was. You have given me favor and caused others to see what You saw. I will always depend on You to customize me to Your specificity. I trust You to mold and fashion me according to the pattern that You have chosen for my life.

I thought of the song that says, "I'm wearing hand-me-down clothes, and that's why they call me Second-Hand Rose." But You, Secret Keeper, are fashioning me like the Rose of Sharon.

By the way, thank You for my new clothes.

Love,

Serita Ann

THE ROSE OF SHARON

Just as the Lord covered the shame of Adam and Eve, He continues to replace our humiliation with humility. We are thankful that He is the one who clothes us. He covers us with His righteousness so that others see that we belong to Him. He is not ashamed of us, but He proudly covers us with His royal robe and stands us before our critics and accusers to boast, "She is mine."

As daughters of the living and only true God, it is time that we clothe ourselves with humility, revealing who we really are. When we enter a room, others should notice our countenance of peace instead of our dress. Our faces should shine with the oil of joy that results from knowing how much God loves us. Our words throughout the day should demonstrate a revelation of God's grace in our lives.

As the bride of Christ, we are each given a wedding gown, provided by Jesus, the Rose of Sharon, himself. He offers an exchange with us, our ashes for His beauty, our grief for His joy, our rags for His garment of praise. He eagerly extends this great exchange so that we will become like Him and glorify the Father by showing the world what a kind and awesome God we serve.

There have been many books on the market to teach us how to dress for success. But the Lord tells us rather to clothe ourselves with Jesus Christ. What would happen if we, His daughters, consciously wrapped ourselves in His robe each morning as we prepared for the day?

What would this "putting on of Christ" look like?

The apostle Paul explains how to do this in Colossians 3:12–17:

> **Therefore, as God's chosen people, holy and dearly loved, clothe yourselves with compassion, kindness, humility, gentleness and patience.**
>
> **Bear with each other and forgive whatever grievances you may have against one another. Forgive as the Lord forgave you.**
>
> **And over all these virtues put on love, which binds them all together in perfect unity.**
>
> **Let the peace of Christ rule in your hearts, since as members of one body you were called to peace. And be thankful.**
>
> **Let the word of Christ dwell in you richly as you teach and admonish one another with all wisdom, and as you sing psalms, hymns and spiritual songs with gratitude in your hearts to God.**
>
> **And whatever you do, whether in word or deed, do it all in the name of the Lord Jesus, giving thanks to God the Father through him.**

In Philippians 2:1–17, Paul further explains how we are to dress ourselves:

> **If you have any encouragement from being united with Christ, if any comfort from his love, if any fellowship with the Spirit, if any tenderness and compassion,**

Then make my joy complete by being like-minded, having the same love, being one in spirit and purpose.

Do nothing out of selfish ambition or vain conceit, but in humility consider others better than yourselves.

Each of you should look not only to your own interests, but also to the interests of others.

Your attitude should be the same as that of Christ Jesus:

Who, being in very nature God, did not consider equality with God something to be grasped,

But made himself nothing, taking the very nature of a servant, being made in human likeness.

And being found in appearance as a man, he humbled himself and became obedient to death—even death on a cross!

Therefore God exalted him to the highest place and gave him the name that is above every name,

That at the name of Jesus every knee should bow, in heaven and on earth and under the earth,

And every tongue confess that Jesus Christ is Lord, to the glory of God the Father.

Therefore, my dear friends, as you have always obeyed—not only in my presence, but now much more in my absence—continue to work out your salvation with fear and trembling,

For it is God who works in you to will and to act according to his good purpose.

Do everything without complaining or arguing,

So that you may become blameless and pure, children of God without fault in a crooked and depraved generation, in which you shine like stars in the universe

As you hold out the word of life—in order that I may boast on the day of Christ that I did not run or labor for nothing.

But even if I am being poured out like a drink offering on

the sacrifice and service coming from your faith, I am glad and rejoice with all of you.

JESUS LOOKS AT OUR HEARTS

Jesus comes to seek us out and save us. He comes looking for the real self who hides in corners and behind new clothes. We see Him searching for someone who is hiding when He went through Samaria on His way to Galilee. This particular route was not unusual from a geographical perspective. Going through Samaria was the shortest way. But Samaria was normally avoided by Jews.

For over 700 years, religious and racial prejudice had separated the Jews from the Samaritans, who were the descendants of the surviving Israelites from the northern kingdom and who intermarried with the newly imported Gentile population after the fall of Samaria in 722 BC. Samaritans worshipped God as the Jews did. They studied the five books of Moses (Genesis to Deuteronomy) but not the rest of the Old Testament. They awaited the coming of a prophet like Moses. But Jewish hatred for the Samaritans sprang more from historical and racial considerations than from any fundamental difference of religion.[1]

However, Jesus was not like the other Jews. He decided that He must go through Samaria on this particular day. His beloved disciple John recorded the event in John 4:4, noting that Jesus had to go through Samaria. I like the way the *King James Version* states it, **And he *must needs* go through Samaria.** But *The Amplified Bible* says, **It was *necessary* for Him to go through Samaria.**

I believe it was *necessary* so Jesus could invite a certain woman at Jacob's well to be part of His family, which also illustrates His love for you and me. It was necessary for Jesus to meet this particular woman so that we could understand that His offer of salvation and hope is open to people even like

---

[1]*Eerdman's Handbook to the Bible*, David Alexander, Pat Alexander, Eds. (Grand Rapids: William B. Eerdmans Publishing Company, 1973), 497, 537.

us. Jesus wanted this Samaritan woman to know that she was included on His guest list. She was invited to drink from the rivers of living water He offers to everyone.

Jesus was tired from His journey, so He went to the well where this woman came for water. He knew she would come to the well at a time when the other women from the city would not be there. This woman didn't have a lot of money or she would have sent someone else to draw the water for her. She was "nameless" as far as the story goes, but she was most definitely a memorable woman. She didn't have a lot left to offer anyone—after all, she had already been used by several of the men in town.

Almost everyone in Samaria knew her, but they usually referred to her as "that woman." The tone in their voice and the sideways glance of their eyes clearly revealed they meant this woman whose name was not mentioned in nice family homes. No one ever walked up to her and said, "Hi, Zema." Instead, they would murmur under their breath when she passed them, "Hmmm, who is it this month? Who is it this year? What are you into now?"

Jesus comes to seek us out and save us. He comes looking for the real self who hides in corners and behind new clothes.

This woman's secrets alienated her from the women who came to the well together. No, this nameless woman had five secrets that had left her so devastated, she didn't even want to come to the well when the other women were there. Besides, she thought no one could relate to all that she had experienced.

Have you ever found it difficult to go to a ladies' meeting at church where other women don't know your name, but you think they know what you have done? Maybe you felt that no one else who went to those meetings had done what you had done. Maybe you could see that they were thirsty for some refreshment to quench their parched soul, but you could not see that their dryness was as severe as your own.

Who could you trust to know who you really are? Who would really understand the struggle it is for you to come into a room full of women whom you feel have it "all together." Surely those women at church who lead the ministries, who attend all the conferences, who drive nice cars, and who are not on welfare, wouldn't understand what you are going through. In one of my meetings, I once challenged a room filled with thousands of women to stand up if they had less than five things they didn't want somebody to know about them. No one stood, but they all applauded my discovery.

The Samaritan woman came to the well that eventful day and walked right into the very thing she had been running from. She walked head-on into Truth. She wanted to get something to drink because she was thirsty in more ways than one. A man was sitting at the well, and she had learned to be cautious of men who sat beside wells and found her alone. Such a scene reminded her of all of her past mistakes. Mistakes could have led to babies out of wedlock; mistakes could have led to rape; mistakes today could lead to new mistakes.

But on this day the man sitting at the well was waiting to let her know that she was not forgotten, and God had a new image for her to wear. Jesus let her know that He knew everything about her. He knew about the man she was living with who wasn't her husband. He knew about the husband she had had before him, and before him, and before him, and before him. He knew the emptiness that these relationships had left. He knew she was the one who thirsted for something to quench the dryness in her spirit. He knew He was the only one who could quench her thirst. He waited by the well for her.

When she came, He asked her for water. Surprised that a Jew would talk to a Samaritan, she asked Him how it was that He would ask her for water. "If you only knew the gift of God, if you knew who I am, you would ask Me to give you water, and I would give you living water so that you would never thirst again. The water that I would give you would become a spring of water welling up, flowing and bubbling continually within you unto eternal life" (John 4:10–14).

YOU'RE AT THE WELL, SO DRINK!

Memories will never quench our thirst or put fresh, clean clothing on our souls. We need access to fresh water every day. We need to be loved every day. Memories are not enough to really satisfy us. If all we have to quench our thirst for love is from the memories of those five experiences in our past, or twenty-five, or one, or none, we will quickly dry up and die from our thirst. We need access to fresh, living water from a well that never runs dry. If parched, waterless memories hold us in bondage from our future, it's time to receive the gift of God.

The woman at the well sat down beside the Truth and was sanctified, clothed with righteousness, and set apart for special use in the kingdom of God. God didn't change her past to make her a messenger of Good News; He used her past to prove His unconditional love for her.

The woman at the well comes to our churches on Sundays. She comes to women's meetings. She reads this book. She doesn't need to be nameless anymore. The Father knows everything about her, wraps her in His robe of humility, and proudly calls her His own.

Jesus, the Incarnate Word of God, said to the woman at the well, "Give Me something to drink." The Word still says to us today, "Speak what you know to Me. Show Me how much of My Word you have hidden in your heart." Jesus still says to the woman who comes for water at the well, "Worship Me, say something to Me to let Me know that you want a relationship with Me. Say something to Me that will quench My thirst for you."

And the woman at the well says, "Why are You asking me for something to drink? Shouldn't You have something with which to get Your own water?"

And the Lord says to the lady, "If you only knew who you were sitting with, it wouldn't matter what you have done. What would matter is that you are thirsty, and I can satisfy your thirst."

If you have never told the Lord that you are thirsty for Him, I implore you to stop reading this book and get alone with Him right now. Tell Him that you need Him to direct your life. Ask Him for that gift of God that He promised to the woman at the well. Your past is not worse than hers. Jesus purposely sought out the woman at the well to prove to you that He cares about your thirst too.

If you truly don't know how to talk to Jesus in your own words, then pray this prayer with me.

> *Lord, I am thirsty for Your living water. I confess that I am not proud of my past, but realize that I do not have the power to break away from the bondage of my memories without Your grace to set me free.*
>
> *I surrender my heart to You.*
>
> *I surrender my past to You.*
>
> *I thank You that my identity no longer aligns with who I have been but with who You are.*
>
> *I give You my future and choose not to be anxious about it anymore, knowing that You will lead me to green pastures and still*

waters where I will be cared for like a lamb with a loving shepherd.

Thank You for filling me with Living Water that will keep me from thirsting again. Thank You for removing my filthy clothes and covering me in Your beautiful robe of humility and righteousness. Thank You for dressing me as a princess and revealing to others who I really am.

His divine power has given us
everything we need
for life and godliness through our
knowledge of him who called us by
his own glory and goodness.

2 PETER 1:3

CHAPTER SIX

Find Your Own Way to the Dance

LIFE IS LIKE A FAIRY TALE!

Cinderella's relatives wouldn't take her to the party with the family horses,
so she took a taxi, better known in those days as a pumpkin pulled by mice.
Where do you need to go?
Whose permission are you waiting on?
Have you checked the Yellow Pages for a ride?

Cinderella could have indulged herself in self-pity because her evil relatives had told her to stay home and refused her a ride to the ball. If she had waited for permission to do the right thing, she never would have married the prince. If she had stayed angry toward her evil sisters, she would not have enjoyed the party once she got there.

God lets us know right from wrong, and He gives us a way of escape from the evil that is plotted against us. He gives us the freedom to do the right thing. Hebrews 8:10–12 confirms this promise:

> **This is the covenant I will make with the house of Israel after that time, declares the Lord. I will put my laws in their minds and write them on their hearts. I will be their God, and they will be my people.**
>
> **No longer will a man teach his neighbor, or a man his brother, saying, "Know the Lord," because they will all know me, from the least of them to the greatest.**

For I will forgive their wickedness and will remember their sins no more.

God gives us permission to forget our past and the understanding to live our present. He said He will remember our sins no more! King David had many regrets. His past was full of sins and secrets, but look at what he discovered about God's love and recorded for each of us:

For as high as the heavens are above the earth, so great is his love for those who fear him; as far as the east is from the west, so far has he removed our transgressions from us.

PSALM 103:11–12

But there is still an enemy of God who wants to steal your freedom from you. The devil wants to keep you in the cinders of who you were to keep you from enjoying your inheritance. He loves to see you sitting in the corner, where you can become his easy prey. Not too long ago I nearly became the easy prey of the enemy. Without the comfort of my Secret Keeper and the prayers and love of my husband, family, and church family, I could have been trapped in the valley of the shadow of death.

Dear Secret Keeper,

When I received the phone call about my mother's condition, I knew I had to rush to her side. They had already put her in the intensive care unit. I was miles away at one of our conferences and would have to fly through the night to get home to her.

Early that next morning I drove to the hospital and, when I stepped out of the elevator, I looked into the eyes of a lady who had sat through the night outside the door of Mother's room. She looked so worried that my heart immediately began to sink. As she escorted me to the room where Mother was, there was a gloominess in the air.

When we arrived at the door, I felt the person I saw had to be another patient. I walked with horror past the bed to a window that had no view. My mother lay with IV poles all around her. An oxygen tube running to her nose insisted that she breathe. But the most devastating piece of hospital equipment in the room was the respirator, the life support system that sustained her life!

How did this happen? How did this happen to Mother? When did this happen? I struggled for my sanity as I stared into nothingness. This is my mother!

Oh, Secret Keeper, I could not find a prayer!

I backed toward the bed and stared into the face of one who had loved me all of my life. She slowly opened her eyes and stared at her baby.

"Mother, I didn't know. I'm here! Mother, I'm here." She couldn't speak at all. Only her eyes spoke of the terror in her heart. For the first time in my life, I saw fear on Mother's half-masked face. She was so afraid. I had not been there to help her like she had helped me countless times.

Secret Keeper, I felt so guilty.

The nurse touched me on the shoulder and told me visiting hours were over. Over? I could only stay thirty minutes with the woman who had given me life?

In the waiting room, the doctors came to inform me of Mother's condition. It was Gillain-Barre, a rare disease that was as antiquated as polio in its derivation. It was a virus that resulted in paralysis from the neck down. The respirator was there because Mother's lungs were not functioning.

They shared with me that the virus was reversible barring any complications from an extended stay on the respirator. Let the fight begin! During the day, phone calls were made to my brothers and sisters. My husband left midway through the conference to join the vigil at the CCICU. Our extended family took shifts supporting us and staying through the night for updates on Mother's condition.

One night as I drove home, my spirit was so heavy. My tears mixed with the raindrops falling on my windshield to further obstruct my vision. I asked You a question, "Are You going to take her?"

I will never forget the sound of Your answer. You, my omniscient Passenger said, "Yes!" And I knew that You would do so. I wanted so much for You to say, "Not yet!" Or even, "Not now!" But I knew Your voice.

For the next day or two, visitor after visitor came to stand by Mother's bed and pray for her. I looked in their faces to see if they sensed the urgency that I felt over her condition and her expected end. They were most comforting in their presence and in their remarks. I think everyone loved her with the same hope of her recovery. But I remembered Your answer, Secret Keeper.

That morning that I arrived to go in to Mother, her kidneys had failed. Dialysis was their prescription. Fifteen minutes into the procedure, I heard a page for Mother's doctor to report to CCICU station! As though I were one of the doctors, I began to run toward her room. As I rounded the wall, I saw the response team pull her gown open and apply pressure to her heart.

Her heart had arrested and so had mine. I remembered Your answer and knew that You had come to take her. The nurse reassured me that they had a heartbeat. I inched toward her side to look into eyes that were set on You. They started the procedure again for someone who had already been stolen from her body. I went back to the waiting room only to hear the doctors being summoned again. No one came to notify the family this time.

Without their invitation, I went to the room that once housed Mother to face a nurse whose nod from side to side affirmed what I already knew—she was gone with You, Secret Keeper. She received her healing in Your presence. Despite my prayers and the prayers of others, Your desire to have her with You prevailed. I fell to my knees in submission to Your will.

I cried unto the Lord with my voice; with my voice unto the Lord did I make my supplication.

I poured out my complaint before him; I shewed before him my trouble.

When my spirit was overwhelmed within me, then thou knewest my path. In the way wherein I walked have they privily laid a snare for me.

I looked on my right hand, and beheld, but there was no man that would know me: refuge failed me; no man cared for my soul.

I cried unto thee, O Lord: I said, Thou art my refuge and my portion in the land of the living.

Attend unto my cry; for I am brought very low: deliver me from my persecutors; for they are stronger than I.

Bring my soul out of prison, that I may praise thy name: the righteous shall compass me about; for thou shalt deal bountifully with me.

PSALM 142:1–7 KJV

The next few services were appearances only. I stared longingly at the front pew where Mother always sat rejoicing before You, but I saw no one. The rejoicing around me did little to breach the gaping split in my heart. Mother was gone, and my prayer for healing seemed to have been denied.

Souls came to the altar awaiting my hands and arms to touch their brokenness, but my heart was overwhelmed. Who would believe that I could pray and agree with them for healing. After all, Mother had died before my eyes. Fear gripped me every time the altar call was made because I knew that many would come to seek healing.

My courage to defy the diagnosis of doctors hemorrhaged from my spirit. I could not maintain eye contact with parishioners who reached out to me for fear they would summon me.

The enemy laughed and mocked me silently before countless thousands. "Now what are you going to do, Miss Healing Hands? Everyone knows what happened to your mother!"

My husband watched my struggle and rescued me again from my despair. He beckoned for me to come to lay hands upon and agree with a sister who had been diagnosed with a terminal disease. With every ounce of faith that I could muster, I stared death in the face and commanded it to flee in the name of Jesus!

I felt something break by the anointing of the Holy Spirit, something that had been bound. The chain that held me captive snapped and worship flooded my heart. The pain and guilt that made my cage melted in the presence of God.

Where, O death, is your victory? Where, O death, is your sting?

The sting of death is sin, and the power of sin is the law.

But thanks be to God! He gives us the victory through our Lord Jesus Christ.

Therefore, my dear brothers, stand firm. Let nothing move you. Always give yourselves fully to the work of the Lord,

because you know that your labor in the Lord is not in vain.

I CORINTHIANS 15:55–58

I looked on Mother's pew and saw that death had lost its sting and the grave held no victory. Weeks later the sister received a report of total healing. Testimony after testimony of God's healing has been shared after I stepped out of Mother's room, closed the door, and let her rest with You, Secret Keeper.

God gives us permission to forget
our past and the understanding
to live our present.

HIS TRUTH IS OUR SHIELD

Because God's enemy seeks to destroy our peace, we should commune with the Lord daily about the things we're going through. He will give us wisdom and grace to do the right thing in times of trial. When we feel like the *prey*, a victim of evil pursuit, it's time for us to *pray* and take action against our predator. Prayer is the most assertive action we can take in writing a happy ending to our own life stories. Prayer gives the situation over to God to work out on our behalf. The Bible says, "You have not because you do not ask God" (James 4:2).

Prayer empowers you to find your own way through life without simply reacting to whatever the devil may throw at you. Prayer invites the Holy Spirit to whisper in your ears what it is the Father wants for you. Prayer establishes your faith and provides a shield around you that protects you from the fiery darts of the evil one. Prayer builds courage within your soul to say no when no is the right thing to say. Prayer keeps you aware of the loving arms of your Lord and cuts a path to victory. In another passage, God tells us what He will do for the one who depends on Him:

He who dwells in the shelter of the Most High will rest in the shadow of the Almighty.

I will say of the Lord, "He is my refuge and my fortress, my God, in whom I trust."

Surely he will save you from the fowler's snare and from the deadly pestilence.

He will cover you with his feathers, and under his wings you will find refuge; his faithfulness will be your shield and rampart.

You will not fear the terror of night, nor the arrow that flies by day,

Nor the pestilence that stalks in the darkness, nor the plague that destroys at midday.

PSALM 91:1-6

Notice verse 5, which reads, **You will not fear the terror of night, nor for the arrow that flies by day.** God promises psychological help with fear that creeps up on us at night and concrete help with real danger in our lives. This promise of God should revive, renew, and strengthen our hearts and minds. Trust God to give you bread for your daily journey. Ask the Holy Spirit to bring God's Word to your remembrance so that you will stand strong against the buffeting of the devil's lies. Yield yourself completely to Him and admit your need of Jesus. Then thank Him for His faithfulness.

IF YOU FEEL LIKE *PREY*, IT'S TIME TO *PRAY!*

The next time the enemy taps you on the shoulder, tempting you to look at your past, you will be able to resist him in prayer. You will ignore him and draw closer into the safety of the Father's arms. Satan doesn't like forcing you into the arms of God. When the devil sees that his flaming arrows of deceit cause you to get closer to the Father instead of deeper into retreat, he will withdraw his weapons. What a victory you will have against the enemy of God through prayer!

The word "pray" is a verb, an action word. Since English was my favorite subject in school, it made me sensitive to the sounds and meanings of words. There is an understood subject when you use a verb alone. The subject is YOU! *You* pray! *You* take action over the situation. *You* make it happen! To pray is to implore earnestly!

The homonym of pray is "prey." The noun "prey" is the person who falls victim to someone or something. The prey is the target of the game, the booty or plunder of the one who chases, the one who is about to be captured by the hunter.

So, you pray to avoid being the prey again. Take action over this situation. The dictionary defines "pray" as an appeal, to beg, to petition, and to plea. Believers know that it means to make our requests known unto God. We are to commune with Him daily about the things we're going through. The "prey," the victim, needs to commune with God, to stay in contact with

God about what the hunter, the devil, is trying to do.

Are you the victim? Are your children his current target? Have your parents become the devil's prey? Or is it your ministry, your marriage, or your family? Is your reputation under fire? Pray to the Father in heaven for deliverance from the enemy, the devourer of your soul who has made you or your loved ones a target. You may have been a victim, but you are not without hope! You can pray to God in secret and He will answer you publicly (Matthew 6:6).

In Psalm 91 we are reminded of what we have when we stay in constant communion with God. We are safe under His protection. It's a privilege and a comfort to know that if we abide under the shadow of the Almighty, even though the enemy comes against us like a flood, the Spirit of the Lord will lift up a standard against him. Whether it's during the storm or during the sunshine, we're safe under the shadow of the Almighty.

I will say of the Lord, He is my refuge. Others make idols their refuge— some women make their looks their refuge, and some women make money or their position in society their refuge—but we who have become prey to the enemy know that God is our refuge. God is our fortress.

The psalmist says, "In Him will I trust." There's no reason to question God's ability to keep us safe. However, the enemy keeps right on bumping up against us, making us doubt whether we're secure in God. The psalmist goes on to tell us that there is no disappointment in Him, no shadow of turning. We can be greatly encouraged with the knowledge that God's promises are sure. They're true, they're accurate, and whatever He says He'll do, He's faithful to do it. He's the only one who's not going to change His mind about us. Something can happen to us today that will alter our destiny for life, but God never changes. He's faithful and surely He will deliver us.

Our comfort is in knowing that God's promise of protection will not waver through our temptations to doubt Him. Though trying times will come, though our health may fail, though our finances may weaken, still our security is in knowing that God will not waver on our behalf. He's not worried about what we're going through. He's not nervous, anxious, or upset because He has us in the palm of His hand.

SO WHAT IF THE TRUTH WERE KNOWN?

Anxiety in the heart of a woman weighs her down. The battle with "What if's" is a waste of time and energy.

What if my worst fear happens?

What if they find out about my past?

What if the company goes bankrupt?

What if my husband doesn't come home?

What if my daughter gets pregnant?

What if I lose my job?

What if. . . ?

Always in front of us is some type of cloud, some opportunity for anxiety over something to fear. But that possibility is what the Scriptures call the snare of the fowler. If you are familiar with hunting, you know that the snares are laid in the woods where the prey will most likely be walking. Traps are hidden so the normal eye wouldn't even see them, lest they be easy to avoid.

Often even our spiritual eye does not see the ambushments the enemy has set for us. We can be walking along and suddenly find ourselves trapped with some part of us stuck in a device that we didn't even know was in our path.

The trap may have been disguised in a relationship, an opportunity to get fast money, or a chance to go out with someone we've been wanting to know for years and years. We don't even see that it's a trap. It's set up for the prey, for the target, for the victim, and as we walk along, we don't even know that something terrible is about to happen to us. Suddenly, we are caught in the snare because we were not alert to the ways of the enemy.

The truth is, the Lord has made a way for us to escape the wiles of the enemy! Read carefully our promises defined in 2 Peter 1:2–8:

> **Grace and peace be yours in abundance through the knowledge of God and of Jesus our Lord.**
>
> **His divine power has given us everything we need for life and godliness through our knowledge of him who called us by his own glory and goodness.**
>
> **Through these he has given us his very great and precious promises, so that through them you may participate in the divine nature and escape the corruption in the world caused by evil desires.**
>
> **For this very reason, make every effort to add to your faith goodness; and to goodness, knowledge;**
>
> **And to knowledge, self-control; and to self-control, perseverance; and to perseverance, godliness;**
>
> **And to godliness, brotherly kindness; and to brotherly kindness, love.**
>
> **For if you possess these qualities in increasing measure, they will keep you from being ineffective and unproductive in your knowledge of our Lord Jesus Christ.**

How many times have you said, "How in the world did I get myself in this mess? I knew better! The Holy Spirit warned me!" But you let yourself be prey to the enemy of your soul. Remember, he's trying to defeat your purpose because he doesn't want you to reach the hope of your calling. But he's a liar.

It's time for the truth to be known. You need to know that no weapon formed against you will prosper! No weapon, whether you see it or whether you don't see it, will succeed in taking you out from under the protective wing of God. God will always provide the way of escape and give us everything we need for life and godliness.

You can take authority over your enemy by telling him,

> *"The Lord rebuke you, Satan! You tried to defeat me, you tried to shut me down, you tried to stop me. People perish for the lack of knowledge, but be informed today that your snare won't work on me, your trap won't work on me. It won't work, because my Lord has made a way for me to escape you, just like a bird that flies through the air without a care in the world."*

GOD IS NOT MOCKED!

The enemy would like for me to grow weary from the disappointments of my past, but I have learned that the past does not reflect the future plans God has for me. When I prayed for God to heal my mother, I did not get the answer I was wanting. But He gave me the grace to trust Him again, so that I could keep sowing faith for healing in new situations. We must trust God's sovereignty and not grow weary of doing what is right and good.

> **And let us not be weary in well doing: for in due season we shall reap, if we faint not.**
> **As we have therefore opportunity, let us do good unto all men, especially unto them who are of the household of faith.**
>
> GALATIANS 6:9–10 KJV

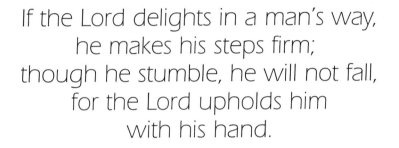

If the Lord delights in a man's way,
he makes his steps firm;
though he stumble, he will not fall,
for the Lord upholds him
with his hand.

PSALM 37:23-24

CHAPTER SEVEN

Kick Off Your Shoes

LIFE IS LIKE A FAIRY TALE!

Cinderella was so eager to obey her fairy godmother, she left her beautiful shoe behind as she fled the party to be home on time. What do you need to leave behind in order to be obedient to God's plan for you?

Everything Cinderella had ever hoped for was given to her, but there was one condition: She needed to be home by midnight. Even the princess in the fairy tale was given instructions which she was expected to obey.

I said in the beginning of this book that I am setting out to prove that life is like a fairy tale when we put our trust in God. He guarantees that we will live happily ever after in heaven, and if we obey Him in this life, we can expect blessings today as well. He sets before us the choice to love and obey Him. When we do, He promises to work all things together for our good. (See Romans 8:28.)

The proof of this promise was greatly tested when my husband and I suffered injuries from a deadly car accident. Here is the story of when I was a barefoot princess.

SHE WORE ONE SHOE

If the Lord delights in a man's way, he makes his steps firm;
though he stumble, he will not fall, for the Lord upholds him
with his hand.

PSALM 37:23–24

Dear Secret Keeper,

Anyone other than a family member who passed by and saw me sitting on the floor in front of my closet that day would have thought, "She must be straightening her shoes." But my family would have thought, "Oh no! She has fallen! What in the world is she doing in the front of her closet sitting with her shoes?" But only I knew how long I had lain in my bed, staring at the ceiling, rehearsing the words I had heard, "She can only wear one shoe."

Nearly six months had passed, and the car accident seemed as though it were yesterday. The sound of the sirens still rang in my ears as I recalled watching the emergency rescue team make certain that my husband, my mother, and my two-year-old twin boys were all okay. I had never before heard the term "jaws of life," but the team who had been dispatched to remove us from the car called for them.

It was as if I were watching a movie. Right before the impact, I saw the Jeep approach the intersection and prepare to make its turn. Surely they saw us. Certainly they won't make that turn right in front of us.

But they did! My husband's cherished Silver-Anniversary Edition Trans-Am plowed into the front of the Jeep. The battery from our car was projected like a bullet through the air. My husband's head cracked the windshield. My mother's shoe landed on the folded dashboard from the backseat of the car as she cradled the boys in her arms. The trim around the stereo knobs dangled like hoop earrings.

My husband beat against the door on the driver's side in an attempt to open it, disregarding the blood that trickled down his face. He kept urging me, "Get out of the car!"

I whispered to him that I couldn't. Before I knew it he had climbed through the bucket seats into the backseat, forced the passenger door open and stood by to assist us out. The boys were jumping up and down with the excitement only children can manifest. Mother, somewhat shaken, stood nearby while my husband stared with disbelief at my right foot. As he lifted me from the car he saw the blood oozing from my ankle where the bone protruded.

Upon closer scrutiny, the ambulance attendant saw that my entire heel cap had been dislocated to the side of my foot. Without my saying a word, the nearly unbearable pain that I felt was evidenced by the tears that streamed down my face. They whisked me into the back of the ambulance with my husband up front peering at me through the window.

I felt the jolt of every pothole in the highway. They seemed to appear from nowhere to add more agony to my pain, as if it were possible. On the stretcher in the hall of the emergency room, I laid for what seemed like years. Nothing and no one could have ever prepared me for the words that the doctor on call spoke to my husband. He lifted the sheet, and with compassion of an ice cube, informed us that I would never walk again!

For the Lord is good and his love endures forever; his faithfulness continues through all generations.

PSALM 100:5

Never is a long time when you lay in bed month after month after month. You confront many issues when your faith comes to trial, and you ask many questions. How will I take care of my family? How will I be attractive to my husband? Do I really want to be a burden? Will I ever feel like a woman again? The voice of the tormentor affirmed anything and everything that would deflate my ego. And I accepted his words that added to the defeat of my self-esteem.

I could not walk without crutches. With crutches, my spirit still could not walk. As the months of recovery passed, each phone call from heartless congregation members who easily dismissed me from their presence intensified my feeling of rejection and helplessness. Whoever I was to them hindered their need for constant attention from their pastor, who happened to be my husband.

Then came the day when I lowered myself from the bed to the floor and began to scoot on my bottom toward the closet. My journey took some time because the path I had so often walked seemed longer through teary eyes. "Never walk again! Never walk again!" This was the music that paced my nonambulatory cadence. My destination was my closet floor. I began to pull from the pile of pumps and sandals my right shoes. I lined them up in front of me and to each side. The one shoe represented my destiny: Never to walk again; if so, with a metal brace and a cane.

I would have to wear one shoe.

(Now in earlier times in Israel, for the redemption and transfer of property to become final, one party took off his sandal and gave it to the other. This was the method of legalizing transactions in Israel.)

RUTH 4:7

My husband interrupted my pity party. He extended his hand

to me as I sat on the floor wallowing in depression. I stood resting against his strong chest as his heart beat with his love for me. In my ear he whispered my hope for the days to come. He assured me, "If you never walk again, I will push your wheelchair, and I will never leave your side."

This man had written on my cast, "The steps of a good man are ordered by God." That day was the first day of my deliverance. His love for me insisted that I close the mouth of the enemy who was robbing me from believing God for my healing. My hero stepped back from me and took my hands. He looked from his tears into mine and said, "Just take one step."

With the agility of an elephant, I picked up my foot and it landed like a club. My hero told me that I had "done good."

"Take one more step. That's good!"

"Take another step. Now rest."

Every day my hero would hold my hands and, with loving therapy, applaud my efforts to move my club foot. He fought the enemy of our marriage for my restoration. My steps began to turn into brief walks from the chair to the couch and from the couch to the table.

In a matter of time, love lifted me! My husband, my pastor, my friend, taught me how to walk again!

Since ancient times no one has heard, no ear has perceived, no eye has seen any God besides you, who acts on behalf of those who wait for him.

ISAIAH 64:4

My confidence and my dignity were gradually restored. I returned to the tasks that I am so very fulfilled in doing: caring for my family. Every now and then, I have trouble with my ankle.

But I am so thankful for the reminder of the Lord's miraculous healing power.

When I left my shoe, the Prince of Peace found it and placed it on my foot.

Today I can wear beautiful shoes again. There were times during my recovery when other women we knew made cruel jokes about my crutches. I felt ashamed of my unattractive gait and single shoe, but I learned that I could walk barefoot in the presence of my Lord and my lover whom God had given to me.

TAKE OFF YOUR SHOES

When Moses stood in the presence of God on the mountain, God told him to take off his shoes because he was on holy ground (Exodus 3:5). Perhaps God didn't want anything to separate Moses from His presence. Don't you think it's time to get rid of whatever keeps you from walking into the presence of God?

The story of Ruth and Naomi illustrates a wonderful truth that surpasses the make-believe of Cinderella. Ruth began her life in hardship, like the princess in our fairy tale, but she inherited all the land upon which she once walked barefoot.

Look at her story in the book of Ruth.

During a time of famine in Bethlehem, Elimelech took his wife Naomi and his two sons to the country of Moab. His sons were named Mahlon (meaning "invalid") and Chilion (meaning "pining") who took wives after their father died. The wives, Orpah and Ruth, lived with their husbands and Naomi for about ten years until their husbands also died.

Naomi decided to return to her homeland and encouraged her daughters-in-law to go back to their homes to find husbands to care for them. But the young women didn't want to leave her. Eventually, Orpah heeded Naomi's advice and returned to her parents, but Ruth said, "I can't leave you.

Don't even ask me to leave you because, wherever you go, I will go, and where you lodge, I will lodge. Your people shall be my people, and your God, my God. Where you die, there I will be buried. The Lord do so to me, and more also, if anything but death parts me from you" (Ruth 1:16–17).

So one daughter went back to who she used to be, and the other one, even though it meant going to a strange land, decided to follow Naomi. Ruth loved Naomi and felt that this woman could teach her the ways of her God.

God does not want us to prove
ourselves but to prove Him.

When Naomi and Ruth arrived in Bethlehem, Ruth said, "Let me glean from the field of your wealthy kinsman, in whose sight I might find favor" (Ruth 2:2). So Naomi bid her to go. Ruth asked permission to glean in the fields after the reapers had passed through. She came early in the morning and worked with only a little rest.

When Boaz, the owner of the field, saw Ruth he told her to glean in his fields and offered her both protection and water when she was thirsty. At his demonstration of kindness, she fell on her face, bowing to the ground before him, and asked, "Why have I found favor in your eyes that you should notice me, when I am a foreigner?"

Boaz said to her, "I am fully aware of all you have done for your mother-in-law since the death of your husband and how you have left your father and mother and the land of your birth to come to a people unknown to you before. May the Lord recompense you for what you have done, and a full reward be given you by the Lord, the God of Israel, under whose wings you come to take refuge" (Ruth 2:8–12).

Boaz invited Ruth to eat with his reapers and made sure that she was allowed to glean where there was plenty of grain left. She continued to work in his fields until the end of the harvest. Naomi, recognizing Boaz as next of kin, instructed Ruth on how to approach Boaz with her request for their continued protection.

When Boaz became aware of Ruth's request, he blessed her for the loving-kindness she continued to show her mother-in-law. He pointed out that she could have become the wife of any man she sought, rich or poor, but she wanted someone who would also look after her mother-in-law. What Boaz said to Ruth is very important for all of us daughters of the King of Kings to understand. He said,

Fear not. I will do for you all you require, for all my people in the city know that you are a woman of strength (worth, bravery, capability).

RUTH 3:11 AMP

Ruth was a noble woman whose humility lifted her to great honor. She could have returned to her homeland and quickly married someone who would provide for her. She could have married a young man in Bethlehem and left Naomi to fend for herself. But Ruth served her mother-in-law and offered to serve Boaz as his maidservant in exchange for protecting and providing for Naomi.

Ruth's humility did not belittle her, but elevated her position to the highest level that a woman in Bethlehem could hold. She followed Naomi and the God of Israel. In so doing, she moved from being the wife of an invalid to the wife of the man who owned the fields she had walked upon. She was brave, capable, and highly valued, yet willing to serve her mother-in-law, her God, and her fellowman. She was the great-grandmother to King David, ancestor of Jesus.

SUBMIT TO PROTECTION

Let's look again at ways we can learn from Ruth. We can learn how to approach both our Lord and our lovers. When she approached Boaz, she asked him to spread the corner of his garment over her, because he was her nearest kinsman and her rightful redeemer. *The Amplified Bible* says that she asked for his wing of protection over her.

Today's society has pushed for women to become independent and self-serving. Independence was never God's original plan for women. He wanted us to be totally dependent upon Him. Eve's attempt to find wisdom apart from His guidance was the reason she fell from His grace.

Ruth demonstrated the highest act of godliness that a woman can present to her Lord. She said, "Please help me, for it is not good for me to be alone." God does not want us to prove *ourselves* but to prove *Him*. His ways confound the world because His Word demonstrates that truth is the opposite of what the world teaches.

In chapter 4 of the book of Ruth, Boaz carefully followed the law in order to legally take Ruth as his own. There was another kinsman who had more right to her than he did, so he presented himself to the other kinsman first. The first heir forfeited his right and confirmed the promise by giving Boaz his sandal. The covenant of passing the sandal to the other symbolized the promise, "I will not tread upon your territory."

Then Boaz went to the elders and told them of his intent. This is where Boaz received a blessing because of Ruth. They said to him,

> **We are witnesses. May the Lord make the woman who is coming into your home like Rachel and Leah, who together built up the house of Israel. May you have standing in Ephrathah and be famous in Bethlehem.**
>
> **Through the offspring the Lord gives you by this young woman, may your family be like that of Perez, whom Tamar bore to Judah.**
>
> RUTH 4:11–12

The elders saw that good things were in store for Boaz if he took Ruth as his wife. Through her willingness to submit to the council of Naomi, the protection of Boaz, and the plan of God, Ruth brought blessing even to you and me. She helped to continue the line of Jesus Christ.

JESUS CONTINUES TO SPREAD HIS WING OVER US

Do you see the parallel of Boaz and Ruth to what Jesus has done for us? When we came to the Lord and submitted ourselves to His protection, He could grant our petition because He had followed the law to legally win the right to be our Redeemer. He confronted Satan, who had first right to us because of the fall, with the price He had paid for us, and Satan could not object. He looked at Jesus and said, "I cannot tread upon Your territory."

We are under the protection of our Kinsman Redeemer, Jesus Christ. Why would we ever want to live our life apart from Him? Why would we ever want to prove our independence from the very one who loves us more than His own life? We are the Bride of Christ, heirs to the kingdom of God. We walk as heirs on ground owned by the one who owns the universe!

Kick off those painful, high-heeled shoes, Princess, and enjoy the feeling of holy ground beneath your feet!

Brothers, I do not consider myself yet to have taken hold of it.
But one thing I do: Forgetting what is behind and straining toward what is ahead, I press on toward the goal to win the prize for which God has called me heavenward in Christ Jesus.

PHILIPPIANS 3:13–14

CHAPTER EIGHT

Stay Till the Ball Is Over

LIFE IS LIKE A FAIRY TALE!

Not wanting to miss the fireworks at the end of the night, Cinderella stayed to the very last second of the celebration. Have you been leaving the party too soon? Is there someone you could encourage to come with you?

Cinderella was not eager to leave the ball. She stayed until she heard the last stroke of midnight, fearing she would miss seeing what the Prince would do next.

I look forward to the day when women are able to stay until the dance is over. So many of us rush from one place to another, always having our mind on where we need to be next instead of where we are. There is a place of rest in God that He wants us each to attain. Once found, we will be equipped to pass on our faith to others. As I said earlier, serving others as Jesus serves us is the goal of our Christian walk.

If we stay with the Lord, enduring to the end of His great plan for us, we will enjoy the rest that results from living in the kingdom of God.

The Lord gives us keys to endure, keys that unlock doors to our future and lock doors to our past that we do not want to enter into again.

Let us not be as Lot's wife who did not want to leave her home, even though her life was filled with disgusting invasions of evil. She was like a Cinderella who wanted to stay in the cinders. Remember how Lot's family was so reluctant to leave that God sent angels to pick them up and set them down outside the city before He destroyed it? (Genesis 19:16) They were warned, "Don't look back!" but Lot's wife could not see the future for her past. She disobeyed, and turned to look at her past.

Archeologists have determined that an earthquake and an explosion of gases were the probable cause of the destruction of these vile cities. The Dead Sea now covers the cities that could not be saved from God's judgment. There is no outlet to this sea and the high concentration of salt kills all life in that area. Salt rocks surround the area that were most likely the result of the rain of salt that took place during the destruction of this place. Lot's wife is entombed within one of these pillars as a silent reminder to all of us who are tempted to look back.

ENDURE TO THE END

A wonderful reward is offered to those who endure to the end. Jesus said, **Since you have kept my command to endure patiently, I will also keep you from the hour of trial that is going to come upon the whole world to test those who live on the earth** (Revelation 3:10).

There is no reward for turning back to the rags and cinders. Great sorrow and disappointment await those who turn down their invitation to the wedding supper of the Lord. Luke recorded the warning of Jesus in chapter 17:24–35:

> **For the Son of Man in his day will be like the lightning, which flashes and lights up the sky from one end to the other.**
>
> **But first he must suffer many things and be rejected by this generation.**
>
> **Just as it was in the days of Noah, so also will it be in the days of the Son of Man.**
>
> **People were eating, drinking, marrying and being given in marriage up to the day Noah entered the ark. Then the flood came and destroyed them all.**
>
> **It was the same in the days of Lot. People were eating and drinking, buying and selling, planting and building.**

But the day Lot left Sodom, fire and sulfur rained down from heaven and destroyed them all.

It will be just like this on the day the Son of Man is revealed.

On that day no one who is on the roof of his house, with his goods inside, should go down to get them. Likewise, no one in the field should go back for anything.

Remember Lot's wife!

Whoever tries to keep his life will lose it, and whoever loses his life will preserve it.

I tell you, on that night two people will be in one bed; one will be taken and the other left.

Two women will be grinding grain together; one will be taken and the other left.

Will you still be grinding grain on the great day when the Lord returns for His bride?

LOCK THE DOOR TO YOUR PAST!

Forgiveness is the key for locking the door to your past so that you never return to it. Unforgiveness reopens the door to yesterday's pain every time you entertain it. Unforgiveness causes you to spend all your creative time reliving the torment of the enemy's deception against you. As long as there is unforgiveness in your heart, the devil doesn't even need to bring new accusations against you. As long as he sees that you are still dressing in your grave clothes, the devil knows he can move on to other victims and leave you alone in your misery.

At first, forgiveness is difficult, but it is absolutely essential for a princess to learn how to maintain this virtue in her life. I took my weakness and laid it once again before my Secret Keeper, admitting to Him that I needed both His deliverance and protection from the painful addiction of unforgiveness.

I identified with Paul's letter to the Philippians:

Brothers, I do not consider myself yet to have taken hold of it. But one thing I do: Forgetting what is behind and straining toward what is ahead,

I press on toward the goal to win the prize for which God has called me heavenward in Christ Jesus.

All of us who are mature should take such a view of things. And if on some point you think differently, that too God will make clear to you.

Only let us live up to what we have already attained.

Join with others in following my example, brothers, and take note of those who live according to the pattern we gave you.

For, as I have often told you before and now say again even with tears, many live as enemies of the cross of Christ.

Their destiny is destruction, their god is their stomach, and their glory is in their shame. Their mind is on earthly things.

But our citizenship is in heaven. And we eagerly await a Savior from there, the Lord Jesus Christ,

Who, by the power that enables him to bring everything under his control, will transform our lowly bodies so that they will be like his glorious body.

PHILIPPIANS 3:13–21

Dear Secret Keeper,

I know that I should have gotten over these feelings by now. How could everyone be going on with their lives when I feel like a car stalled on a six-lane highway during rush hour? It's hard to believe that anyone could wrestle with unforgiveness and still be Spirit-filled. But it does happen to the best of us. Harboring unforgiveness is far more damaging than what the perpetrator ever did to me.

It seems as though I am the only one left rehashing the past. It is not that you wish anyone ill will, it is just a gut-wrenching feeling that you get when someone who caused you to question your self-worth never acknowledges the injustice they have done to you. They could walk in and a sunny day would instantly disappear, as if a storm would erupt any moment. Perhaps they don't dignify your feelings with memories of the words they smirked about in corners of restaurants, on phone lines that stretched across the city, or while motoring across the country.

Surely, if they knew that I was privy to their conversations it would result in a series of apologetic incantations. Sometimes, I just wanted to walk up to them and ask out of curiosity, "Why did you make me the brunt of your heartless babble?" And right before I'd open my mouth and insert my foot, You'd peck me lovingly on the shoulder and remind me that I was looking back at days too distant to retrace.

What felt in my heart like yesterday had mysteriously turned into years. It was high time that I went on with my life. Everyone that I am lamenting over has. I need to stop memorializing past pain. It is virtually impossible to drive forward and look backward.

You intended to harm me, but God intended it for good to accomplish what is now being done, the saving of many lives.

GENESIS 50:20

After all, it did not prevent You from having the ultimate say-so in my life. It was time for me to relinquish past hurt and the ghost that held me prisoner so I could take hold of the realities only found by walking hand in hand with You into my destiny. You taught me to use maladies for stepping-stones.

The whisperings they did about me somehow became silent as they watched You prepare a table for me. The one they labeled as "Least Likely to Succeed" felt like the "Teacher's Pet."

Bear with each other and forgive whatever grievances you may have against one another. Forgive as the Lord forgave you.

COLOSSIANS 3:13

It now seems so uncomplicated to wear my coveted title. All of my contenders have disappeared. I now believe with my whole heart that unforgiveness involves only two. It does not matter how many voices there were that made folly of me and my dreams. When it came time for true deliverance, You and I strolled through hall after hall, past faces that had forgotten me and what they'd said. You led me to doors that stood propped open with bitterness and resentment, and I released the handles. I walked out with only the vapors of what used to be tears.

Secret Keeper, the joy of it all is that You never share with others how you had to tarry with me when I wallowed in the bed of unresolved issues. You sounded the alarm and insisted that I get up and go on. I never want to oversleep and miss what You have awakened me for.

Forgiveness is the only lasting deliverance. Others can pray that your life will improve, but only you can forgive those who have hurt you. Forgiveness breaks the power of sin and pulls down walls that separate us from God and others. Jesus taught,

If you forgive men when they sin against you, your heavenly Father will also forgive you.

But if you do not forgive men their sins, your Father will not forgive your sins.

MATTHEW 6:14–15

WHAT IF FORGIVENESS WAS A HABIT WITH YOU?

It excites me to imagine a church full of women who make it a habit to forgive others. How would the habit of forgiveness change us? How would it change our world?

Children would see the principle of unconditional love demonstrated from their parents. Husbands and wives would enjoy the security of knowing that no matter what happens, there is someone at home who will lift them up when others have cast them down. Employees would face each new day with enthusiasm, eager to work as unto the Lord, having already forgotten the offenses of the day before. It would be like having God's will on earth as it is in heaven.

Choose to endure. Lock the door on your past. Endure to the end and stay for the whole party that God has planned for us. Enduring to the end means staying with God's plan long enough to see its reward for your life and its influence on the lives of others.

ARE YOU NAOMI, RUTH, OR ORPAH?

I believe there are three kinds of women who are reading this book. You could be like Naomi, Ruth, or Orpah. Most likely, we all identify somewhat with all three of the women. They all understood what it was to lose everything. They had to leave behind their old churches, their old lifestyles, and their old way of doing things. Through faith, two found a new life better than their biggest dreams, but one lacked courage and retreated to her old way of life.

I hope you are not embracing the attitude of Orpah, who returned to her past and missed what God could have taught her through Naomi. Orpah would have learned everything Naomi taught Ruth, but she could not seem to grasp the vision of new possibilities in God because she was so tied to where she had come from and who she used to be. The unknown intimidated her, and she retreated to the safety of her corner.

Perhaps you are like Ruth, who was eager to learn from Naomi. Women like Ruth will initiate a healthy attachment to women like Naomi, vowing to be teachable and do whatever their mentor tells them to do. Ruth could see that this older woman could teach her the ways of the Lord. With tenacity, she implored Naomi to let her stay at her side and learn from her. She could see gifts in Naomi that Naomi couldn't even see in herself at the time.

If you are like Ruth, you are fully aware that you have more to learn. Find a woman with the qualities of Naomi and learn from her. Let her know that you admire her and need her instruction. Naomi demonstrated the ability to move when it was time to move. She did not let the disappointments of life consume her. Even though she struggled with sorrow to the point of telling everyone to call her Mara (which means bitterness), I find it interesting that everyone continued to call her Naomi. She must have demonstrated more optimism than she was aware of. Who do you know who is like that?

Forgiveness is the key for locking the door to your past so that you never return to it.

There are women who are born to be leaders and mentors, as Naomi was to Ruth. One can look at this "Naomi type" of woman and say, "When I grow up, I want to be just like her." If you already enjoy your title of princess and have learned to lock the door of your past, won't you step forth to help the next generation of young women inherit their titles? Please step forward and help the younger Christian women lift their chins with dignity again and act like daughters of the living God.

Perhaps God is prompting your heart with names of young women who would love to receive a call or a letter of encouragement from you. Perhaps you know that it is time for you to teach others how to dress for God's best as Naomi did Ruth. You will find a new love of life just as Naomi did when she took Ruth's precious baby in her arms and enjoyed being his nursemaid. Ruth told Naomi she needed her, but we can see that teacher also became the benefactor of her student.

God wants women to build up other women:

> Likewise, teach the older women to be reverent in the way they live, not to be slanderers or addicted to much wine, but to teach what is good.
>
> Then they can train the younger women to love their husbands and children,
>
> To be self-controlled and pure, to be busy at home, to be kind, and to be subject to their husbands, so that no one will malign the word of God.
>
> TITUS 2:3–5

If you are a Naomi, you may not even recognize your gift, but younger women will come to you and ask you for advice. If this is happening, it is because they see wisdom in your actions and fruit in your life. Ruth and Orpah could both see that Naomi loved her husband. When her husband died, Naomi grieved because everything she had dreamed seemed to be over.

Naomi was so devastated by the loss of her husband, she felt she was no longer able to do anything. Are you like Naomi? Have you given up on your own goals because the person or thing that you associated your success with is no longer with you? It could have been your husband. It could have been your job. It could have been an association with people from a previous ministry or from your other way of life. Have you given up on leading other women into victory because you've made mistakes yourself?

The body of Christ needs women who are like Naomi. Where are you? We need women who know God intimately and who plan to do exploits in spite of the opposition and circumstances. We need women who won't give up on their ministries even though they have fallen and everybody knows about it. We need women who will assume their rightful position as mothers in the house of God.

Naomi must have looked at those girls and seen herself, both what she had been and what she could have been. In loving them, she did not manipulate or try to control them. She was careful not to deny them their right to choose to be who they were supposed to be. She encouraged them to pursue their own destinies.

We must not live our lives only for ourselves, but realize that the decisions we make are being observed by the Ruths, the Orpahs, and our daughters. We need to endure doing the right thing, so that God's glory is manifested in our churches. As younger women in the faith see the fruit of our decisions, they will want to follow the godly standards they see in us.

Mentorship is not teaching with words, but is by example. Nagging, berating, and ridiculing young women will cause women to look back instead of forward. We must practice carrying ourselves with grace and humility if we want our daughters to be trained to carry themselves like royalty.

Let the younger women hear us praise our husbands publicly. They don't want to hear us swearing at the men in our lives. Young women need to see the blessings that result in the lives of women who are submissive to their husbands. They need to be taught to lift up their husbands and help them to become godly men. They need to learn how to approach men. They need to learn how to love God with their whole heart from just watching you.

Are the women who know you seeing Naomi or Mara? Do they see a bitter old woman who's given up on life? Could it be that Orpah only saw Mara and feared where Mara was starting to lead her? Or did Ruth say, "In spite of Noami's faults, I'm going to stick around, because God knows Naomi's life is so much better than the life I lived without God."

Be a woman who can teach new Christian women godly character. We are about to see the greatest revival that the world has known. God is getting ready to restore women to the place that He first intended for them to be. The church will soon be full of women who have never seen godly examples before.

There will be young Ruths and Orpahs in our midst. Oh, I hope that we will all endure to the end of the dance, and stay to help these younger women find a personal relationship with God. Please don't let them see Mara when they enter the ballroom, the sanctuary of God.

An Orpah will need lots of encouragement. She will say, "I can't do this. I love you, and God knows I've learned a lot, but I don't think I can do what you say I should do. I think I'll go back to what I'm accustomed to doing."

Will we be able to explain to her that God does the changing and all we do is the trusting? Will we have fresh testimonies that we can share with her to reveal how God cared for us yesterday just as He did so many years ago?

Were you ever on the verge of giving up because nobody took the time to tell you about themselves? Nobody took time to tell you, "Baby, God can find a wonderful man to love you and the babies you've had out of wedlock." Did anyone take time to tell you that you could lose your husband and then find a job that meets his income and your income together? Orpah won't go back to what she's accustomed to if she sees the glory of God and the testimony of His power in our lives.

We have to be willing to tell the truth. This may mean revealing some of our "secrets" so she will know that we have had hardships just as she has, but God is able to redeem all that we have lost through our sinful lives. Both the Ruths and the Orpahs need women to teach them how to wash themselves through baptism and enjoy wearing the robe of righteousness.

We will need to be honest before the young women who will be looking to us for standards. Will they think we have always been as wise as Naomi? Or will we take down the facade and admit that we have been afraid before? Will we humble ourselves and admit that we have wanted to run like Orpah did, but because we endured, we found someone who loved us when we were like Orpah?

God is moving in the world. As we lift Jesus, He will draw all men and women unto Him. We must stop lifting our own image before these young women who want to be part of the wedding dance. These women who will soon be coming to us won't be accustomed to being ladies. Like Orpah, they will come from backgrounds which were filled with religious deception, immorality, and lack of understanding about God. They won't know how to serve Him. They won't know they are walking in ungodly ways, and it will take gentleness and love to teach them the way they should go.

If you are a Naomi, the whole creation is anticipating your coming out and helping to guide the young women whom God will bring to you for help.

Where are you, Naomi? The women are dying.

WHERE ARE YOU, NAOMI?

Please don't leave before the stroke of midnight, for there are others who need to learn how to prepare themselves for the prince. Don't go home early and redress in your cinder-covered cloak.

If you have lost interest in the party, focus on someone else who has never even been to the Lord's wedding reception. Look for the Orpahs and Ruths who need guidance in the things of God.

Teach them practical applications:

- Show them where to find those wonderful consignment stores.
- Show them the thrill of yard sales.
- Show them how to decorate one-room efficiency apartments.
- Show them how to keep their homes clean.
- Show them how to freshen themselves.

Teach them spiritual lessons:

- Show them how to wash themselves of bitterness and fear.
- Show them how to put on the garment of salvation.
- Show them how to enjoy a barefoot walk with God.
- Show them how to be first to forgive.
- Show them how to enjoy the provisions of their Father.

Don't leave too soon; there are others who need your friendship. You are not too old to be useful. You don't have too many sins in your past to be used for His glory. You haven't made too many mistakes to be a good counselor. Young women looking for love are having baby after baby, relationship after relationship; and you could give Jesus to them if you don't go home too early.

Stay till the ball is over and help someone else learn to dance with the Lord. Teach them how to tell their secrets to the Secret Keeper. Show them that nothing is too hard for God. He can bring them out of sin and degradation. Show them the Prince of Peace who patiently waits for them.

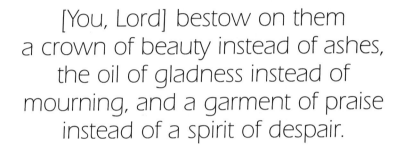

[You, Lord] bestow on them
a crown of beauty instead of ashes,
the oil of gladness instead of
mourning, and a garment of praise
instead of a spirit of despair.

ISAIAH 61:3

CHAPTER NINE

Sweet Dreams Really Do Come True

LIFE IS LIKE A FAIRY TALE!

When Cinderella woke up the next morning, she thought the night before had simply been a dream. Suddenly, there was a knock at her door. Expecting to find a door-to-door solicitor, she was surprised to see her Prince waiting to be invited in. Don't you hear Him knocking at your door?

Her life would never be the same, for Cinderella had danced with the Prince. Now she knew that no one else in all the kingdom could satisfy her longing heart. She regretted fleeing from him so quickly without telling him the truth about who she was. Never in her wildest dreams did she expect him to come looking for her.

Why are we afraid to be honest with the Lord? He came to seek us out. He didn't sit on His throne and wait for us to find Him. He sent messengers ahead to let us know He was looking for us. He sent love letters to decree His intentions toward us. Finally, He came and personally knocked on our door. Jesus didn't care that we weren't dressed up that day. He didn't care that we were wearing our cinder-covered cloak of bitterness. He loved us anyway. As soon as He saw that we were happy to see Him, He swept us in His arms and promised to never leave us. What a love story!

And it is so very true! It's not a fairy tale at all! From the beginning of time, our Father has planned this story for you to understand that *you* are the princess whom He loves. He sent Jesus to find you, to take you as His very own bride, and to live and reign with Him in a kingdom where the ways of God's loving-kindness rule. He came to take you to a place where you will never cry again, feel pain, or be hungry.

We can't even imagine what that will be like. Can you remember a time in your life when you were happy? Can you remember a time when you weren't worried? Imagine feeling that way forever. The most wonderful part of this story is that it begins the day you say, "Yes, Lord, I will be Yours." He doesn't make you wait until heaven to enjoy the provisions that will someday be magnified there.

Jesus said,

The thief cometh not, but for to steal, and to kill, and to destroy: I am come that they might have life, and that they might have it more abundantly.

JOHN 10:10 KJV

The word "life" is translated from the word *zoe,* which is the same life and presence of God He breathed into Adam at creation. Jesus is saying that He came to bring us the presence of God, and not just enough for us to get by, but more than enough, so the abundance of His blessings would overflow from our lives into the lives of others.

Thousands upon thousands of women can give testimony to the provision of the Lord, but please experience His love for yourself. Let Him love you each day. When is the last time you let Him work out a problem for you? You can enjoy waking up to new mercies each morning. Jump out of bed to discover He has made your own dream for happiness come true.

Jesus can make you into a princess, and it doesn't take Him long. It may seem painful at first, because He will take things from you that you thought you had to have. But He *loves* you. He will only ask you to trade your rags for His riches. He will ask you to give Him your secrets, your filthy security blanket, and accept the radiant gown that He made just for you. What will you have to give to Him?

If you are not presently enjoying your inheritance as a princess, there is something that you need to give up in order to receive God's best for you. What is it? If you have to think about it too long, you are probably missing the obvious answer. Nothing will stand out like this memory, this person, this habit that is keeping you from accepting your blessings from God. Maybe it's your dependence on a certain relationship, a certain position at work, or certain material things that preoccupy the goals of your heart.

What have you attached yourself to so tightly that tears well up in your eyes when you think about letting it go? What is it, who is it, what ministry, what job, what pastor, what husband, what wife, what child breaks your heart when you think about letting it go and turning it completely over to God?

God won't share your heart with other idols. He will remove them from your list of "gotta-haves" and prove that you didn't have to have them after all. He will show you that you don't need it. You don't need more money, more recognition, or more acknowledgment. You only need more of Him, and He will give you the desires of your heart. What an awesome trade!

Let's see, I give Him my secret unforgiveness, lust, hatred, greed, and co-dependent tendencies, and He openly gives me forgiveness, love, provision, and transparency before all those who examine my life. Then they will see that I am justified—just as if I'd never done it, been it, or even wanted it. What is this love that surpasses any fairy tale that we have ever read? Doesn't it sound worth trying?

Don't turn back to your secret way of life before hearing how He can take drugs out your system and alcohol off your breath. Yes, He will put you in beautiful gowns that won't come off for strange men. He will give you a new heart that will say, "Yes, it does matter that he's married." He will give you wisdom that tells you to get off the street at three o'clock in the morning. He will give you eyes to see that the person you are looking for will come to you like a prince, not as a thief.

The new heart He gives you will direct you to peace, not to poverty. The Lord will teach you what is right and what is wrong. He will give you a way to escape from the evil that is plotted against you. He will give you the grace and power to do the right thing.

God confirms this promise in His Word:

This is the covenant I will make with the house of Israel after that time, declares the Lord.

I will put my laws in their minds and write them on their hearts.

I will be their God, and they will be my people.

HEBREWS 8:10

God knows your needs, not just your material needs, but also your emotional and physical needs. He will complete the work He has begun in you. He will teach you to walk with dignity, as a princess. He will make you ready to marry a prince.

FAIRY TALES DO COME TRUE!

Dear Secret Keeper,

[You, Lord] bestow on them a crown of beauty instead of ashes, the oil of gladness instead of mourning, and a garment of praise instead of a spirit of despair.

ISAIAH 61:3

Life, with all of its twists and turns can be so unpredictable. I have always loved stories where ugly ducklings become beautiful swans. Little did I know that you were writing a similar story on the pages of my life.

I was born a coal miner's daughter. In my community, known as a coal camp, there were no big I's and little you's. Everybody was somebody because we all knew one another. Our fathers all worked in the same coal mine. When our daddies came out, all their faces were covered with coal dust. They all looked the same.

As I have grown up, I realize now that they looked more alike than the physical eye could detect. They had all experienced the same life-threatening danger that is involved in underground mining.

Side by side they risked their lives, ate out of metal lunch buckets, and provided decent homes for their families. Nearly all of the families bought groceries from the company store, which also provided the children with the latest in modest fashion.

Recently I visited the remains of the land where we played "Red Rover" until the sun bowed and gave the stage to the moon. The dirt roads seemed so broad then, accommodating our stick ball games and hopscotch courts. Today the road only resembles the path to adulthood.

The path is marked with memories of a little girl who played alone with imaginary friends and had tea parties for doll babies. My mama nursed the wounds I received from bike accidents and falls on asphalt playgrounds.

My papa taught me the rewards of allowances earned for dusting the furniture and washing the dinner dishes. And I grew up knowing the importance of earning a decent living and taking care of your family, even if it meant risking your life.

I graduated from our local high school with high honors. It is so ironic that during the commencement exercise, I led the class of 1973 in the "Lord's Prayer." Off to college I went with no idea of what it was all about. I was so lonely during the early years that it is no wonder I ended up in the wrong company.

Soon the experiments began with cigarettes, alcohol, marijuana, and sex. Gee, how else could the coal miner's daughter fit in with these city slickers whom I thought had it going on?

Through it all I knew that this was not Your will for my life, Secret Keeper. I could not get high enough to avoid Your voice, Your warnings. I would go to church occasionally and feel so repentant for my wrongdoings. I would have visions of walking past Mother's door and seeing her kneeling beside her bed. I knew that sometimes she was praying for me. Her prayers prevailed through many mishaps and calamities.

Through a series of secret pal cards, I met the love of my life. From a distance I knew that he was someone I would need in my life. I was a new convert, but he was a pastor. I dare not waltz upon him lest he think I was being carnal. So I admired and observed him from afar.

Secret Keeper, he was so strong in spirit. When he spoke, the revelation of God flowed from his mouth with such accuracy that all who heard instantly received the deliverance for which they had longed. I was so awed by Your presence in his life that I knew I had to be near him every time the opportunity presented itself.

The opportunity was presented sooner than I was prepared to receive it. He came to my church for a revival! I felt like a kindergartner on my first day at school. I had just the day before mailed a card revealing my identity. And now his secret pal was no longer a secret. It was little 'ole me!

The first night of the revival I sat in the corner in the back. I could hardly distinguish the beat of the drums from the pulse of the blood rushing through my skull. I don't even know what he preached or if he preached, all I know is that he knew my name and he probably resented the sight of my invisible face.

You don't need more money,
more recognition, or more
acknowledgment.
You only need more of Him,
and He will give you the desires
of your heart.

The most unfathomable thing occurred right after service. My pastor's wife decided to introduce me! I wanted to crawl under the pew and pray for the immediate return of the Lord. "Even so come Lord Jesus!" While my pastor's wife stood talking to my "no-longer-a-secret pal," she suddenly beckoned for me to come to her. The aisle seemed a mile and half long.

My hero stared at me with eyes that I knew would melt me into the carpet. As I approached him, he began to smile that smile. To me he said, "Do you know where a bachelor can get a home-cooked meal?"

I stuttered, "I'll ask my mother." Gee, I felt so numb and dumb.

The days went by quickly, turning into months. My heart was full of him. We called one another until our phone bills resembled house payments. We talked about everything, often until the sun came up. I loved the sound of his voice, the sound of his laughter, the sound of his silence. I was in love and love was in me.

I don't think that he actually proposed. But somehow his attempt was good enough for me. Our wedding was sacred. Even then, Secret Keeper, Your presence was with us. Words of prophecy came forth to sanction our union and pronounce Your blessing upon us in the years to come. Surely, it was a dream come true!

The dream was threatened when my new husband lost the best job he had ever had. The chemical plant that he worked for laid him off. What were we to do?

Trust in the Lord with all your heart and lean not on your own understanding; in all your ways acknowledge him, and he will make your paths straight.

PROVERBS 3:5–6

My husband had heard the call of the Lord to full-time ministry. Being the responsible man that he was, his first concern was to provide for his family. Backed against the wall, he now surrendered to the voice of the Lord, trusting Him as he'd never trusted Him before. He stepped out on a walk of faith where he had never trodden and began to believe God for the impossible.

The revivals were few and far between. Our income was spasmodic, but the bills were consistently over our head. We were submerged in financial waves until one by one our utilities were disconnected. At first it was just the phone, but then to the phone was added the water, to the water was added the electricity, and all the utilities were disconnected either simultaneously or at intervals too frequent to handle.

We soon started to go to my in-laws for dinner, with or without invitation, only to return to a dark home. We played games with the twins by lighting candles and sending them to bed. The innocence of a child brings glimpses of the faith that can conquer anything.

I know how to be abased, and I know how to abound. Everywhere and in all things I have learned both to be full and to be hungry, both to abound and to suffer need.

I can do all things through Christ who strengthens me.

PHILIPPIANS 4:12–13 NKJV

We sought public assistance through welfare. It was often so degrading to sit and be insulted by the social worker who seemingly mocked our circumstance. My husband began to dig ditches for gas lines to subsidize our lack of income. He would come home to little food and sometimes a boiled water bath. I never saw his countenance fall. With blisters on his hands from the shovel's handle, he would leave morning after morning, returning with generic pampers for the twins and a humble meal of ox tails with rice and cornbread mix.

I don't know how many shovels of dirt brought us out of our despair, but with perseverance my husband dug us out. Full-time ministry rarely begins in ditches, but often in trenches. Strategically, You led my husband through the wilderness of lack to remind him of the Scripture he now says with a greater conviction:

My help comes from the Lord, who made heaven and earth. He will not allow your foot to be moved; He who keeps you will not slumber.

PSALM 121:2-3 NKJV

The invitations for revivals and ministry began to come from coast to coast. The word that he spoke was revelatory and born from experience. The word held such healing for so many that it was noised abroad of the "Boy Pastor from West Virginia" who had not celebrated his thirtieth birthday.

Promotion came from You, Lord. With each revelation came the provision my husband so desperately desired for our family. From a small two-bedroom apartment to a wood-frame home to a split-level mid-entry on the side of a hill to the home that anyone would consider their dream. He disciplined himself and drove his family safely through. In my eyes, he is the greatest hero I will ever know. He taught me how to walk again.

I recall his elevation to the office of the Bishop. It was such an esteemed honor and position. We were all so proud. As I prepared his royal robes for the consecration service, I noticed how regal the purple brocade fabric was. I pressed the half cape that would cover his strong shoulders that had carried his family through financial travesty without complaint. My spirit echoed, "He is royalty. He is a prince in the kingdom. Tonight he receives the crown that will house many jewels."

A prince indeed? If this be so, could it be that I am his princess? Does this make me a princess in the kingdom? Indeed it does! Tonight You reward him openly for prayers that were prayed in his secret place to You.

Secret Keeper, I know that You were the one who dried his tears and calmed his fears. Thank You for giving me this kind, wonderful prince. I will honor him and respect him with every ounce of my being.

Here I sit, unscathed by the innumerable darts of the enemy. One night I exchanged my "Street Van" for a stretch limousine. When our chariot arrived, the doors swung open to a red carpet streaked with roving skylights. My prince, my knight in shining armor, was my husband who had been nominated for a "Grammy."

From the dirt road of a coal mining community to the red carpet rolled out for me across the world I remain the same little girl who talked to imaginary friends and hosted tea parties for doll babies. I don't know whether I was a little girl dreaming I was a princess back then, or whether I am now a princess dreaming I am a little girl. It's like an ugly duckling to a beautiful swan story. It's just like a fairy tale.

Thank You, Secret Keeper, for the promise that we can live happily ever after.

THE LORD GIVES AND GRANTS THE DREAM

More than all else, I hope you see by my testimonies that it is the Lord who performs the great work in you, not you who perform for Him. He has called you to an everlasting love, and He will complete the good work that He has started in you.

When He comes, your prayer may be full of unbelief:

Me, Lord? When I look at the way I was before You came into my life, I wonder, are You talking to me, God? You're loving me, Lord? Your mind is full of me? God, as holy as You are, You're talking to me, God! Not just every now and then, but on a daily basis. You've taken it upon Yourself to speak personally and distinctly and call me by my name. There was no doubt in my mind: You were not talking to somebody across the room, but You were talking to me, God!

I was not looking for the Lord the night He rescued me from my cinder-smudged face and my pitiful corner of self-pity. Everybody around me was looking at me with expressions of surprise, as if to say, "He couldn't be talking to Serita. I know God's not talking to *her*." But the Lord said to me, "Oh, yes, I called you something nobody else had ever called you. I called you unblamable, unreprovable, forgiven, washed, holy, purposeful."

Aren't we grateful to be saved, forgiven, and not forgotten? Though He forgot what we couldn't forget, He didn't forget us. He's already forgotten what we still regret. So many things happen to us during our lives that we wish we could wipe off the slate. We want to start over with a clean board so we won't have to tell our children our secrets. But the slate has been forgiven and erased. God did that for you and me, and we're the only ones who keep bringing up the past. We keep remembering who we were and who we could have been if we hadn't made certain wrong turns with certain individuals, but God is not thinking about that old girl. In the sea of forgetfulness, He's drowned her.

I can remember when I got baptized. I went to church as a favor to my mother. I thought, *Okay, I will go down there with those "sanctified folks." I'll go because I will have time to get out and do what I need to do.* And as I sat there beside my mother, God's anointing began to fall.

I wasn't accustomed to the spirit of prophecy, so when Pastor started prophesying, I was startled when He looked me right in the eye and said, "You dream a lot. You have visions of things that are going to happen before they happen. God has a call on your life."

I started trembling, because I had known there was something I was supposed to do in the kingdom. But for some reason, instead of going left, I went right. Instead of going up, I went down. And instead of listening to the voice of the Lord, I listened to the voices of my peers, those who didn't know or care what was best for me.

As I sat there listening to Pastor, I became uncomfortable. I knew this was my day for deliverance. When he said, "Who wants to get baptized in the name of the Lord Jesus?" my feet hit the floor and, before I knew it, I was up front, bent over, repenting and weeping before the Lord. Afterwards, the deacon baptized me in Jesus' name.

He kept saying, "Serita, look in the water. Whoever you were before you came to this meeting today is in the water. All of your sins are in that water. Look in that water. *Whoever* you were when you came in here, she's in the water. *Whatever* you planned to do when you left this service, she's in the water. God has put a barrier between who you were and who He has called you to be."

I looked in the water and saw dope and sex and a mess. I thought, *God, You did that for me? In a matter of fifteen minutes, You gave me a new life? How could that be? I was sick of me and You set me free.* Nothing changed outwardly. I still had problems that needed to be faced and dealt with. But my mind had changed. I knew that I was brand-new in Christ Jesus, because He had accepted me just by saying, "Yes, Lord, I am Yours." I started leaping and rejoicing.

As special as He made me feel, I am obligated and privileged to tell you that He has the same love letter for you. He's a mighty God. Appreciate Him. Thank Him. Enjoy His presence and His sweet Spirit as He fulfills His purpose in you. Pull down strongholds, cast down imaginations, and put the past under your feet.

Yet the Lord longs to be
gracious to you;
he rises to show you compassion.
For the Lord is a God of justice.
Blessed are all who wait for him!

ISAIAH 30:18

CHAPTER TEN

A Prince Is Waiting for You

LIFE IS LIKE A FAIRY TALE!

Cinderella would never have known
how much the prince truly loved her
if she had continued to hide the fact
that she wasn't really a princess,
but was merely a servant.
He changed her truth and it turned out
that she was a princess after all.
Have you had an honest talk with
the Prince of Peace?

When the prince learned the truth, that Cinderella was poor and desti-tute, he was able to prove his great love for her by saying, "It doesn't matter what you have or what you have done, I love who you are. All that I have is yours, if you will simply say yes." He valued her above his own life and took her to be his bride. Together they served the people in his kingdom happily ever after.

Can't you see the parallel of Cinderella's fable to your own love story with Jesus? Only your secrets keep you hiding when He comes looking for you. He knows what you have done. He knows all about your weaknesses, but He also knows what you do not understand. He knows what the Father has in store for you, and He sees who you will become under the nurturing of His love.

Don't let your secrets create walls that separate you from God! Jesus has paid a great price to tear the veil in the temple of God that once separated us from the Holy of Holies. Remember how it used to be when only the priest could enter into the place where God dwelt? The priest had to wash and sanctify himself with water to enter the room where God was.

Now we are washed and made clean by Truth, and God enters into our very heart. Don't let secrets keep you from telling the Secret Keeper your truth. Be honest with Him and watch the walls that once kept you from enjoying the face of God fall to the ground in ruins.

We are to worship God in spirit and in truth. This means we must take off our mask. It isn't really hiding anything anyway! Take off the mask and see that you are in great company, for we all have had secrets like you. Let Him see the real you. Let Him see your pain. Let Him see your concerns. Tell Him when you are worried, lonely, or hurting. Let Him hear and see your naked, broken life and heal you with His truth.

He will not leave you bleeding on the side of the road. He will not leave you longing for somebody else to touch you. He will give you all you need. He will keep His promises. He won't leave you or forsake you. He won't give up on you. He is a friend who will always remain closer than a brother.

PULL DOWN WALLS THAT KEEP YOU FROM GOD

I read a book by Robert Fulgum entitled *All I Really Needed to Know I Learned in Kindergarten*. Fulgum suggests that serenity and a quiet spirit are very much needed in our noisy society. He tells the story of villagers in the Solomon Islands who go out into the forest, and if a tree is in the way of a path they want to take, they scream at the tree for thirty days to make the tree die and fall. Day in and day out they scream at the tree, and in thirty days the tree begins to wither and die.

Jesus taught the same lesson, that we can speak to trees that aren't bearing fruit and forbid them to live:

And seeing a lone fig tree by the road, He came to it, and found nothing on it except leaves only; and He said to it, "No longer shall there ever be any fruit from you." And at once the fig tree withered.

And seeing this, the disciples marveled, saying, "How did the fig tree wither at once?"

And Jesus answered and said to them, "Truly I say to you, if you have faith, and do not doubt, you shall not only do what was done to the fig tree, but even if you say to this mountain, 'Be taken up and cast into the sea,' it shall happen.

"And all things you ask in prayer, believing, you shall receive."

MATTHEW 21:19-22 NASB

Are there fruitless trees in your life that need to be cursed and cast into the sea? God has given you authority to cast out the things that don't bear life for you. That is part of your inheritance as a princess reigning with Jesus in the kingdom of God.

I think Fulgum made a good point about needing serenity and quiet. He wrote that hollering and screaming at a living thing kills its spirit. If someone or something has been screaming at you, it is time to respond. I beg to differ with the old adage that says, "Sticks and stones may break my bones, but words will never harm me." Cruel, unkind words can stay with us for the rest of our lives if we don't know how to respond to them.

If a tree can die from spoken words, how much more can unkind words kill our spirit? Fulgum listed all the different things that we might scream at during the day: the car that pulled out in front of us, our spouse, our children, and even the computer! He came to the conclusion that we need to study to be quiet, that we must learn self-control so that we do not say things hastily. Most of all, we must learn not to scream.

Perhaps there is something inside of you that needs to be shouted at. I have found that there is a time to scream at that which oppresses me! But perhaps you are screaming at something or someone you shouldn't. Perhaps there is something that makes you feel like screaming, but you can't quite put your finger on what it is.

When you are honest with yourself, what is inside of you that makes you feel like screaming? First, what is that coming out of you that makes you look like you are screaming when you enter a room? What does your posture say about you? What does your walk suggest about you? What does the way that you stare at those who are different from you suggest about you?

And who can others hear you screaming at? What makes you scream at them? Is it the employer who overlooks you? Is it your spouse, who never acknowledges your hard work? Is it your children who cannot be controlled?

What's going on inside of you that only you know about? What's buried under all that wonderful attire, that beautiful dress, that fabulous suit? What's really going on under the superficial smile that turns into tears as soon as someone walks away?

What are you screaming at? Sometimes, unbeknownst to us, others see our prejudice. They see our jealousy, our rebellion, and our indecisiveness. It can only help us if we let ourselves see it too.

What is going on with you?

Oh, Princess, that you would only learn to rest in God! If you could only learn to trust your Savior in all things:

> **This is what the Sovereign Lord, the Holy One of Israel, says: "In repentance and rest is your salvation, in quietness and trust is your strength, but you would have none of it.**
>
> **"You said, 'No, we will flee on horses.' Therefore you will**

flee! You said, 'We will ride off on swift horses.' Therefore your pursuers will be swift!

"A thousand will flee at the threat of one; at the threat of five you will all flee away, till you are left like a flagstaff on a mountaintop, like a banner on a hill."

Yet the Lord longs to be gracious to you; he rises to show you compassion. For the Lord is a God of justice. Blessed are all who wait for him!

ISAIAH 30:15-18

In repentance and rest is our salvation, yet we insist on running away on swift horses. The Lord says that in quietness and in confidence we shall gain strength, but we would not allow that to happen. Even then, the Lord longs to be gracious to us. In rest and in trust shall be our victory. When we learn to just let it go and turn it over to Jesus, He will make everything all right again.

The enemy wants you to keep screaming at your past. He doesn't want you to grow in God. He doesn't want you to reach your potential in God. He'll remind you of the people who abused you, and every time you see somebody who looks like them, something will rise up in you. At that moment, let it go! Let God arise and His enemies will scatter.

If you must scream, scream at the real enemy of your soul. The enemy is not someone who is sitting beside you. When you look in the mirror and see only the person you used to be, tell the enemy of your soul. "NO! I will not let you keep me back! I will not let you hold me down! God has great plans for me, and I am following God!"

When Joshua fought the battle of Jericho, his warriors couldn't see how beautiful Jericho was behind the wall. Palm trees grew in Jericho and it was plush and green, but no one could see it because of that wall.

What gifts and talents are you hiding behind a wall that needs to fall? What attachment are you holding onto from your past that keeps your wall standing? What if we all knew your secrets? Are you afraid we wouldn't love you? Would you still love us if you knew our secrets?

Why do we feel we have to come to church and pretend to be somebody who God knows we're not? He knows all about us. There's nothing hidden from Him, and nothing about us offends Him or causes Him to disclaim us. He knows if our mother is a strange woman. He knows of our peculiar attachments. He knows if we didn't get a good start in life, and if we weren't presented as a debutante. He knows if we were unwed mothers at sixteen. He knows . . . but He's called us, "Jericho, beautiful, beautiful, Jericho, surrounded by a wall. You belong to Me." God claimed Jericho as His own.

GOD KNEW JERICHO WAS BEAUTIFUL

The wall of Jericho was much wider than the walls of forts we see in the movie reenactments of our Wild West. The wall around Jericho was so wide that Rahab the harlot was able to build her house in the wall itself. A community, not just her alone but her whole family, lived with her in the wall.

If we live in a wall, everyone related to us becomes entrapped in our wall. No one gets to see inside of Jericho as long as we are content to stay within its confines. Every time we are reminded of our shame, we put another layer on top of the wall. Every time someone does something to us that reminds us that we were raped or molested, or every time we see the boss who stood in our face and said, "You're nothing," another layer is added to our wall.

It's time to bring down the wall that is hiding the beauty of who you really are. Joshua was told to simply walk quietly around the wall and wait for the moment that God said to shout. We too are invited to walk quietly with our Father; and, if there is any screaming to be done, it is to celebrate that He has brought down that wall that has separated us from Him and from each other. Jesus has given us authority to trample on snakes and scorpions. There is no more worthy snake to put under our feet than Satan. Let's agree that the wall has come down.

Satan, we picket your wall, we march around the wall, we refuse to allow you to lock up the promises of God behind the wall. There is a good marriage behind the wall. The real gift of our ministry is behind the wall.

Our children will be healed when they get through the wall. Our lives will be better when we get through the wall. God has promised us Jericho. He said to be strong and courageous, for, "I am with thee, to deliver thee, whithersoever thou goest."

Operation "mission impossible" is to tear down the wall, brick by brick, course by course, line by line, memory by memory, struggle by struggle, doubt by doubt, and fear by fear. We pull down the memory of what they said, what we heard, what we went through, what happened when we were nine, what happened when we were twelve, what happened when we were thirteen.

Satan, in the name of Jesus, we are tearing down this wall. We won't live behind the walls anymore!

The anointing pulls down strongholds and destroys the yoke. The yoke isn't somewhere across the street; it's on us. We don't need to destroy a yoke next door; we need to break the yoke off our own neck, off our ministries, off our relationships, off our marriages, off our ability to love others. We can't love others or accept love when walls separate us. The name of Jesus pulls down the wall.

The enemy tried to sabotage our youth, he tried to mess us up, because he knew God wanted to use us. He tried to ruin our alpha to destroy our omega, but the devil is a liar. He knows we can't help where we've been, but we can change where we're going. We can't help how we started, but we can change how we end up. We can rewrite the ending to our own story.

The people of God got together and said, "We've seen the other side of the wall, and we're going to march around it until we get a breakthrough!" What they did seems silly, but it was a divine strategy. It came from the

Captain of the host himself. For six days they marched around the wall, saying absolutely nothing at all. They just assessed the situation.

When you really get ready to be healed, you have to assess the damage. You have to look at the situation and say, "Why am I like this? Why do I keep running people out of my life? Why am I afraid people will get too close to me? Why do I shut doors on myself? Why is it that when God gets ready to use me, I can believe Him to use everybody else, but I can't believe God to use me?"

For six days they silently inspected the wall. So, take a minute right now and look to see if you have a wall that separates you from others. If so, what is holding you back from possessing what God says is yours? Take a look at it. Israel spent more time looking at the wall than they did screaming at it. For six days, they just assessed it. How did I get like this? What in the world happened to me?

No doubt there are things in your past that are so terrible you can scarcely utter them. Behind all of the pretense of maturity, most of us are battered children who grew up. We're still dealing with childish issues of rejection and abuse. But our real enemy now is this wall.

We are to worship God in spirit
and in truth. This means
we must take off our mask.
It isn't hiding anything anyway!

If you can get through this wall, the anointing is going to rain on you. If you can get through this wall, healing is going to rain on you. If you can get through this wall, you're going to lay hands on the sick and they shall recover. If you can get through this wall, demons are going to tremble when you get up in the morning. If you can get through this wall. . . .

Perhaps you have become so discouraged with the wall that you have contemplated suicide. You wouldn't tell anybody, because it's embarrassing, but sometimes the wall has been so thick that you secretly wished you were dead. Bishop and I come together to speak life to you! You shall not die. You're going to live.

To tear down the wall and live, you will need to give the greatest offering that you have ever given. No, you won't need your checkbook to make this offering. This offering is more than money; it's an offering of *honesty*.

Honesty is an offering people hardly ever give, because we dare not admit to anyone that we're in trouble. We worry about what others might think if they knew that what they see is not who we are. Who cares what they think? The truth is, everyone else is so worried about their own secrets that they aren't even thinking about us. But we are often in trouble and yet resist the one thing that will set us free. Truth will set us free.

God wants to heal you. Won't you let His power pull down the wall?

AND THE WALL CAME TUMBLING DOWN

Some years ago, I was taught a term that I find most befitting for the journals I have shared with you. During a psychology class in college we were introduced to the phrase "territorial bubble." A territorial bubble is described as an invisible wall which individuals erect to shield themselves from the people with whom they come in contact. This invisible barrier causes people on an elevator to stare upward at the changing floor numbers to avoid eye contact with one another.

This bubble prevents people from getting too close to you. I would even venture to say that a territorial bubble can shield your heart from would-be intruders who seek to find out your dreams and the secrets that are hidden in your heart. The fear is that if they invade your bubble, your invisible wall, they will mock your desire to live happily ever after.

When the trumpets sounded, the people shouted, and at the sound of the trumpet, when the people gave a loud shout, the wall collapsed; so every man charged straight in, and they took the city.

JOSHUA 6:20

Walls, whether visible or invisible, are mechanisms of self-defense. They are used to keep the uninvited out. They ward off would-be assassins and enemies. The concept of walls is timeless. Throughout history, specifically in the Bible, walls represented safety. Some walls were so wide that communities were built on top of them. Those who resided in these communities had the strategic advantage of seeing on either side of the wall. They could see both what was hidden inside the protection of the wall and what was prevented from coming inside.

No doubt, those who resided on top of the wall longed to come down to enjoy the pleasures kept behind the wall but were too intimidated by the impending danger on the other side. How could they enjoy the beauty inside the wall, knowing that enemies lurked outside who might find a way to break in at any moment? They remained trapped on top of their fortress. Sometimes, to protect the ones I loved, I have extended them a rope to come join me on top of my wall of safety.

Recently while walking on the campus of a maximum-security women's prison where I was ministering, I was drawn to the many different walls that existed. The visible walls were obviously intimidating. They imposed such finality as they entrapped us, daring us to try to go beyond them. There were cinderblock walls and fenced walls all around me. The only way to get beyond the wall was to have an escort assigned to us that took us from point A to point B. Without instruction, I knew how far I was allowed to go.

Through a fenced wall I watched the women during what was referred to as their period of outside recreation. Some walked, some ran, and some waved and greeted us warmly. Others made enticing comments inappropriately addressed to their same sex.

Walls were all around us. I could stare at them and they at me and none of us could get out. None of us were able to get in. These walls were a direct result of one's own conduct or actions. However, the walls were reinforced by the actions of others.

I would sometimes allow people inside my self-erected walls; however, it was by invitation only. I felt compelled to protect my heart from anyone who tried to get too close to the secret place.

When you have only shared the tormented pain of the past with the Secret Keeper, you often, without realizing it, construct a wall. Like a princess in a fairy tale, you are kept in an ivory tower atop a wall, waiting for Prince Charming to rescue you from the impending doom that accompanies the hush-hush of secrets.

Many come to retrieve you, but they can only get so far up the wall. They either grow weary with their attempts to get to know you, or they tire of the invisible wall that appears without warning and often without cause.

The Lord is close to the brokenhearted and saves those who are crushed in spirit.

PSALM 34:18

What only the Secret Keeper knows is the misery that is involved in being the princess who has lost her shoe. The shoe you leave behind is such a significant part of you. It determines who you are and who you will become. Your true identity is undeniably connected to experiences in your yesterday.

Deliverance finally comes when you confront your past and put it in its proper perspective. It happened to you but *it* is not you. You survived the trauma; you too can walk again. Could it be that you are to share your secrets so that you can come from behind the wall and allow others to come in?

My husband recently took me to Jerusalem. We visited many historical sights that are so vividly portrayed in the Scriptures. Of all of the places I walked, the most impacting was when I encountered the Wailing Wall. There were tiers of history, layers upon layers. From a distance I could perceive the height and breadth of the wall. It was vast, more than the eye could encompass without panning from side to side and from top to bottom.

In front of the wall were women. Some of the women were in wheelchairs while others were in strollers. All ages and stages of life were represented. There were those who had head coverings and others who had nose rings. All of us encountered the wall for different reasons.

I thought of the studies I had done on the Court of the Women, which was situated near the entrance of the temple. The Wailing Wall flanked one side of the court. It was one of the sights frequented by the Secret Keeper, the place where He sat and observed the activities of the women.

It is said that it was the place to which the woman caught in adultery was dragged by her accusers. It could be where the widow cast in her mite. Both women's real actions were known only by the Secret Keeper, who said of one, "She has given all that she had," and of the other, "Let him who is without sin condemn her." Perhaps men saw and knew what these women had done, but the Secret Keeper knew *why* they did what they did. With this knowledge comes deliverance.

My little children, let us not love in word, neither in tongue; but in deed and in truth.

And hereby we know that we are of the truth, and shall assure our hearts before him.

For if our heart condemn us, God is greater than our heart, and knoweth all things.

1 JOHN 3:18-20 KJV

You see, dear reader, when I came to the realization that the Secret Keeper had already forgiven what I could not forget and that He had already forgotten what I still regretted, there was such a release. The walls I had built to protect my feelings and to hide the guilt of the past became less and less needful. All along I felt I was keeping people from getting in, but in actuality I was prohibiting myself from getting out. An invisible wall trapped me.

Only the Secret Keeper could rescue me, and He has!

Standing at the Wailing Wall with other women who were just like me, I confronted the real wall. I began to release tears of gratefulness. Ironically, the ugly duckling in me came face-to-face with something life-altering and symbolic. Each step that I had to take to reach the wall represented memories in my life that I sorely needed to release. Instead of the wall getting smaller, with much intimidation it loomed above my head.

It was so high I could not see the top. That is how my secrets had held me captive. It is customary for those who visit the Wailing Wall to write prayer requests on paper and press them into the cracks of the wall. Thinking of all the issues that were in my heart, I began to search for something to leave in the wall. With a tearstained face, I reached inside my purse and found my one and only business card. It was to become more than just a prayer request, because I did not need to write anything on it. It already had my name on it, and that engraving held all that the Secret Keeper had bid me to become. On the card was printed my name, Serita Ann. "Serita" is translated "Sarah," which means "princess." "Ann" means "grace," and the Lord was calling me to be "Princess Grace."

Brethren, I do not count myself to have apprehended; but one thing I do, forgetting those things which are behind and reaching forward to those things which are ahead, I press toward the goal.

PHILIPPIANS 3:13 NKJV

I folded my request and found a small opening in the wall. On this opening that held my heart's desire, I laid my head and began to worship. I lost all consciousness of those around me. More women began to move into the space I had occupied alone for so long. It didn't matter that they were close enough to hear my cry, because they were crying too.

I needed no walls to protect me from people who were basically just like me, battling shame and guilt in their minds. It was time to walk out of my past into my future. The beautiful swan had to fly. There was a princess within, and the Prince of Peace was waiting for me!

In all your ways acknowledge Him, and He shall direct your paths.

PROVERBS 3:6 NKJV

I am so thankful. I don't know how or when, but dear reader, I slipped through the wall!

To contact First Lady Serita Ann Jakes, write, call, or e-mail:

Serita Ann Jakes

6777 West Kiest Boulevard

Dallas, Texas 74214

214-333-6315

www.tdjakes.org

T.D. JAKES
Speaks to Women!

DELIVERANCE FROM THE PAST,
HEALING FOR THE PRESENT.

by
T. D. Jakes

Introduction

Few church leaders are ministering God's message of deliverance and restoration to the needs of women today like T. D. Jakes. Bishop Jakes' biblical message on the true nature of womanhood and his soothing words to the used and abused are a clarion call to the church.

We have tried to capture some of T. D. Jakes' most inspiring messages on womanhood in this convenient quote book. Whether it is read at home, or during a break at work, it is our hope that these bite size nuggets of wit and wisdom will encourage women everywhere to celebrate their womanhood. Celebrate your womanhood—with T. D. Jakes!

My daughters are in their springtime,
my wife is in the middle of summer,
and my mother is walking through autumn
to step into winter. Together they form a chord
of womanhood—three different notes creating
a harmonious blend.

It is important to remember that for every person,
there will be a problem. Even more importantly,
for every problem, our God has a prescription!

The more you medicate the symptoms, the less chance you have of allowing God to heal you.

Clinging to people is far different from loving them.... It is taking and not giving.... God proved His love, not by His need of us, but by His giving to us.

It is wonderful to be self-sacrificing, but watch out for self-disdain! If you don't take some of the medicine you are healing others with, your patients will be healed while you are dying.

The glory of God is manifested only when there is a balance between grace and truth.

It does not matter if you have been oppressed socially, sexually, or racially; our Lord is an eliminator of distinctions.

Every woman has something she wishes she could forget.

Forgetting isn't a memory lapse; it is a memory release! Like carbon dioxide the body can no longer use, exhale the past and let it go out of your spirit.

Children are living epistles. They stand as evidence to the future that the past produces it.

We can build all the churches we want. We can decorate them with fine tapestry and ornate artifacts. But if people cannot find a loving voice within our hallowed walls, they will pass through unaltered by our clichès and religious rhetoric.

Every time you see a woman who has
unnatural fear in her eyes, low self-esteem,
or an apologetic posture, she is saying,
"Carest thou not that I perish?"

You may right now be looking child abuse in the
face. If you think it's ugly, you're right.... But if you
think it can't be healed, you're dead wrong!

You are standing in a stream with water rushing
around your ankles. The waters that pass you by
at that moment, you will never see again. So it is
with the misery that has challenged your life.
Let it go, let it rush on by.

The only hospital for wounded souls is
the church.

We must maintain a strong boundary line
between our past and present. God is present.

We will never know who a person truly is until we understand where they have been.

Facing the past is the secret of being transformed from a vulnerable victim to a victorious, loving person. Be responsible enough to face your weaknesses and pains.

There is a call out in the Spirit for hurting women. . . . No matter how many men have told you, "I don't want you," God says, "I want you." He says, "I've seen you bent over. I've seen you at your worst in the aftereffects of what's happened to you. And still, I want you."

Allow God's power and anointing to touch your hurting places. God knows the woman you would have been, should have been, and could have been. So let Him heal and restore you as you call out to Him.

Forget how many times you've been married. Put aside those who mistreated you. You can't change where you've been, but you can change where you are going.

Women are open beings by nature and design. Men are closed. So be careful who you open yourself up to. Those who seek your help may drain your power.

There is a special conflict between the woman and Satan. He is attracted to you because he knows that you were designed as a receptacle to help meet someone's vision. If he can get you to help meet his vision, you will have great problems.

Until the desire to go forward becomes greater than the memories of past pain, you will never hold the power to create again.

Too often we starve the embryo of faith that is growing within us. Put God's truth in your spirit and let it feed. Allow it to nurture and grow.

Celebrate who you are. You are the image of God.

God wants us to understand that just because we can't see it, doesn't mean that He won't do it.

God will reward those who persevere in seeking
Him. He may not come when you want Him to.
But He will be right on time.

Why should you allow your vision to be
incapacitated for lack of a man? Cling to the truth
that God is doing a good work in *you*. Each of us
needs our own vision and walk with God.

Woman, you do make a difference. The world would be a different place if it were not for you.

Often, unmarried women complain of their need for a husband. But rarely does a single woman boast about the kind of relationship she is free to build with the Lord. So before you ask God again for a man, take care of Him.

The Scripture calls unmarried women virgins because God is of the opinion that if you do not belong to a man, you belong strictly to Him. Single women ought to be the most consecrated women in the church.

When you confront your husband, don't make him feel interrogated. Remember, you could win the argument and still lose the man.

Men created in the likeness of God respond well to praise. A woman who knows how to talk to a man is difficult to withstand.

If you are looking for someone to be your everything, don't look around. Look up!

A truly good relationship is a spicy meal served on a shaky table, filled with dreams and pains and tender moments. Moments that, in those split-second flashbacks, make you smile secret smiles in the middle of the day.

Many see Jesus as a way to heaven and the
solution to spiritual problems. But they fail to see
that He is the solution to *all* of life's problems.

Faith is more than a fact—faith is an action.

Woman, God wants you to believe Him. Make a
quality decision and stand on it.

Regardless of your social position or your past, God raises people up equally.

If you have blown it, know that God is in the business of restoring broken lives.

If you believe your past can keep you from moving forward with God, you underestimate the power of faith.

If you want the enemy to release you, remind him Whose daughter you are.

God is no respecter of persons. Faith is based on equal opportunity.

The power to get wealth is in your tongue. You shall have whatever you say.
And all things, whatsoever ye shall ask in prayer, believing, ye shall receive. Matthew 21:22

It's not what people think and say about you that makes you different. It's what you think about yourself and what your God has said about you that really matters.

Before your attitude is corrected, you can't be corrected.

Your attitude affects your situation—Your attitude will give you life or death.

God will reach into the mess and pull you out when you're in trouble. Just allow Him to keep you strong enough not to let people drag you back into it once He gets you out.

Love is eternal. It is not limited by time. When you commit yourself to loving someone, you make that commitment to *all* the person is.

We are not valuable because we love God. We are valuable because He loves us.

Woman, you need to recognize what God has put *in* you. When God made you, He didn't just decorate the outside. He put some things into your feminine spirit that a man needs more than anything God put on your outside.

The inner beauty that makes you valuable to God will also make you valuable to others. Some may just take longer to notice it.

Perhaps you feel scarred by the past. Maybe you think you are unattractive and unworthy. Nothing could be more untrue. God painted a wonderful piece of artwork one day. And that painting is you.

God always has more for you today than what you went through yesterday.

The sinful things you may be fighting to maintain are not worth the price they cost to maintain.

God never extends our days beyond our purpose.

Those who allow their identity to be lost in circumstances will have to change with them.

No matter what age you are, you have never seen it all. There are no graduations from the school of life other than death.

Be careful about setting your own watch. God's
time is not your time. He may not come when
you want Him to. But He is always right on time.

Your past is paid for, even though the wounds of
it have left their scars. The scars are only there to
remind you that you are human. Everyone
has scars.

Hidden inside of you is a great woman who can do great exploits in His name. He wants that woman to be set free. Dare to believe that He will do what He said He would do. Unleash your faith.

Most men get their feelings hurt when they feel they have changed, because the change is not accepted by the woman in their life.

Men and women are very different. We were brought forth at different stages. The woman was the crescendo of the creation. God outdid Himself when He brought her forth.

There is nothing wrong with being emotional. There is nothing wrong with being able to feel. Just don't let your emotions lead you.

God wants you to pray about things you can feel. Because if it doesn't move you, chances are it won't move Him.

God gave you feelings to light His altar of incense.
When you burn about something in prayer by
putting your feelings into it, it's like lighting the
incense in the tabernacle. It goes up toward God
as a sweet-smelling savor. No two prayers
smell the same.

When somebody says, "I messed up, I had a baby
out of wedlock, I've been divorced three times,"
God's not going to be touched by their holiness,
He's going to be touched by the *feelings* of
their infirmities.

The biggest obstacle to *really* ministering to hurting people in the church is that we look on the outside of people. Don't let the clothes fool you.

Start a rumor that Jesus is coming. Then let your problem hear the rumor.

The real issue is, can a woman with a past touch a God in the present Who is able to change the future? It can be done!

The very pain that's been tormenting and traumatizing you could be the very pain that pushes you to touch God.

As Jesus was on his way, the crowds almost crushed him. And a woman was there who had been subject to bleeding for twelve years, but no one could heal her. She came up behind him and touched the edge of his cloak, and immediately her bleeding stopped.
Luke 8:42–44 NIV

Whatever it is that you need from God, it can be done! In spite of your circumstances, it can be done.

Like the woman with the issue of blood, when justice says you can't get to Him ... mercy says, "Let her by."

Bring your bondage, secrets, nightmares, and childhood trauma to the altar and let the blood of Jesus touch them. He is able to deliver you.

Don't give your life to Jesus and then go back to where you came from. He wants to set you free and *keep* you free.

Secrets are killing the church because there has been no platform created for us to *just be real.* There is too much fear of being stoned.

Wholeness doesn't come from having another person; wholeness comes from being tied in with God. Wholeness comes when He does for you what no one else could do. You are complete in Him.

Let the child in you cleave to the Father in Him.
Be a child in the presence of God.

Sin is not the real issue ... sin is merely how you
medicate the problem.

Never allow another person's actions to control
how you see yourself.

Don't let life kill you … Live! If you can't run, walk. If you can't walk, crawl. But *Live!*

Even the worst sinner is inwardly drawn to God, even if he doesn't serve Him.

There is something about going through dilemmas and crises that lets us discover things about God that we would not have known under any other circumstances.

Many of us have tried to use God for personal gain. We have viewed God as a spiritual Santa Claus and have talked to Him only when we need something from Him. This is why many of us are constantly in problems.

There are times when we are so obsessed with our destination, that we forget we must go through various phases to get there.

If you want to get to victory, you must be willing to go through the wilderness. This is where the people who really want to do something for God are weeded out from those who have a momentary, superficial, mundane relationship with Him.

Are you aware that the more the enemy fights you, the greater the indication that blessings are on the way? The enemy fights those who know who they are, and Whose they are.

God is a God of plans. He is a God of order. As the God Who knows all things, He is never surprised by the attack of the enemy. He has already made a way of escape for you.

When the Scripture talks about a peace that passes all understanding, it is referring to a peace that is anointed. When people look at your situation, and then look at you, will they be confused?

God loves music. When Saul was possessed with demons, David would play on his harp until the demons leaped out of Saul. There is something about the anointed music of the Holy Spirit. . . . That is why you must be very careful about the type of music that you allow to enter your soul.

Don't allow anyone to take your song from your lips. Paul demonstrated that if you have a song, you can sing your way out of the jail.

Whatever we worship is what we ultimately end up serving.

When put into a place of prominence, many of God's children forget Who brought them there.

To fall is bad enough. But to fall and not cry out for help, refusing to repent for your sin, is worse than the fall itself.

We sometimes find ourselves in need of not only divine but also human assistance. In fact, God usually sends other people to help us in our time of need.

God is not deaf—nor is He hard of hearing. He can hear your thoughts afar off. He can hear a snail sliding through the grass in the middle of a rain storm. He knows what you are trying to say even before you say it.

Satan may bring false accusations against you
during the trial of your faith. His perjuring
principalities may bring condemning indictments.
But you can't lose with the lawyer I use. Jesus
has never lost a case.

God is looking for people who have enough
compassion to stop and ask, "How are you
today?" and then stay long enough to
hear the answer.

Quit acting as if you've made it on your own.
God's grace and mercy have brought
you through.

Whatever God declares or decrees, He has the
power to perform.

We cannot do anything without God. Don't let
Satan deceive you into believing that you can
make it on your own. As soon as you fall, Satan is
right there whispering, "You will never get up."

Asking "why?" is not necessarily a rebellious attempt to question God's authority. "Why" is simply wanting to understand and be at one with God's reasoning.

Just because the vision tarries doesn't mean God has changed His mind or given up on you. The timing of the situation may not be right for God to get the ultimate glory and benefit out of your trusting in Him.

The problem with most Christians is that we are far too impatient. If God doesn't speak in the first five minutes of our prayer time, we get up, shake ourselves off, and concede that God is not talking today.

If God has spoken to you about your life and has shown you a glorious end, wait on it. If, in your waiting, you exercise faith, prayer, and patience—the vision shall surely come to pass.

Patience, contrary to popular belief, is not the same as waiting. Waiting is a passive posture. Patience is an active principle. It is based on the scriptural principle of persistence and perseverance.

We ask for strength and God sends us difficult situations. We ask for a favor, and God gives us responsibility.

God desires for us to know His will even more
than we want to know it.

Knowing God's divine purpose for your life is one
of the greatest assets you can possess.

When you know your purpose, you won't sit and
passively allow things to occur in your life that are
contrary to God's purpose and vision.

When you are assured of your purpose, you are not fearful of men or of external personal conflicts that attempt to hinder you.

God says, "I'll do it backwards for you. I declare the end from the beginning. I make the beginning work into the end. I establish purpose— then I build procedure."

God's response to you is simple. Anything that is made well is made slow. "The quality must go in before His name goes on it."

Things that seem impossible in the natural come to pass when we walk by faith, believing in God's prophetic Word.

The calling of our lives has already been determined in heaven. Your purpose in the sight of God is already an accomplished thing awaiting its fulfillment.

Man is inconsistent. God is consistent.

You may ask God why He allows us to go through trials and temptations. If you're not tempted by evil, how do you know you can resist evil?

Temptation, in and of itself, is not sin. It is *surrendering* to temptation that is sin.

If Jesus had not specifically called Lazarus by
name, everyone and everything everywhere
would have risen.

You need to pursue your destiny by the will and
grace of God. But understand and know
assuredly that your destiny has a price. It costs
you everything.

Never allow another person's opinion to be your goal. They may not like you.

When God gets ready to bless you, He doesn't ask anybody if He can do it. He just blesses you anyway.

Don't go to a church that won't let you praise God.

When God makes an *appointment with you,*
something awesome is going to happen.

No power can hold you, no demon can stop
you. . . . Give God what He wants and He will
make every enemy leave you alone.

Fear traps time and holds it hostage in a prison of
icy anxiety.

It is He alone whom we must trust to see the very worst in us, yet still think the very best of us. It is simply the love of a Father.

I believe the church has confused *conviction* with *condemnation.... Conviction* leads us to a place of deliverance and change. *Condemnation* leads us to the gallows of despair and hopelessness.

We are properly draped and dressed to come into the presence of a holy God only because His accepted Son, Jesus Christ, has wrapped us in His own identity.

I began to realize the great truth that the blood of Christ doesn't just reach backwards into the bleakness of my past debauchery—it also has the power to cover my ongoing struggles!

When Mary, the sinner, came and washed Jesus'
feet with her tears, some mocked Jesus and
discredited Him. . . . It wasn't that Jesus didn't
know the hands that washed His feet had done
wrong. . . . It was that He didn't care!

We need to lay ourselves before Him and seek His
face in the beauty of holiness—the holiness that
produces wholeness.

The greatest place to preach isn't in our great
meetings with swelling crowds and lofty
recognitions. The greatest place to preach is in the
trenches, in the foxholes and the hogpens of life.

Oh, thou man or woman of great passion, driven
by intense feelings and desires, you often wrestle
with your ambitious nature. Hear me and hear
me well: You don't want to kill your passion—you
just need to redirect it toward a godly vision.

If we exist without passion, we slump into a state of stagnation that hinders us from achieving the purpose of God in our lives.

It is the burning effect of a vision that causes us to escape destruction.

There is absolutely no substitute for the syrupy nectar of human experience. It is experience that seasons the future relationships God has in store for us.

To never trust again is to live on the pinnacle of a tower. You may feel safe from life's threatening grasp, but you will be so detached from life that you may soon lose consciousness of people, places, dates, and events.

If the angels were to stroll through the earth with the Creator and ask, "Which house is yours?" He would pass by all the mansions, cathedrals, temples and castles. Then unashamedly, He would point at you and me and say, "That house is Mine!"

The very best of us camouflage the very worst in us with religious colloquialisms that reduce Christianity to more of an act than an attitude.

The renewal of the old man is a daily exercise of the heart. It progressively strengthens the character day by day, not overnight!

It is when we strip away the facade of the superficial and ask God to bring about the supernatural that we experience the real power of God.

We must learn how to be as open about our failures as we are about our successes. Without this kind of honesty, we create a false image that causes others to needlessly struggle.

When you find someone who can see your
flaws and your under-developed character,
and love you in spite of it all, you are blessed.

Repentance comes because of the unfailing love
of a perfect God, a God Who cares for the
cracked vases that others would have discarded.

It is to the distraught heart that seeks so desperately for a place of refuge that we extend soft hands and tender words.

This "dippity-doo, a little dab will do you" mentality that we preach is not scriptural at all. We need God's treatment every day. We are not a finished product.

Jesus' love was so *awesome* that it could only be depicted by the morbidity of His dying.

Our ministers are dying of loneliness because they feel obligated to maintain some false image of perfection in order to be of service in our society.

Can you imagine what the disciples thought when Jesus ended supper and laid aside His garments? How could a person of His stature stoop so low? I tell you, He never stood as tall as He did when He stooped so low to bless those men whom He had taught.

Every person who finds real purpose will sooner or later go through some series of adversities that will cause them to let go of the temporal and cleave to the eternal.

True worship is born when true sacrifice occurs.
When we lay upon the altar some bleeding
object that we thought we would keep
for ourselves, that's worship.

Your ministry truly becomes effective when you
know that there is precious little difference
between the people you serve and yourself.

With joy we draw water from the wells of
salvation! But what good is that water if we fail
to use it to wash away the weariness of
someone's journey?